Old Main

Interior, Old Main

Littlefield House

Old Engineering Building

THE UNIVERSITY OF TEXAS: A PICTORIAL ACCOUNT OF ITS FIRST CENTURY

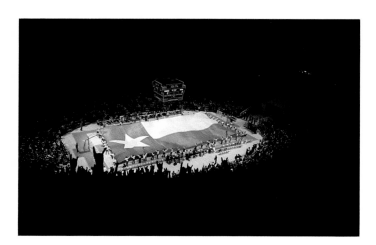

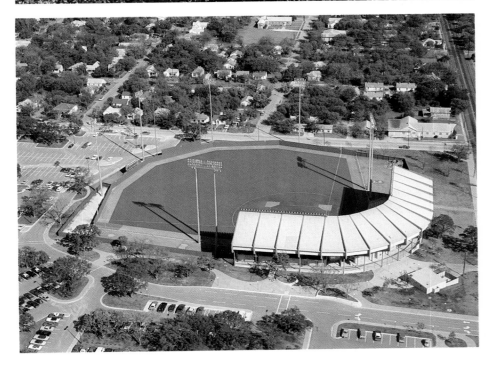

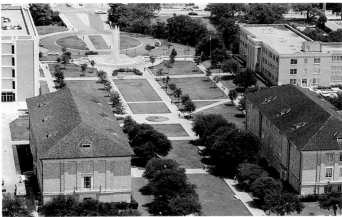

The University of Texas
A Pictorial Account of Its First Century

By Margaret C. Berry

University of Texas Press
Austin and London

International Standard Book Number 0-292-78508-9
                    (special edition) 0-292-78509-7
Library of Congress Catalog Card Number 80-53005
Copyright © 1980 by the University of Texas Press
Printed in the United States of America

Requests for permission to reproduce material
from this work should be sent to
Permissions, University of Texas Press,
Box 7819, Austin, Texas 78712.

To Harry Huntt Ransom

Who, *"in an era and a region where the investment of time and money in stadiums may in some locales exceed that in libraries, . . . stood firmly for the library as a center of the higher learning enterprise."*
> —Logan Wilson, former president of The University of Texas at Austin and former chancellor of The University of Texas System

Who *"for a moment . . . showed us a view from the mountaintop, showed us how exciting our academic valley could be."*
> —Joe B. Frantz, professor, Walter P. Webb Chair in History

Who *"for more than a third of a century . . . symbolized all that is good and true and beautiful about The University of Texas."*
> —Frank C. Erwin, Jr., attorney, former chairman of the Board of Regents, The University of Texas System

Whose *"creative achievements are now part of our inheritance. They live on in us, even as the man known as Harry Huntt Ransom will continue to live in us and in those who come after."*
> —Donald L. Weismann, University Professor in the Arts

The above quotations are from tributes made at a commemorative assembly honoring the memory of Chancellor Emeritus Harry Huntt Ransom on May 4, 1976, in the Lyndon Baines Johnson Auditorium on The University of Texas campus at Austin.

Contents

Foreword

This effort to present the first one hundred years of the University in pictures is a product of Harry Ransom's vision and Margaret Berry's dedication and loving persistence. In the notes Harry Ransom assembled before his death, there is the admonition that a pictorial account should not be burdened with an elaborate text. He took pains to distinguish an "illustrated history" from a "pictorial account." Margaret Berry has been mindful of the Ransom concept. The temptation to include a long text dealing with people, places, and events has been stoutly resisted. This book is a visual experience—scenes of the past, faces of those who built an institution and faces of those who came, worked, played, and laid a foundation for life. For many, this will be a nostalgic book. But behind the nostalgia is the evolution, recorded in images, of a great institution. Publication of this pictorial account comes most appropriately one hundred years after the 1881 session of the Legislature of the state of Texas on March 30, 1881, said:

Be it enacted by the Legislature of the State of Texas, that there be established in this State, at such locality as may be determined by a vote of the people, an institution of learning, which shall be known as The University of Texas.

Peter T. Flawn, President
The University of Texas at Austin

Preface

Chancellor Emeritus Harry Huntt Ransom was commissioned by the Board of Regents to prepare a history of The University of Texas after he retired as chancellor. He was the ideal choice for the task, because for almost a half-century he had known the University from the bottom rung of the academic ladder to the chancellorship. He wisely decided that the history should be multivolume and that the first volume should be a pictorial account of incidents in the colorful history of the institution. When he died suddenly in April 1976, I was asked, after a considerable time lag, to complete the pictorial volume.

Chancellor Ransom had wanted the pictorial book to show the importance of people shaping the University. I have tried to carry out this wish, because I am also a believer in the significance of the roles of individuals in shaping institutions. The product, perhaps, is not what Chancellor Ransom would have published, nor is it what I would have published if I had begun, on my own, at the beginning. The final decisions are mine nonetheless, and the blame for any inaccuracies, omissions, or distortions must be placed on me.

This book is not a pictorial history. It is a pictorial account of events that have been of significance during the University's first century. I hope that the viewers and readers who are former students can enjoy reviewing the institution's past while revelling in the heady nostalgia of their own days on the campus and that those who do not know the campus can acquire an appreciation for a campus culture that is tied to the larger culture but that has become more complex because of diverse representation. The geographical setting, the people, and the pervasive traditions are all considered.

This volume is prepared with love for an institution that is constantly changing, developing, and growing in quality, as well as in size. It is prepared with appreciation for the University, for its diversity, its traditions, its culture. It is prepared as a keepsake for those who have been here, who have dreamed of its greatness and seen those dreams realized, who have gone their separate ways and yet are held together by the nostalgic memories of University days.

More than one thousand photographs, a few as old as the University itself, are presented to portray events of the past century and to remind all of us of some of the people who are representative of the many who together have made this great University.

Acknowledgments

Harry Ransom had collected hundreds of photographs for a pictorial account of the history of The University of Texas, but his sudden death in April 1976 left his successors with no way of knowing everyone who may have made contributions. I express appreciation to an unknown host of helpers and shall make no attempt to acknowledge personally the individuals who lent him assistance in putting the story together.

Most of the photographs belong to the University. They came from the University Archives, the University Writings Collections, Texas Student Publications, University News and Information Service, Sports News, and various University departments. The Ex-Students' Association also provided files of its pictures, and several individuals on the faculty and staff offered photographs. I have no way of saluting individually all the photographers who through the years have taken the pictures reproduced here.

Outside the University, we had assistance from the Austin–Travis County Collection of the Austin Public Library, Audray Bateman, director; photography collections at the Department of Public Safety and the Texas Highway Department; Lynn Segall at Aerotech, Commercial Aerial Photography; Lou Maysel; and Jack's Party Pictures. A rousing tribute to our neighbors is in order.

Although listing individuals is asking for trouble, the services of several were significant during my tenure with the project. I think especially of Joe B. Frantz, Ralph Elder, Helen Tackett, Martha Boyd, Joe Coltharp, Buddy Barnes, Maud Ann Armstrong, Loyd Edmonds, Pauline Hannah, Audrey Slate, Larry Kolvoord, Frank Armstrong, and Loraine Jackson, but there were others.

In the University History Project office the services of Esther R. Moore were invaluable. She had worked with Dr. Ransom and provided the continuity the project needed. Michael Holle and Carol Johnson, each of whom also helped Dr. Ransom, and Ruth Mathews, Jan Haney, and Katrina Platé, who arrived later, were of special assistance.

THE UNIVERSITY OF TEXAS: A PICTORIAL ACCOUNT OF ITS FIRST CENTURY

Sec 10 ——— The Legislature shall as soon as practicable establish, the maintenance, support and direction of a University of the by a vote of the people of this State, and styled, "The Univers motion of literature, and the arts and sciences, including an Ag department ———

Sec 11 ——— In order to enable the Legislature to perform t foregoing Section, it is hereby declared that all lands and set apart, and appropriated, for the establishment and main of Texas", together with all the proceeds of sales of the sam hereafter to be made, and all grants, donations and appr be made by the State of Texas, or from any other source, shall consti University fund ———

And the same as realized and received into the Treasury of t sum, belonging to the fund, as may now be in the Treas Bonds of the State of Texas, if the same can be obtained, if not, and the interest accruing thereon, shall be subject to appropriation -plish the purpose declared in the foregoing Section ———

Provided, that the one tenth of the alternate sections of the lands gran the State, which were set apart and appropriated to the establishmen by an act of the Legislature of February 11th 1858, entitled "an act to Texas", shall not be included in, or constitute a part of the permanent Universi

Sec 12 ——— The land herein set apart to the University fund shall -ons, at such times and on such terms as may be provided by law; provide for the prompt collection, at maturity, of all debts du lands, heretofore sold, or that may hereafter be sold, and sha the power to grant relief to the purchasers ———

Sec 13 ——— The Agricultural and Mechanical College of Tex of the Legislature passed April 17th 1871, located in the cou made, and constituted a Branch of the University of Texa culture, the Mechanic Arts, and the Natural Sciences connected t shall at its next session, make an appropriation, not to exceed forty construction and completion of the buildings and improvemen furniture necessary to put said College in immediate and s

Sec 14 ——— The Legislature shall also when deemed practicab for the maintenance of a College or Branch University for the Youths of the State, to be located by a vote of the people be levied, and no money appropriated, out of the general revenue, for the establishment, and erection of the buildings of the Univers

Sec 15 ——— In addition to the lands heretofore granted to is hereby set apart, and appropriated, for the endowment mainten University and its branches, one million acres of the unappropria

Introduction

The Legislature shall as soon as practicable establish, organize and provide for the maintenance, support and direction of a University of the first class, to be located by a vote of the people of this State, and styled, "The University of Texas," for the promotion of literature, and the arts and sciences, including an Agricultural, and Mechanical department.

—Constitution of Texas, 1876
ARTICLE VII, SECTION 10

When members of the Constitutional Convention of 1876 adopted the present Constitution of Texas, the idea to establish a university was not new. The origins of The University of Texas reach back to 1827, when Texas was still part of Mexico. Article 216 of the 1827 Constitución de Coahuila y Texas provided that "the seminaries most required for affording the public the means of instruction in the sciences and arts useful to the state . . . shall be established in suitable places, and in proportion as circumstances go on permitting." However, no action was taken to implement this provision. Certain leaders of the Texas Revolution complained in the Texas Declaration of Independence of March 2, 1836, that Mexico "has failed to establish any public system of education . . ." These Texans declared in the Constitution of the Republic, adopted March 17, 1836, that "it shall be the duty of congress, as soon as circumstances will permit, to provide by law, a general system of education."

President Mirabeau B. Lamar of the new Republic of Texas spoke of the need for education and for a university to help provide it when he made his first speech to the Texas Congress on December 20, 1838. His words are an important part of the intellectual history of Texas:

If we desire to establish a Republican Government upon a broad and permanent basis, it will become our duty to adopt a comprehensive and well regulated system of mental and moral culture. Education is a subject in which every Citizen, and especially every parent, feels a deep and lively concern. It is one in which no jarring interests are involved, and no acrimonious political feelings excited; for its benefits are so universal that all parties can cordially unite in advancing it. It is admitted by all, that [a] cultivated mind is the guardian genius of democracy, and, while guided and controlled by virtue, is the noblest attribute of man. It is the only dictator that freemen acknowledge and the only security which freemen desire. . . . Let me therefore urge it upon you, gentlemen, not to postpone this matter too long. The present is a propitious moment to lay the foundation of a great moral and intellectual edifice, which will in after ages be hailed as the chief ornament and blessing of Texas. . . . Postpone it a few years, and millions will be necessary to accomplish the great design.

Only two weeks after President Lamar's address, Ezekiel W. Cullen made a long report on behalf of the committee on education for the Republic of Texas. Attached to this report was a bill providing that "each county of this Republic shall have three leagues of land surveyed and set apart for the purpose of establishing a primary school or academy in said county" and, further, that twenty leagues of land should be set apart for the establishment and endowment of two colleges and universities, one in the eastern part of Texas and the other in the western part. The amount reserved for a college or university was changed from twenty to fifty leagues before the bill became a law on January 26, 1839.

An act locating the capital of Texas was passed on January 14, 1839. When the streets were laid out and the land for Austin was apportioned, forty acres almost a mile north of the location of the new capitol were designated as "College Hill."

Not until two decades later did the Texas Legislature, in 1858, set aside for a university (1) the sum of one hundred thousand dollars of United States bonds in the state treasury "not otherwise appropriated" and (2) the fifty leagues of land reserved for each state to encourage construction of railroads in Texas. The Act of 1858 was never implemented, for the Civil War ensued and part of the money was used for war expenses. Once the war was over, in 1865, the Texas Legislature voted to replace all university funds that had been borrowed.

The 1866 Constitution of Texas provided for the maintenance of the university fund and directed that "at an early day" the Legislature make provisions, by law, for the organization and operation of a university. The state still took no action for the next fifteen years, although boards of administrators were appointed from 1866 to 1873.

In 1871, the Texas Legislature took advantage of the opportunity provided by the Morrill Act (1862) passed by Congress and established the Agricultural and Mechanical College of Texas at College Station on the Brazos River. While plans for implementing the college moved forward slowly, the state Constitution of 1876 called for the creation of The University of Texas, yet to be located. The Agricultural and Mechanical College, scheduled to open in the fall of 1876, was designated as a branch of the University.

Through the 1876 Constitution, the state took away from the endowment the railroad lands that had been added to it by the Act of 1858. On the other hand, it designated one million acres of unappropriated public domain in West Texas and in 1883 added another one million, with the income from sale or grazing rights on the two million acres to go to The University of Texas and the Agricultural and Mechanical College of Texas.

On March 30, 1881, the Texas Legislature ordered an election for the purpose of locating the University. By this same enabling act, a governing board of eight (later nine) regents, selected from different portions of the state, was authorized. The Legislature granted to the regents the power to regulate courses of instruction, to prescribe books and authorities used in the several departments, and to confer degrees. They could appoint professors and remove them when "the interests of the University should require it." The act also stipulated that the admission fee should never exceed thirty dollars, that the University should enroll male and female on equal terms without charge for tuition, that religious qualifications for admission to any office or privilege in the University should be banned, and that no course of a sectarian character should be taught.

The University, unlike many other schools, has remained at its original location. Several Texas cities campaigned vigorously for the honor of being selected as the site of the proposed University. On September 6, 1881, Austin was selected for the "Main University" and Galveston for the "Medical Department." The Austin campus was located on College Hill, that forty-acre plot set aside for the University in Republic of Texas days. Two months after the site was chosen, Governor O. M. Roberts called the first meeting of the Board of Regents.

Ashbel Smith, a life-long bachelor, was the first president (not called chairman until later) of the Board of Regents. He worked vigorously to recruit the best men available so that the University might begin with a recognized reputation for scholarship. He wanted a good faculty to come first; residence halls, gymnasiums, and administrators could come later. The University, modeled after Thomas Jefferson's University of Virginia, had no president for its first twelve years. The faculty chose a chairman to guide it loosely and do the paper work, while the regents served in a supervisory capacity and held the primary responsibility.

Oscar Henry Cooper, a native Texan from Panola County, who graduated from Yale in 1872 but had no official position with the University, made the establishment of the University his special project. In July 1880 he attended a meeting of the State Teachers Association in Mexia chiefly for the purpose of getting a memorial committee appointed on the organization of the University. As chairman of that committee, he went to Austin and worked untiringly at his own expense to get the enabling legislation passed in 1881. He joined Ashbel Smith in urging selection of a scholarly faculty without regard to political or religious beliefs. Late in his life, he became a member of the faculty of the University as a part-time professor of the history and philosophy of education (1928–1930).

With legislative guidelines provided by the Act to Establish The University of Texas, passed on March 30, 1881, and with a constitutional directive to be "first class," University founders laid the cornerstone of the Main Building on November 17, 1882, and almost a year later, September 15, 1883, the University formally opened with a ceremony in the new but unfinished west wing of the Main Building.

Thus, The University of Texas began in Austin, a small town of only 11,500 residents in 1883. To John William Mallet, a former professor at the University of Virginia who was chosen by Ashbel Smith to be the first chairman of the faculty, Austin was truly a frontier outpost. He wrote that he noted a "Texas spirit" that caused local people to believe they could do things beyond their capacity.

The University experienced delays in construction of the Main Building in 1883. A strike by bricklayers and the death of a contractor made it obvious that the building would not be ready for classes in September. Governor John Ireland granted permission to the faculty and the regents to use the Temporary Capitol at the corner of Congress and Eleventh that first fall and to erect temporary partitions within it to make lecture rooms. Smith Ragsdale, the first proctor of the University and the only nonteaching staff member that first year, reported a sufficient number of accommodations for all prospective students at twenty dollars per month, room and board. Under authority of the regents, the academic and law branches were organized first, and registration continued throughout the fall.

Teaching the first University students in the Temporary Capitol was an unpleasant experience for the faculty. The makeshift partitions were not soundproof, and the noise was at times unbearable. Worse yet, the students were not prepared for university work. Mallet wrote, "These young Texans were characterized by a great lack of formal school training . . . combined with a certain quite notable maturity of mind derived from early contact with and participation in the activities of adult life." Austin citizens were congenial, but the faculty had difficulty finding housing and Austin's weather that fall was unusually hot, dry, and dusty. The eight men on the faculty had little reason to enjoy their first year.

The Medical Department (later Medical Branch) was opened in 1891, following the donation of the John Sealy Hospital to the state by the city of Galveston. The School of Pharmacy was added in 1893 but was moved to the Main University at Austin in 1927.

Counting former chairmen of faculty and presidents ad interim, the University has had twenty-five chief administrators, with tenure averaging almost four years. Leslie Waggener, who had the longest tenure, was chairman of the faculty for ten years, gave up that position during 1894–1895 to Thomas S. Miller, and then returned in 1895, when the regents established the presidency, for another year as president ad interim. Harry Yandell Benedict was president for ten years, from 1927 to 1937; he died in office, collapsing from a heart attack outside the University YMCA on Guadalupe Street. More recently, Harry H. Ransom might also be eligible for a longevity award for more than a decade of service, first as president of the Main University and then as chancellor of The University of

Texas System. (See the Appendix for a complete list of presidents and their terms.)

The University developed within a culture that still clung to "the collegiate way of life," that aspired to build a "university of the first class," that accepted the "elective principle" of education, that gave at least lip service to equal education for women, and that felt the influence of the Progressive movement. Large divisions in the University were first called "departments," and subject divisions were called "schools," as was the case at the University of Virginia. Texas also followed Virginia in departing from the old university tradition of including religious studies in the curriculum. Texas emphasized the need to prepare young men to serve the state as lawyers, judges, diplomats, and other public officials. The University stressed science instead of relying solely on traditional classical studies, following the lead of Charles W. Eliot of Harvard, who championed an expanded curriculum.

Through its affiliated schools program, summer schools, and extension work, the University encouraged young people throughout the state to further their education. Beginning in 1884, all high schools that met certain academic standards could affiliate with the University. The graduates of the affiliated high schools, if at least sixteen years of age, could enter the University without taking entrance examinations, but graduates of nonaffiliated high schools had to pass entrance examinations that varied with the applicant's choice of department.

In 1894, the Department (later called College) of Engineering was inaugurated; the University had announced the degree of civil engineering for the first time in 1892. A summer session was first held in 1898. Other major divisions of the University were organized as follows: in 1905, the School (now College) of Education; in 1909, the Division of Extension (now Continuing Education); in 1910, the Graduate School; in 1922, the School (now College) of Business Administration; in 1924, the College of Physical Activities, merged into the School of Education in 1925; in 1938, the College of Fine Arts; in 1948, the Graduate School of Library Science; in 1950, the Graduate School of Social Work, now the School of Social Work; in 1951, the School of Architecture, formerly a part of the College of Engineering; in 1965, the School (now College) of Communication, formerly part of the College of Arts and Sciences. In 1970, the Lyndon B. Johnson School of Public Affairs admitted its first students. In 1971, the College of Arts and Sciences was divided into the College of Humanities, Natural Sciences, and Social and Behavioral Sciences, and the Division of General and Comparative Studies. In 1977, the administration of the Hogg Foundation for Mental Health (located on the Austin campus since 1940) was transferred to The University of Texas System. In 1979, the College of Humanities, the College of Social and Behavioral Sciences, and the Division of General and Comparative Studies were combined to form the College of Liberal Arts.

The University of Texas System was established gradually. When the chancellorship was created in 1950, the University consisted of the Main University in Austin; Texas Western College in El Paso; the Medical Branch in Galveston; the M. D. Anderson Hospital for Cancer Research, the Dental Branch, and the Post Graduate School of Medicine, all in Houston; and the Southwestern Medical School in Dallas. The branches at Arlington, Dallas, San Antonio, Permian Basin, and Tyler, plus the upgrading of Texas Western College to The University of Texas at El Paso, lay ahead. James Pinckney Hart occupied the chancellorship from the time it was created until his resignation on December 31, 1953. On January 1, 1954, President Logan Wilson became president and acting chancellor until September 30, 1954, at which time the chancellorship was abolished by the Board of Regents.

In September 1960 the position was re-established, and President Logan Wilson became chancellor of The University of Texas. On the same date, the title of the chief executive officer of the Main University was changed to president of the Main University, and Harry Huntt Ransom assumed the position. Logan Wilson resigned as chancellor on April 1, 1961, to become executive director of the American Council on Education in Washington, D.C. The regents named Harry Ransom chancellor, and he continued to serve as acting president of the Main University until the appointment of Joseph R. Smiley as president on May 31, 1961. Harry Ransom resigned from the chancellorship on December 31, 1970, and became chancellor emeritus on January 1, 1971, the date of the appointment of Charles A. LeMaistre as chancellor.

Authorized by the Legislature in 1959, South Texas Medical School, located in San Antonio, was first founded in 1961. In 1967, The University of Texas Nursing School became a Systemwide school. In 1972, it comprised components at Austin, El Paso, Fort Worth, Galveston, Houston, and San Antonio. Effective September 1, 1976, The University of Texas System School of Nursing was reorganized to place each of the six schools under the administrative jurisdiction of other System institutions, and the school at Austin became the School of Nursing of The University of Texas at Austin.

In 1967, when Frank C. Erwin, Jr., was chairman of the Board of Regents, the Sixtieth Legislature changed the names of the component institutions: The University of Texas became The University of Texas at Austin; the Medical Branch became The University of Texas Medical Branch at Galveston; the Dental Branch became The University of Texas Dental Branch at Houston; the M. D. Anderson Hospital and Tumor Institute became The University of Texas M. D. Anderson Hospital and Tumor Institute at Houston; South Texas Medical School became The University of Texas Medical School at San Antonio; Texas Western College became The University of Texas at El Paso; and Arlington State College, which had been transferred from the Texas A&M University System to The University of Texas in 1965, became The University of Texas at Arlington.

The Sixty-first Legislature, in June 1969, authorized additional System components: The University of Texas at San Antonio, The University of Texas Dental School at San Antonio, The University of Texas at Dallas, The University of Texas of the Permian Basin, and The University of Texas Medical School at Houston. The University of Texas Institute of Texan Cultures, originally established as the official state of Texas exhibit at the 1968 San Antonio World's Fair (HemisFair), was transferred to the Board of Regents in 1969. Under University auspices, it continues as a center of history and culture of the people of Texas. It had component institution status from July 10, 1970, until February 1973, at which time it became part of U.T. San Antonio. In September 1978, it was returned to component institution status.

In October 1972, the Board of Regents of The University of Texas System reorganized the biomedical units at Dallas, Galveston, Houston, and San Antonio into four Health Science Centers. In addition, the Regents created The University of Texas System Cancer Center, the purpose of which was to coordinate University-wide programs in cancer studies. The Sixty-fifth Legislature transferred jurisdiction of the East Texas Chest Hospital to the Board of Regents of The University of Texas System, effective September 1, 1977; its name became The University of Texas Health Center at Tyler. The Sixty-sixth Legislature transferred Texas Eastern University at Tyler to The University of Texas System, effective September 1, 1977; its name became The University of Texas at Tyler.

On September 1, 1977, Everitt Donald Walker was appointed president and chief operating officer of The University of Texas System. On March 3, 1978, Chancellor LeMaistre was appointed president of The University of Texas System Cancer Center; by action of the Board of Regents on April 7, 1978, President Walker was named president and acting chancellor of the System. On October 20, 1978, he was appointed chancellor of the System, and the position of president of the System was abolished.

The University derives the greatest portion of its income directly or indirectly from the state. The two million acres of land in West Texas granted to the University in 1876 and 1883 have been leased since 1884 at varying rates for grazing and other purposes. The expectation first was that income from the lands would provide ample support for the University, but income was quite small and insufficient. The 1876 Constitution prohibits appropriation from the general revenue for the erection of buildings, but appropriations for equipment and operating expenses have been made in varying amounts by each legislature since the first appropriation in 1889. In 1923, oil production began on the western lands when the Santa Rita well "blew in," and since that time the receipts from oil leases and royalties have become a part of the permanent fund. Approximately one-third of the income from the permanent fund is apportioned to Texas A&M University, while the remainder of the income is available for current operating expenses and permanent improvements at the University. To legislative appropriations and income from land and bonds are added fees paid by students and the proceeds of endowment funds donated by individuals and groups.

Certain surges of change have had sweeping effects on the culture of the University. Advances in technology, improvement in the public school system of Texas, increase in the state's population, and political controversy and decisions are factors effecting social change at the University. More specific events, such as the installation of a new president or chancellor, the term of a highly motivated regent, the action of a faculty committee, or the construction of a new building, have also had significant impact on the campus society. Some of the identifiable events causing change at The University of Texas during its first century have been (1) Helen Marr Kirby's appointment as lady assistant and her consequent influence as a "mother figure" and guardian of student morals; (2) the appearance of the automobile, which changed social patterns, increased mobility, made possible the commuter student, and quickened the pace of student life; (3) the women's rights movement, accompanied in the teens and the twenties by such visible changes as shortened skirts and women marching and yelling at football games and in the 1960s and 1970s by demands for equal rights; (4) World War I, World War II, and the Korean War, with the emotional problems accompanying each and the impact produced by worldwide social changes during and after each war; (5) the striking of oil on University of Texas lands in West Texas, producing revenue with which to make physical changes on the campus of tremendous importance to the future structure of the campus society; (6) the beginning of Plan II, an honors program that enhanced the intellectual development of its participants and served as an academic standard for other areas of the University; (7) the dismissal by the regents of Homer Price Rainey, accompanied by heated debates, protests, and investigations; (8) the Heman Sweatt case and the subsequent integration of the University in all its divisions; (9) the appointment to the presidency and later the chancellorship of Harry Huntt Ransom, under whose leadership the University made great strides academically, especially through faculty recruitment and in the development of libraries and special collections; (10) the Vietnam War and the nationwide student protests that brought sweeping changes in politics, enrollment, and standards; (11) the splitting of the old College of Arts and Sciences into three colleges and a division and the eventual re-creation of a College of Liberal Arts. Certainly these changes are not the only ones that have been of significance, but they serve as examples of the events in the University's history that have had repercussions, produced change, and helped to make the University what it is today.

As the University approaches its one hundredth anniversary, it has cause to celebrate its growth in size and quality. From that humble beginning on September 15, 1883, when it had 1 building, 2 departments, 8 faculty members, and 221 students on a forty-acre tract north of the Capitol, U.T. Austin has grown to become a city within a city. With more than 1,800 faculty members, support personnel numbering approximately 10,000, and over 40,000 students, the University now has a campus made up of 316 contiguous areas with 121 major buildings. A recent assessment of graduate training in the leading professional programs in the United States in law, education, and business ranks those programs at U.T. Austin in the top ten among public institutions. No other institution—public or private—in Texas or the Southwest achieved ratings in any of the categories. Another recent study, comparing research in thirty-five major state universities in the nation, shows U.T. Austin ranking among the top institutions of higher education having the strongest research programs in the physical sciences, engineering, chemistry, and the life sciences. A previous survey of doctoral education (the Roose-Anderson Report of the American Council on Education in 1970) showed that four U.T. Austin programs (linguistics, German, Spanish, and botany) ranked among the top five in the United States. Four other programs (population biology, civil engineering, classics, and geology) also were among the top ten. In that report, a total of twenty-three U.T. Austin Ph.D. programs placed in the leading categories of their respective fields. The University's library ranks ninth among all academic libraries in the United States, having experienced during the past decade a growth rate almost four times that of the other members of the top ten. The library now holds well over four million volumes.

In addition to the research projects conducted on campus, U.T. Austin also maintains important teaching and research units located miles from Austin: the Marine Science Institute, which has a marine laboratory at Port Aransas and a geophysics laboratory at Galveston; the McDonald Observatory atop Mount Locke in West

Texas and the Radio Astronomy Observatory about forty miles south of McDonald near Marfa; the Winedale Historical Center at Round Top; and the Dobie Paisano Ranch.

As U.T. Austin has grown in faculty, staff, and students, so have its academic programs. About four thousand courses are offered in the University's eight colleges, six schools, and fifty departments. Facilities are among the finest in the country. The current faculty is an assemblage of scholars that includes twelve members of the National Academy of Sciences, fourteen members of the National Academy of Engineering, a Pulitzer Prize winner in history, a Nobel laureate in chemistry, and holders of ninety-three endowed chairs and professorships.

The time is right for significant academic development. The University's future is in the hands of those with the potential to move it toward achievement of the excellence commanded in that 1876 Constitution—"a university of the first class."

THE UNIVERSITY OF TEXAS: A PICTORIAL ACCOUNT OF ITS FIRST CENTURY

1. The University Environs

Although the geographic center of Texas is near Menard, Austin is as conveniently located as any city in Texas.

Travis County, with its natural beauty and moderate climate, is a crossroads. Throughout the known history of the area, those who passed through or settled commented on its hills, its streams, and its woodlands to the west of the Colorado River and its grassy prairies and blacklands to the east. The early Spaniards, the Indians, and explorers from other colonies found the area to be rich in the charms of nature. It is located astride a major geologic occurrence, the Balcones Fault, or Escarpment, which extends in a curved line across Texas from Del Rio to the Red River. From the limestone cliffs of the escarpment, water is forced to the surface by artesian pressure, producing numerous natural springs in the area.

In July 1832, Reuben Hornsby settled at the bend of the river about ten miles below Austin, where he, his wife, Sallie, and their six sons started the first settlement in Travis County. Stephen F. Austin scouted the region around present-day Montopolis in the spring of 1830, looking for an appropriate spot to locate a town that would fulfill Moses Austin's dream. He died in 1836, but machinery was in motion for the location of the capital city of the Republic of Texas. In 1838, General Edward Burleson started the settlement of Waterloo, where Austin is now located, to provide a ford over the Colorado River at the mouth of Shoal Creek.

The president of the Republic, Mirabeau B. Lamar, came to the area for a buffalo hunt in the fall of 1838. The next year, five commissioners, appointed by Lamar to select a permanent site for the seat of government, reported to him on April 13, 1839, that they had selected the town of Waterloo. The name of the site was changed to Austin as a tribute to Moses and Stephen F., who for a decade had dedicated themselves to their dreams for Texas.

Austin had less than twelve thousand residents when The University of Texas was founded in 1883, but the natural charms of its environs enchanted students then as they do today. Students like to dream of the future while lazing by Austin's streams beneath the broad cypress, pecan, and hackberry trees or while broiling a steak beneath a spreading liveoak on a rocky overlook.

Austin is indeed a pleasant place!

Two early maps of Austin show the importance of the Colorado River and two of its creeks, Shoal and Waller, in the location of the capital of the Republic of Texas.

An act of the Congress of the Republic, in January 1839, provided for the selection of the site for the capital, to be named Austin, and for an agent to lay out the town so that the most valuable lots would be set aside for the Capitol and state buildings and the remainder, not more than half, would be sold at public auction.

Judge Edwin Waller was the agent appointed by President Mirabeau B. Lamar to lay out the town. He and surveyor William H. Sandusky arrived in Austin in May 1839 and set up camps for construction crews on Waller Creek and at Durham's Spring, near present

Sixth and Nueces Streets. Sandusky surveyed an area about a mile square, laying it out in lots and setting aside space for such important places as the Capitol, the president's house, and even a university. Sandusky's original map, drawn in 1839, shows Uncle Billy Barton's house by the creek that was later named for him. On the map it is called Spring Creek.

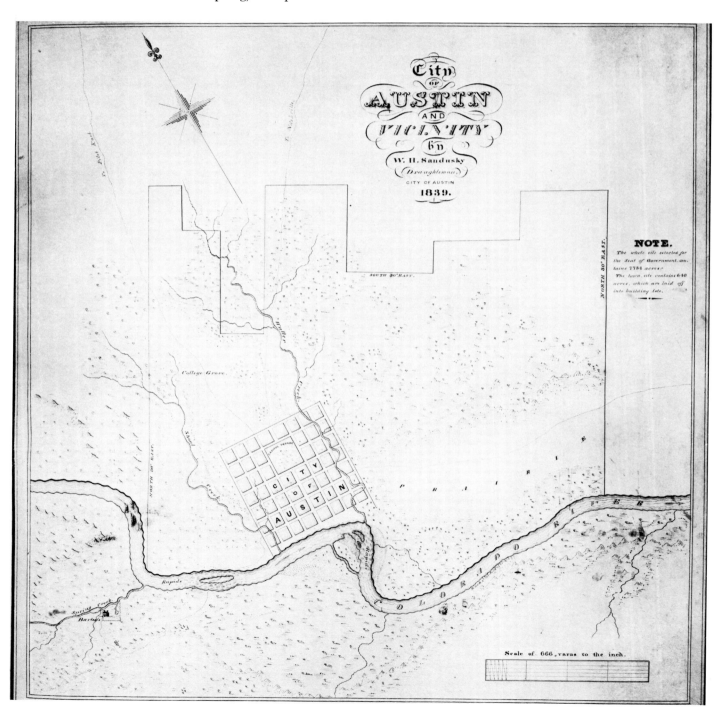

The plan of the city used by Judge Waller, who became the first mayor of Austin, is shown in greater detail. The proposed locations of specific buildings are on this map.

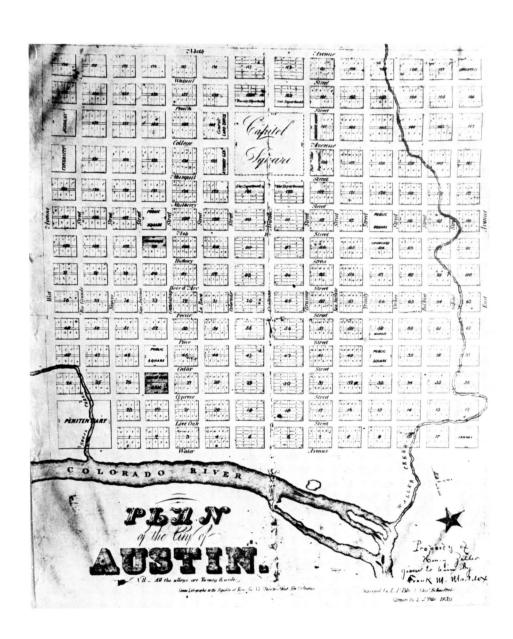

Bull Creek flows for only eight miles from the hills northwest of Austin into the Colorado River, but it forms an indelible memory for University students who recall picnics, car washes, stream wading, fraternity initiations, and other events in its waters or along its banks. The winding road through the hills from the University to Bull Creek is like a mountain road to students from Texas' flatlands. Tradition says that Mormons first built it in 1846.

Thirty-two miles to the west lies Hamilton Pool, a natural pool within a cave where Basin Creek catapults ninety-five feet downward on its way to join the Pedernales.

Around 1916, the cold waters of Deep Eddy under tall cottonwoods older than the University could be reached by streetcar. Had the University moved to Brackenridge Tract in the 1920s, as proposed, Deep Eddy would have adjoined the campus.

This view of Austin's skyline from the hills is readily recognized by generations of students. The skyline changed little from 1937 when the Tower was built until the mid-1960s. The tower of the Main Building and the dome of the Capitol were principal landmarks.

Austin has been know as "the city of the violet crown." At sunrise, at sunset, or during the daytime when the sun's rays are broken by puffy, cumulus clouds, a violet haze or glow hangs like a crown over the hills to the west of the city.

Looking north on Congress Avenue in 1876, one could
see the first stone Capitol, which was built in 1853 and
burned in 1881. Austin had a population of less than
ten thousand when this picture was made.

Millett's Opera House (1878) and the Hancock Building (1880), converted into an opera house in 1896, were important to the cultural life of Austin and the University. Traveling entertainment groups presented opera, theater, lectures, phrenology readings, and numerous other programs. Sarah Bernhardt, Edwin Booth, and John L. Sullivan came to Austin. Millett's (*top left*) was used by the Legislature in the 1880s. Both buildings were designed by F. E. Ruffini, the architect for the Old Main Building at the University.

The Hancock Opera House (*top right*) later became the Capitol Theater, at first a second-run movie house and then a sleazy cinema palace.

Looking west on Pecan (Sixth) Street about 1888 (*bottom*), one sees the multibalconied Driskill Hotel, built two years earlier. By the 1930s, Sixth Street had fallen into decay, but by the 1970s it was an intermittently restored, rather attractive area of restaurants, townhouses, and antique shops.

The Temporary Capitol (*top left*), built in 1883, was located at the southwest corner of Congress and Eleventh Street. It was hastily constructed for use while the magnificent new Capitol was being built. University classes were held in this buiding from September through December during the year the University opened. It burned in 1889.

The ground breaking for the new Capitol was on February 1, 1882, but construction lagged. The cornerstone was laid March 2, 1885, the forty-ninth anniversary of Texas independence. By the summer of 1886, the first-story walls were completed, and by that fall the walls of the second story neared completion. The dome,

made in Charleroi, Belgium, was set in place, and by January 1888, the roof was completed.

Approximately a mile from the University campus, the Texas Capitol was dedicated with a week of celebration in May 1888. It is constructed of pink granite from neighboring Burnet County. Inside, Texas woods—oak, pine, cedar, ash, cherry, and walnut—are used. On February 26, 1888, the "Goddess of Liberty" was in place on top of the dome, and on April 21 the building was opened to the public.

Austin became the city of eternal moonlight in 1895 when it acquired the tower system. Constructed from cast and wrought iron, the triangular-shaped towers are 165 feet tall and are mounted on smooth 15-foot steel poles to discourage climbers. Of the thirty-one original towers, nineteen still stand, one of them on the U.T. campus, but they are soon to be dismantled because they are no longer structurally sound.

The E. M. House residence, shaped like a ship with many porthole windows, stood on one of Austin's high hills. Built in 1892, it was razed in the 1960s. Here, many a political campaign was organized and prominent visitors to the state were entertained. Years later,

the residence became the home of the Delta Chis and then the Lambda Chis. Many old Austin homes were used by fraternities before most of the groups built their own.

Scholz Garten, dating from 1866, with Saengerrunde Halle, thirteen years younger, has been a rendezvous of politicians and University students for over a hundred years. It is now listed in the National Historic Register.

Beautiful homes in Austin, some of which have been demolished, are reminders of the beauty and charm of the city throughout the years.

Abner Cook built a number of these distinguished homes, one of which was Woodlawn (*top*) built for James Shaw but bought by Governor E. M. Pease in 1859 and years later by Governor Allan Shivers, who also served the University as chairman of its Board of Regents. Governor and Mrs. Shivers restored the mansion and recently willed it to the University.

Colonel J. L. Driskill, who built the hotel bearing his name, lived in a house several blocks north of the University campus on Whitis (*center*). His home was later used as the Faculty Women's Club and served as home for a number of faculty women.

Across the street from his own house, Colonel Driskill built a home for one of his sons (*bottom*). The house was later bought by J. M. Day, Driskill's brother-in-law, and, later still, by the Episcopal Diocese of Texas as a residence for Bishop Kinsolving. It was used even later as a sorority house.

The big new dam (*top left*) on the Colorado River was completed on May 21, 1893, when the University was barely ten years old. Students rode streetcars to the dam site for picnics, and a military band often played concerts nearby. A flood broke the dam in 1900, loosing a torrent of water all over the city.

The dam was rebuilt in 1913, only to flood downstream again in 1935. Residents had to use the well on the Capitol grounds or drive out north of Austin to the Travis Tourist Courts, which had an artesian well, to get water for drinking and cooking.

The Tom Miller Dam (*bottom*), completed in 1940, was located away from the center of the fault line and has endured for forty years.

The Christmas lights on Congress Avenue have warmed the hearts and spirits of thousands of University students. The best place to view the lights is from some halfway point up the rise on South Congress Avenue.

Few students have missed browsing in the antique and junk shops and used furniture stores along Red River Street. Urban renewal projects cleared out a few of the shops, but others are still around for collectors and bargain hunters.

William Barton moved to Travis County in 1837 and named two springs near which he settled for his daughters, Parthenia and Eliza, only to have the springs later renamed for him. Barton's, where the water holds steady at 68°, has been a favorite spa for students throughout the years. Pictured here are visitors to the springs at the turn of the century and swimmers in the big pool after the construction of a dam and sidewalks years later.

Another nostalgic spot (not pictured) for students of the late 1920s and 1930s was Dillingham's pasture, located eight miles north of the University on the Georgetown turnpike. For twenty-five cents, students had the privilege of parking undisturbed; about thirty minutes before the dormitories would close, owner H. N. Dillingham would get on his old dark bay horse and, accompanied by three black dogs, would ride from car to car ringing his big bell to warn the students that it was time to go back to the campus.

The road to Mount Bonnell was once unpaved and rocky. Today it is paved and lighted and lined with expensive homes.

Hippie Hollow on Lake Travis has become a popular retreat for "skinny-dippers" since the 1960s.

The Hike and Bike Trail along Shoal Creek provides students a quiet place to enjoy solitude or to walk hand-in-hand with a friend. In recent years, it has become popular with joggers.

Wooldridge Park, near the center of town and across the street from the old Austin Public Library, has long been the site of picnics, political rallies, and band concerts.

Waller Creek, an intermittent stream rising in the northern part of the city and flowing south five miles into the Colorado River, was named for Edwin Waller, first mayor of Austin (1840). The creek, which runs through today's campus and is shaded with cypress and liveoak trees, was about two blocks east of the original Forty Acres. In recent years, a beautification project has included the creek and has made it a pleasant area for picnicking, hiking, studying, or dreaming.

2. The Campus

Locating the University by Vote

"In accordance with his powers, Governor O. M. Roberts proclaimed an election to be held on October 15, 1881, for the purpose of locating The University of Texas. Despite the extensive campaigns of ten other communities, the results placed the Main University at Austin and the Medical Branch at Galveston by a large majority."

—*Cactus*, 1933

One can easily become nostalgic about the U.T. Austin campus. In the early years, the Old Main Building stood in the center of the original Forty Acres, a high-lying tract between Twenty-first and Twenty-fourth Streets and between Guadalupe and Speedway. In the fall, a slow rain soon turned the dead needle grass into a green meadow; in the winter, an occasional snow transformed the whole place into a fairyland; in the springtime, the mesquites turned lacy green, and bluebonnets covered the campus. Few students failed to take a walk down to Waller Creek on a sunny fall day to pick up pecans or to kick stones into the water or to take a stroll around the Peripatus on a spring evening.

The grounds today consist of 316 acres at the main campus. Included are the original 40-acre campus; a small 5-acre tract at Twenty-fourth and Speedway known for many years as Clark Field, purchase of which the Thirty-seventh Legislature provided in 1921; the Little Campus (formerly the Blind Asylum, used during World War I by the School of Military Aeronautics, and later home of the Extension Division), located between Eighteenth and Nineteenth Streets and Red River and East Avenue, given to the University by the Thirty-ninth Legislature; the Texas Wesleyan College property, a 21-acre tract northeast of the campus, purchased in 1931; the Episcopal property, consisting of about 4 acres north of Littlefield Dormitory, purchased in 1931; the Littlefield Home, occupying about one-half a block, bequeathed by the late George W. Littlefield; and the recent acquisitions north, east, and southeast of the campus, extending across Interregional Highway 35. In addition, the U.T. Austin campus includes the 444-acre Brackenridge Tract along the Colorado River presented to the University by George W. Brackenridge; 476.2 acres at the Balcones Research Center, north of Austin; 25.6 acres at the Gateway Apartments; the 60-acre field for intramural sports north of the campus on Guadalupe; and 32.85 acres at the Bee Caves Research Center. The University also owns 66.9 acres on which the Marine Science Center at Port Aransas is located; 130 acres at Winedale, near Round Top; the 400-acre site of McDonald Observatory in West Texas; and the 254-acre Dobie Ranch near Austin.

The photograph of the west wing of the Old Main Building (*top*) was taken from the middle of Nineteenth at University Avenue by Paul McCombs in the summer of 1883, the year the University opened its doors.

In 1898, Old Main was still incomplete, as was B. Hall on the right (*bottom*). This view of the campus was from Guadalupe at Twenty-first. The Chemical Laboratory is on the left. The Forty Acres were enclosed by a wooden fence to keep cows out. Admission to the campus was through turnstiles, which the cows learned to operate.

This photograph, made from the Capitol about 1895, shows the Old Main Building with its completed (1888) middle section, including its auditorium. To the left of Old Main stands the new Chemical Laboratory (1891). Guadalupe Street is the street to the left of the Chemical Laboratory.

The Peripatus (called Perip for short) was the walk around the Forty Acres made possible when Major George Littlefield gave $3,000 to the University in 1901. The walk was not paved until 1913. In the top-left picture below, a student is shown walking north on the Guadalupe side of the campus in 1909. The Woman's Building can be seen through the trees on his right.

The University band played concerts on Saturday nights from the bandstand located in the southwest part of the campus. Students sat on the grass to listen or took a walk on the Perip.

Three co-eds are shown sunning in a field of bluebonnets on the campus early in the century. They are sitting on the approximate site of today's West Mall Office Building. In the background (*left to right*) are the Woman's Building, the Chemical Laboratory, and the old water tank.

The Car Shed, which for many years early in the century stood near the end of the present West Mall at Guadalupe, was a good place to wait for a streetcar, especially on a cold day, as in this photograph made in the 1920s. It was also a popular meeting place for students who were going on picnics or excursions.

Beck's Pond was a shallow puddle under the trees along the graveled walk at the northwest side of the library (now Battle Hall). It was created by Harry Birk Beck, superintendent of grounds, who stands beside the pond. Crude as it was, it was a popular spot on the campus until 1932 when a tunnel from the Power Building to the Architecture Building cut through the pond.

Tennis was a popular sport at the turn of the century. In 1910, the clay tennis courts back of Old Main were surrounded by bluebonnets in the spring. In the background can be seen (*right to left*) the back of the auditorium, the Power House, and B. Hall.

From the old Law Building, which stood where the Graduate School of Business is today, the Old Main tower was imposing during the 1920s.

The top photograph is a view of the campus taken from the Capitol in 1904. One can see Old Main (*center*) after the East Wing had been completed in 1899. To its left are the Chemical Laboratory (1891) and the Woman's Building (1903). Behind the West Wing is the Littlefield Home (1894). To the right of Old Main are the Engineering Building (1904) and B. Hall (1890). The street on the extreme left is Guadalupe; the one on the extreme right is Speedway.

The mesquites and tall grass provided a pastoral setting during the University's early years.

New acreage was not added to the original forty, clearly defined in the October 1918 photograph below, until the Board of Regents decided during that year not to move the campus to the Brackenridge Tract on the Colorado River. The row of buildings on the right and those at the top were temporary structures, commonly called "shacks," built before the big oil discovery on University lands in West Texas. After the regents decided not to move, the purchase of additional land began.

This row of temporary structures (*bottom*) was built during World War I to house the cadet corps. Within a week after Congress declared war on Germany, the entire male enrollment was organized into three battalions, the largest cadet corps in the Southwest.

The transition from the old to the new . . .

The new Littlefield Fountain in 1933, more neo-classic than Texan, replaced the circular drive and bluebonnets leading up to the Old Main Building. The fountain has been a campus landmark for nearly half a century.

The back portion of the new Main Building, sans tower, had been completed when this picture was made in 1934, but Old Main was still standing, as the tips of its towers indicate.

The West Mall in 1943 had far less traffic, was covered with green grass in the spring that usually turned brown in the summer, and was not framed by a walled bed filled with azaleas.

In 1929, cars could drive to the front of Old Main, but few students had cars. This picture was taken from a window in Garrison Hall.

These aerial views of the University campus indicate growth and change by decades.

In 1933, Paul Philippe Cret proposed a plan for the future development of the campus (*top*) that had more impact on the University than did earlier plans. Spanish Renaissance was already established as an architectural theme at Texas. At the end of that year, twenty-eight permanent buildings were on the campus. Nine were dedicated as the University celebrated its fiftieth anniversary. In the drawing, the light-shaded buildings had been completed; the darker ones were proposed.

Few new buildings were constructed in the 1940s, because of World War II. This aerial view (*bottom*) was made after completion in 1942 of three buildings—the Chemical and Petroleum Engineering Buildings, flanking the proposed East Mall, and the Music Building near Littlefield Fountain.

A photograph of the campus made in January 1954 (*top*) indicates the extent to which Paul Cret's design for the campus was followed.

By 1963 (*bottom*), the Undergraduate Library and Academic Center had been completed, as had Kinsolving and Blanton Dormitories, the Business-Economics Building, and the new Drama and Art Buildings. University enrollment had passed 20,000.

University enrollment increased from 24,001 in the fall of 1964 to 41,841 in the fall of 1974. Fall enrollment in 1979 was 44,102. To accommodate the students, new buildings were constructed and new wings were added to old buildings. This photograph and map show how the campus changed.

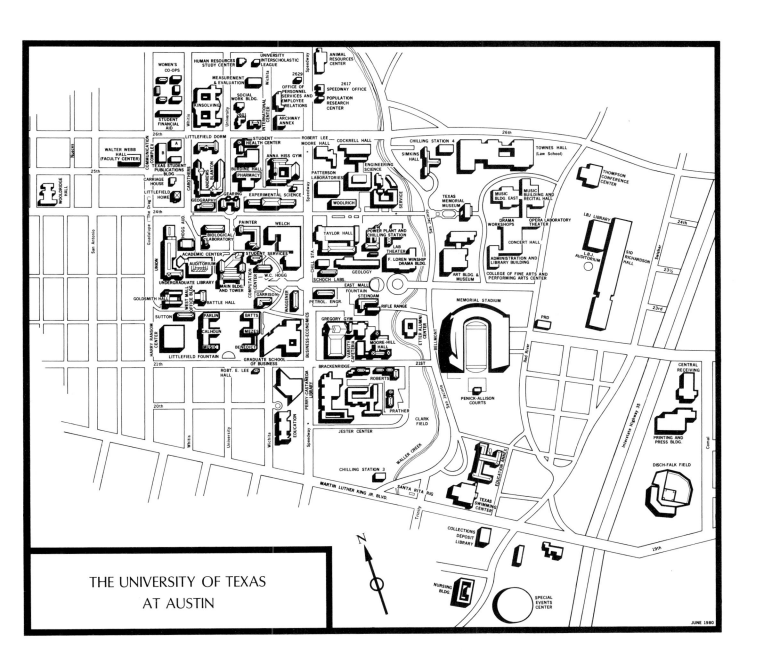

THE UNIVERSITY OF TEXAS
AT AUSTIN

JUNE 1980

45

1914: As one looked up University Avenue toward Old Main, only one vehicle could be seen. H. J. Lutcher Stark, in 1911, was the first student to own a car.
1959: A photograph taken from the same site indicates that automobiles had created a parking problem.

In November 1979, the Parking and Traffic Division reported 19,364 car registrations on campus.

In 1900, students rode bicycles, but not until the 1960s did bicycles and motorcycles become a common mode of transportation for students. Bicycle lanes were created along the edges of busy streets.

The expense and hazard of driving automobiles on campus popularized motorcycles, and several large parking areas for them now exist.

These two trees, called the Battle Oaks, were photographed in the 1920s. They still stand on the northwest corner of the campus back of the Texas Union. According to folklore, former ad interim President W. J. Battle is credited with having saved the trees from destruction when the Biological Laboratory was under construction.

A native liveoak tree east of Carothers Dormitory is the largest and oldest tree on the campus.

Austin is blessed and sometimes cursed with a variety
of weather . . .
    Rain and drizzle.
    Balmy sunshine.
    Occasional snow.

In 1929, drugstores along the Drag provided curb service to lucky students with cars. One would drive to a reserved parking space in front of the store and honk the horn; a carhop would come out and take the order for a cherry coke, a lime phosphate, a cup of java, or whatever happened to be the "in" drink.

In 1980, food vendors found a ready market for their wares. They competed with the numerous fast-food services that replaced the old drugstores on the Drag.

Another familiar vendor in the University area is Gordon Knight, who has been active for forty years.

Since the mid-1960s, street vendors have lent a cosmopolitan atmosphere to the Drag. Students bargain at the Renaissance Market on Twenty-third with the vendors, who are often students themselves, for all kinds of wares, particularly art, jewelry, and handcrafts.

The Brackenridge Tract along the Colorado was given to the University by Colonel George W. Brackenridge in 1910. He had hoped the main campus would be moved to that 444-acre site.

After World War II, army barracks were moved to the tract to serve as temporary housing for the numerous married students who came to the University. These barracks are still used as student housing, although, at the time of this writing, they are scheduled for demolition.

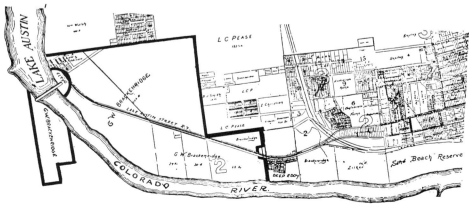

The University owns 476.2 acres at the Balcones Research Center in north Austin. The picture below, looking north, shows the east tract of the research center.

Paisano Ranch, fourteen miles southwest of Austin in the Texas hill country, was the 254-acre country place of J. Frank Dobie. It now serves as a retreat where Southwestern artists and writers who hold Dobie-Paisano fellowships can live and work for a specified period of time. Shown below are the entrance gate and house.

Winedale Stagecoach Inn near Round Top in northeast Fayette County was restored and given to U.T. Austin in 1964 by Miss Ima Hogg. The compound has housed a variety of programs, from James Ayres' "Shakespeare at Winedale" to James Dick's music festival to old-fashioned oompah bands. The old inn has been given an official historical medallion by the State Historical Survey Committee. The plaque tells the story.

The old inn first began to take form about 1834 when William S. Townsend built a large room with a sleeping loft and a fireplace. Six years later the property was sold to John York, and in 1847 it was sold to Samuel K. Lewis, who enlarged the inn to its present form. Miss Ima Hogg, recognizing the historic value of the inn, acquired the property in 1963 and immediately launched a restoration program. Although an expert on American architecture in her own right, Miss Hogg also sought the services of others, including Blake Alexander, architectural historian at U.T., and Wayne Bell, restoration architect at the University. A bedroom in the inn is shown here.

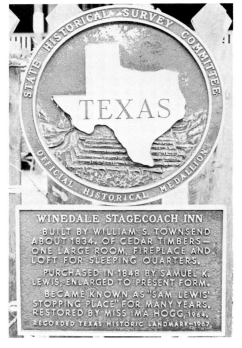

More than four hundred miles to the west of Austin, the McDonald Observatory is operated by the faculty of the Department of Astronomy. It houses a 107-inch telescope, the third largest in the world when it began operation in 1969. An 82-inch reflector was installed in 1939. The observatory is located at an altitude of 6,800 feet on Mount Locke in the Davis Mountains upon 400 acres of land donated to the University.

The Marine Science Institute, with laboratories and boat facilities on the Gulf of Mexico at Port Aransas and Galveston, is a unit of The University of Texas at Austin. It functions academically through the College of Natural Sciences and the Graduate School. The Port Aransas Marine Laboratory, founded in 1941, stands at the entrance of the main ship channel to Corpus Christi, with access to a wide variety of beach, bay, Gulf shelf, and open Gulf environments. A $3 million expansion program completed in 1974 provides excellent new facilities.

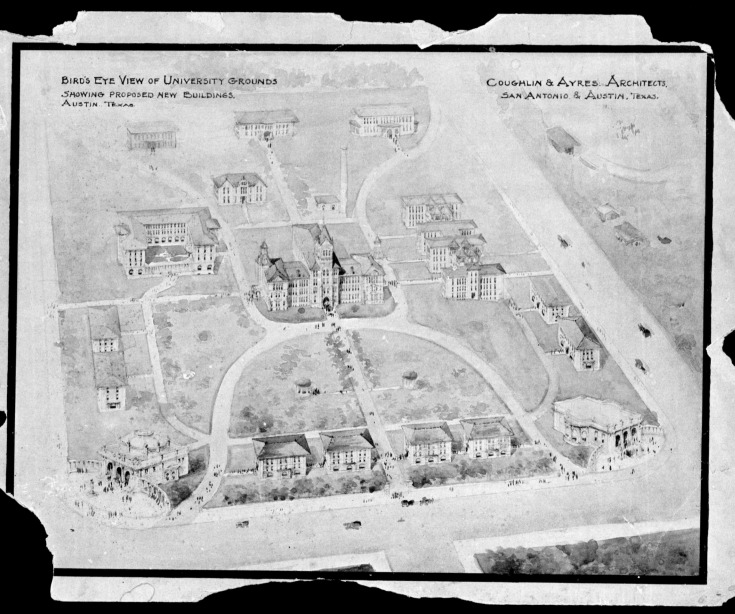

BIRD'S EYE VIEW OF UNIVERSITY GROUNDS
SHOWING PROPOSED NEW BUILDINGS.
AUSTIN. TEXAS.

COUGHLIN & AYRES. ARCHITECTS.
SAN ANTONIO & AUSTIN. TEXAS.

3. Building Development

A turn-of-the-century design for future development of the original Forty Acres was prepared by Coughlin and Ayers, San Antonio architects, who were also architects for the Woman's Building. The plan was not followed, however; even the size of the Woman's Building was altered. The only buildings completed when the design was drawn were Old Main, the Chemical Laboratory, B. Hall, and the old Heating Plant.

At the formal opening of classes on September 15, 1883, Ashbel Smith, in the principal address, said, "A university is a temple of knowledge; is pre-eminently entitled to buildings of solid structure, graceful architecture, with convenient rooms and all the minor appliances, such as we trust to have for the University of Texas in time—but bricks and mortar do not make a university."

At first no particular plan existed for building development on the Forty Acres. F. E. Ruffini, architect for Old Main, sketched its placement on a piece of lined notebook paper, placing the building at approximately the center of the campus, with the central arch of the south façade framing a view of the Capitol dome. The Victorian Gothic taste was for a natural, informal arrangement and so none of the early buildings was "placed" in accordance with a plan.

Few of the original University buildings remain. Old Main was taken down only thirty-six years after its east wing was completed. Its auditorium had been condemned long before. The old Chemical Laboratory and the Woman's Building burned. B. Hall, the Law Building (later Pearce Hall), and the Power House (later Radio and TV Building) succumbed to the wreckers to make room for new structures. Of the buildings constructed before 1920, only three remain—the Engineering Building (now the Student Services Building), Battle Hall, and Sutton Hall.

The University's oldest buildings were not constructed for it at all. The Littlefield Home, now housing offices of the Development Board, was the residence, completed in 1894, of Major and Mrs. George W. Littlefield and was willed by Major Littlefield to the University. The other two oldest buildings originally housed the Blind Asylum and later became part of the University's Little Campus, several blocks southeast of the Forty Acres.

Cass Gilbert, consulting architect from 1910 until 1914, drew up a master plan for the campus. The revival of the Renaissance style of architecture had created a desire among University leaders for a more formal and planned campus, and Gilbert's plan divided the campus into four parts with three malls that have remained in all future schemes.

Paul Cret, who served as consulting architect from 1930 through 1942, designed a plan for the campus in 1933. Not only did he function as chief planner and coordinator, but he also designed several buildings. Between 1930 and 1933, nine new buildings were begun, and an over-all plan and decisions on style were essential. Cret's greatest talent was his sensitivity to the spaces around and between buildings. His personal interest in the buildings themselves was in the creation of the present Main Building with its tower and the six South Mall buildings designed as a visual frame for the Main Building.

The important decisions on style made in the 1930s had a long-lasting effect on University architecture. Spanish Renaissance was already established as a theme at Texas and was greatly in vogue throughout the country during this period. Even though a violent change in architectural style occurred nationally between 1930 and 1940, Paul Cret's own buildings in Washington, D.C., and the 1937 Texas Memorial Museum at The University of Texas are unique examples of "traditional architecture" of the twentieth century, in which reuse of forms borrowed from the past was popular.

A new era of architectual style began on the campus in 1958 when the Engineering Laboratories Building (now the E. P. Schoch Laboratories) was designed with no reference to Spain or the Renaissance. A reluctance to break too abruptly with preceding style restrained the design in a few 1960s buildings, but change was obvious. Some conscious repetitions of the familiar themes were still noticeable, but by the 1970s, the break was complete. Three materials—brick, cream limestone, and Texas shell stone—have been used in all of the buildings since 1911. The dark gray granite columns of the Academic Center are an example of the successful blending of a new material with the basic three.

The "Master Plan Development Report" of March 3, 1964, stated the intention to "organize, arrange and orient the building and land use elements to each other and to the site in a fashion which facilitates logical expansion resulting in a total composition which appears organized, natural and correct." Stated objectives were "anti-commercial type buildings with contained views of the outdoors, interesting and varied work spaces, areas providing complete isolation when needed, and a free flow of circulation to all parts of the development by its inhabitants."

When, after the Civil War, General George A. Custer was sent with federal troops to preserve order in Texas, he and his family were housed in one of the buildings of the future Little Campus, used since by the University for various purposes. In this old photograph, Custer is on the steps with his wife, Libbie, and their dog. Others on the porch are officers and friends. The house, built in 1860 by Abner Cook and later remodeled as shown below, was preserved by a vote of the regents in the spring of 1978 and is to be restored as a landmark.

On November 17, 1882, the cornerstone of the Old Main Building was laid in the presence of an assemblage of over three thousand spectators, who heard speeches by Governor Oran M. Roberts, Colonel Ashbel Smith, and the Honorable J. H. McLeary, Attorney General of Texas and Ex-Grand Master of the Grand Lodge of Masons of Texas. The stone is preserved in the current Main Building and may be seen to the right of the main entrance.

On September 15, 1883, the University was formally opened, although the west wing of Old Main (*top left*) was still incomplete. Classes were conducted in the Temporary Capitol until January 1884. F. E. Ruffini, an Austin architect, designed the west wing and chose the placement of the building, on a knoll slightly north of the center of the Forty Acres, site of the present Main Building. The style was Victorian Gothic, the most popular style for college buildings at the time. The building contained stained-glass windows, central and flanking towers, steeply pitched roof, buttresses, and the parapet of medieval fortifications.

The central section of Old Main, including the rotunda and the auditorium (*top right*), was added in 1889. Burt McDonald, the architect, changed Ruffini's earlier design only slightly. To complete the auditorium seating two thousand, the Twenty-second Legislature in 1891 appropriated $25,000.

The east wing, also designed by McDonald, was not added until January 1899. Even then, furnishings and heat were not immediately provided. Step by step, Old Main became a reality and served as the focal point for University activity until razed in 1935.

President William L. Prather's office in Old Main in 1904 was not an example of sumptuous interior design, but University appropriations for that year were only $165,148.34.

The president's conference room in Old Main at the turn of the century had electric lights, a luxury not provided for students in the library until 1905.

Helen Marr Kirby, lady assistant who later became dean of women, set up a special study hall for the young ladies near the library on the first floor of Old Main (*top left*). Here they could gather between classes to study.

The offices of two female faculty members in 1904, (*right*) reflect their interest in art. Lilia Casis was adjunct professor of Spanish with a salary of $1,800. Jessie Andrews, the first female graduate of the University, was instructor in German. Her annual salary was $1,200.

A corner in the Greek Room in Old Main (*bottom left*) is a reminder of the important role played by William J. Battle, professor of Greek during the early years. His classroom, filled with statuary and Greek artifacts, resembled a museum. More than sixty of these casts have recently undergone a vigorous restoration and are on permanent exhibition in the Michener Gallery. The Battle Collection, acquired between 1894 and 1923, is one of the most representative collections of casts of classical Greek and Roman sculpture in the United States and is thought to be in the best state of preservation.

Classes at the turn of the century were far more formal than they are today. Note the men in coats and ties and the women in hats (*top left*).

The rotunda in Old Main (*top right*) was a meeting place for students in the days before a Texas Union or student lounge. Lack of sufficient heat in University buildings caused students to gather around radiators (not visible here). In fact, radiators in the corridors were to students "what the coffee houses were to Addison; they are the gossip corners, the lounging places for small talk."

The zoology classroom (*center left*) and the botany laboratory (*bottom left*) were exemplary in their day. None of the classrooms had lights.

The auditorium in Old Main (*center right*), with a seating capacity of two thousand, was described in 1896 as "one of the largest and most beautiful halls in the state." It was condemned because of structural problems before the 1916–17 session.

The University Co-Operative Society was organized in 1896 by students and faculty so that students might save money in their purchases of books and supplies. The Co-Op was originally located on the first floor of Old Main.

The original B. Hall, as it stood from 1890 until 1899, was constructed at a cost of $17,000, donated by Colonel George W. Brackenridge. Built especially for "poor boys," it had rooms for 42 students and a dining room for at least 150. Each room was furnished with "two beds with mattresses, dresser, bookcase, wardrobe, table and two library chairs." Boys in four rooms shared a bathroom, "supplied at all hours with hot and cold water, and a marble-top washstand with hydrant attached." Rent at first was $2.50 per student per month.

In 1900, an Austin architect, James L. O'Conner, covered the plain and severe façade of the original B. Hall and added wings. The remodeled building accommodated 125 students.

Grandiloquently dubbed the "Citadel of Democracy" and the "Tammany Hall of the University," B. Hall thrived on its independence. As one governor of Texas asserted, "the laws of Texas stop" at its doors. Here the Barbs (barbarians or nonfraternity men) of the student body ran their campus politics. After a big freshman-sophomore fight in 1925, B. Hall was closed as a dormitory. In 1952, after several big cries by aging alumni, it was razed. In the interim, it housed the student health service, offices of the dean of student life, and several other services.

Four architecturally undistinguished buildings were constructed after Old Main and B. Hall. They were the Chemical Laboratory (1891), the Woman's Building (1903), the old Engineering Building (1904), and the old Law Building (1908). They reflected the growing interest in Renaissance-style architecture current throughout the country at the time.

Shown in the top picture, the Woman's Building (*left*), completed at a cost of $83,000, was opened to students at the beginning of the 1903–04 session. After it was closed as a dormitory in 1940, it was used for teaching modern languages and, later, drama until it burned in 1959. The Twenty-second Legislature appropriated $25,000 for a Chemical Laboratory (*right*), built during the summer and fall of 1891 and described as one of the most complete and serviceable in the South. It burned in 1926.

The old Engineering Building, built in 1904, has seen a variety of tenants from speech to journalism to student life. Now ivy covered, it is called the Student Services Building. It is the oldest building still standing on the original Forty Acres.

The Power House (1910) represented the beginning of a new era for University architecture (*top left*). Architects were George Endress and Frederick M. Mann, who designed the old University "Y." The red Spanish tile roof was to become a standard feature on University buildings for the next three decades.

The Law Building (*top right*), constructed in 1908, was renamed for James E. Pearce, the anthropologist, when the Law School moved to its new location on the east side of the campus in 1953. The old building was removed in 1972 to make room for the new Graduate School of Business Building.

The first library building (1911), designed by Cass Gilbert, set the general architectural style of the University as Spanish Renaissance and is still one of the most beautiful buildings on the campus. The outside of the building is decorated with signs of the zodiac. At the beginning of the 1950s, the Board of Regents renamed it the Eugene C. Barker Texas History Center and promised that it would be "a corner of forever Texas." After the Barker Center was moved to Sid Richardson Hall in 1971, the old library building was renamed Battle Hall for Professor William J. Battle.

The Episcopal church, under the leadership of Bishop George Kinsolving, opened the Young Ladies Church Institute in September 1895 and offered a church home for a limited number of women who attended the University. This dormitory, later known as Grace Hall, was first occupied by students in the fall of 1897. It had accommodations for thirty young women. Telephones were not installed, because the "matron" thought the ringing of the bell would disturb the students when they were studying. Parlor dates were not permitted, and callers were prohibited during the week. Students could go out on Saturday and Sunday nights but were required to be in by ten o'clock; hall lights were turned out at eleven o'clock. The Colonial Ball, with only women in attendance, was the big annual event. The building was renovated in 1923 at a cost of $75,000, and its capacity was increased from thirty to forty-two. It was finally razed in the late 1960s.

Many students, both men and women, lived in boarding houses near the campus. Mrs. Whitis' House was one of the early ones for women. A group of University students were in her sitting room in April 1904 when this photograph was made.

Shacks covered the campus before oil was discovered on University lands in West Texas. Erected as inexpensively as possible, they housed classrooms and other campus facilities. One of the wooden structures was the University Commons, called the Caf (*center left*); another was the first men's gymnasium (*top*), located on Twenty-fourth at Speedway. The women's gymnasium was adjacent to the Woman's Building, near the site of the Academic Center auditorium today.

The "shack-o'tecture" era lasted until the big building program of the 1930s. Temporaries were to rise again after World War II (*bottom*) and some would remain until the early 1970s, but their cream paint and red roofs were less offensive (*center right*).

Sutton Hall (*top left*), also designed by Cass Gilbert, was built in 1918 and was called the Education Building until 1930, when the name was changed to honor William S. Sutton, the first dean of the College of Education. Animal designs decorate the outside of the building. The College of Education moved out of Sutton Hall in 1975, and the building is now used by the School of Architecture.

No permanent buildings were started from the time Sutton Hall was built until after oil was discovered on University lands. The Biology Building, now Biological Laboratory (*bottom left*, 1925), was designed by Herbert M. Green, who, with partners LaRoche and Dahl, would eventually design eighteen University buildings.

Taylor Hall (*bottom right*, 1930) was named for Thomas U. Taylor, founder and first dean of the College of Engineering. It was one of nine buildings dedicated in 1933 when the University celebrated its fiftieth anniversary.

The Hal C. Weaver Power Plant, named for the chairman of the Mechanical Engineering Department, was completed in 1928. Several additions have been made since, and it remains the principal source of power generation on the campus. It was the first building completed off the Forty Acres.

Construction of Garrison Hall was completed in 1926. Named for George P. Garrison, who was appointed history instructor in 1884, the building houses the Department of History. Under the eaves of the outside walls are figures of famous Texas cattle brands. Also on the outside walls are the names of six famous Texas pioneers—Austin, Travis, Houston, Smith, Lamar, and Jones.

The "new" Brackenridge Dormitory was completed in August 1932, accommodating 137 men. Each room included a large study table with a study lamp, built-in bookcases, two closets, and a built-in dresser.

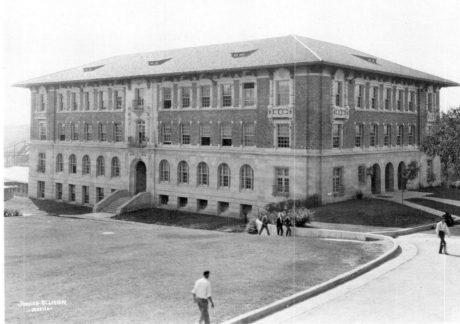

Waggener Hall (*top*, 1931), named for Leslie Waggener, first president of the University, originally housed the College of Business Administration. On the exterior of the bulding are shown Texas products produced in sufficient quantity for export. This photograph was taken from Gregory Gymnasium when Waggener Hall first opened.

The Physics Building (*left*, 1933) and the Chemistry Building (*right*, 1931) are shown in the center picture as they were originally constructed. Now T. S. Painter Hall (since 1974), the old Physics Building with its 1959 addition presently houses the Department of Computer Sciences. Robert A. Welch Hall (since 1974), formerly the Chemistry Building, was enlarged in 1961 and again in 1978. The original part of Welch is currently being completely renovated. On the outside of the building are inscribed names of great scientists.

Goldsmith Hall, formerly the Architecture Building (*bottom*, 1933), has an enclosed patio. Exterior designs symbolize various architectural fragments—columns, arches, shields, and lintels. Plans are underway to add a wing to this building.

The Will C. Hogg Building (*top left*, 1932) was the Geology Building until 1968, when the Geology Department moved. Offices for the Hogg Foundation for Mental Health are on the top floor, and the dean of the College of Natural Sciences occupies the first floor. The outside still bears the decorations of a geology building—a geologic frieze and inscription, "O Earth, what changes hast thou seen."

Mary E. Gearing Hall (*top right*, 1933), dedicated to the pioneer women of Texas and formerly known as the Home Economics Building, was renamed in 1976 to honor Mary E. Gearing, first chairman of the Department of Home Economics. A small, simple fountain is in the courtyard.

The Texas Union, built in 1933 and remodeled in 1958 and again in 1976, has served as a center for student activities and for student and faculty interaction. The Union quickly became the social center not only of the University but also of Austin. The dining area was probably the best in the city in 1933, and an orchestra played there every evening. Upstairs, the grand ballroom was considered the ultimate in opulence. Ligon Smith, who led a Dallas society orchestra based at the Peacock Terrace in the Hotel Baker, played for the opening dance.

Despite protests from loyal alumni, Old Main was taken down during the 1934–35 school year to make room for the present Main Building with its tower, which was completed in 1937. The new building was designed by Paul Cret of Philadelphia. Built of Bedford, Indiana, limestone, its style, like that of so many other buildings of its period, is modified Spanish Renaissance. It was roundly denounced at first as an abomination in the sight of Texans. J. Frank Dobie, for instance, thought it should be laid on its side. Nevertheless, the Tower has become the symbol of the University.

Batts (*top left*), Mezes, and Benedict Halls, all built in 1952, flank the South Mall on its east side. Named in honor of Judge Robert L. Batts, regent and ex-professor of law, Batts houses the Departments of Germanic, Romantic, and Slavic languages and a large auditorium for lectures and films.

The Music Building (*top right*), on the west side of the South Mall, was opened in 1941. Its recital hall was made acoustically sound with spring floors, resonating walls, and suspended ceilings. The Music Department has outgrown the facilities and eagerly awaits space in the new Fine Arts complex.

The Experimental Science Building (*bottom*) was completed in 1951. When it opened, it was one of the largest buildings in the United States dedicated to scientific research. T. S. Painter, U.T. president from 1946 to 1952, crusaded for it. In the background (*center*) are Anna Hiss Gymnasium and (*left*) the Pharmacy Building, which was under construction and which, in 1980, is getting a nine-level addition to its south side. This picture was taken from the University Tower.

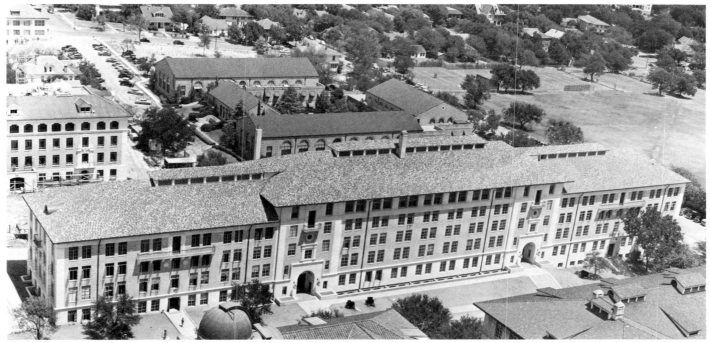

The School of Law moved from its old building on the original Forty Acres in 1953. The present building was named Townes Hall, honoring John C. Townes, who was dean of the Law School from 1902 until 1923. The new addition, started in 1977, is shown here.

The old Longhorn Band shack, north of Memorial Stadium, was razed in 1969 when the band moved to its new home, Music Building East. The new hall has special doors, approximately 14 feet by 10 feet, to accommodate Big Bertha, the world's largest drum.

Built in the late 1800s, the K. C. Miller home had the best view in the University area. A typical Southern mansion, it was home to the Kappa Alpha fraternity for awhile. The University of Texas Press moved in for a ten-year period (1958–1968) before the house was razed to make room for landscaping the grounds south of the Lyndon Baines Johnson Presidential Library.

Below is the new (1977) Printing and Press Building. The Printing Division of the University is on the right, and the Press is on the upper level, at the left.

A gymnasium . . .

In Old Main at the turn of the century.

And in L. Theo Bellmont Hall today.

Registration was held in non-air-conditioned Gregory Gymnasium from the 1920s to 1973. Spending five to fifteen hours in a registration line was once considered normal. Before Gregory Gym, students lined up to register in the old Law Building; from 1973 until summer 1978, they used Bellmont Hall, which is air-conditioned but was too crowded; beginning in June 1978, the spacious Special Events Center became the site of registration. With five to ten times as many students as fifty or more years ago, registration takes only a fraction of the time today.

Underneath the upper deck on Memorial Stadium is Bellmont Hall, the home of intercollegiate athletics for both men and women, the Department of Physical and Health Education, the Athletic Ticket Office, and the U.T. Police Department. The building also provides research space for Physical and Health Education, facilities for physical education classes and for men's and women's physical training and intramural sports, and areas for gymnastics, handball, squash, weightlifting, and other sports activities. The top of the building provides additional seating space in Memorial Stadium for fourteen thousand spectators.

The Special Events Center opened its doors on November 29, 1977, with a basketball game between Texas and Oklahoma. Its prime purpose is to be the finest basketball stadium in the Southwest, perhaps the finest college basketball facility in the world. Whatever its official name or primary use, the students and media call it the "Super Drum." The multipurpose facility is used not only for sports events, but also for cultural and entertainment programs, registration, speakers, banquets, and receptions.

The Nursing Building, located on Red River between Seventeenth and Eighteenth Streets and overlooking Waller Creek, was completed in 1973. Designed to accommodate future increases in student enrollment and faculty, the building has fourteen classrooms of varying sizes, including two which have glass-enclosed observation areas for one-way viewing; seventeen seminar rooms; seventy-four faculty offices; and three conference rooms. A special feature is a large learning center on the fifth level, with facilities ranging from a simulated hospital area, complete with hospital beds and several manikins, to a videotape viewing room.

The Texas Swimming Center, facing Red River Street at Martin Luther King Boulevard, contains a 50-meter indoor swimming pool and a separate 25-yard-square diving pool. The facility's viewing stand accommodates 2,150 persons in armchair seats, and the facility has been used for several college commencement exercises since 1977, the first year it was open.

Formerly the Journalism Building, the Geography Building (constructed in 1952 and renamed in 1974) houses the Department of Geography.

At the southwest corner of San Jacinto and Twenty-sixth, some engineering and science buildings reach skyward. From left to right in this group are the Engineering-Science Building (1964); Ernest Cockrell, Jr., Hall (*foreground*, 1974); and Robert Lee Moore Hall (*extreme right*, 1972), first called the Physics-Math-Astronomy Building, which now houses the Fusion Research Center's Texas Experimental Tokamak (TEXT), a device used in studies furthering understanding of nuclear fusion.

The Business Administration–Economics Building (BEB), built in 1962, houses the undergraduate College of Business Administration, the Department of Economics, and the Bureau of Business Research. The new Graduate School of Business Building, completed in 1975, joins BEB on the left. This complex is located on the southeast corner of the original Forty Acres.

The Geology Building was completed in 1967 and was dedicated by Secretary of the Interior Stewart Udall. The building houses a large library and lecture hall, the Bureau of Economic Geology, and the State Geological Survey offices.

The beautiful and functional Joe C. Thompson Conference Center was a gift to the University from the former member of the Board of Regents (1957–1961) for whom it is named. Constructed in 1970, the Conference Center is used for continuing education and professional development. The foyer of the center is shown on the right.

The $44 million College of Fine Arts Performing Arts Center is the largest construction project ever undertaken by The University of Texas at Austin. The Center, which will become fully operational in 1981, will include, in addition to administrative offices and a library, numerous performance spaces and such support facilities as properties, scenery, and costume shops and storage; sound studios; rehearsal rooms; a graphic arts studio; and public relations and publicity offices. The Center's major performance areas include the Concert Hall (3,000 seats), Recital Hall (700 seats), and Opera Laboratory Theater (400 seats). The Fine Arts complex forms something of a campus within the campus. The three departments of the college (Art, Drama, and Music), the Art Museum, and the Performing Arts Center occupy buildings in which the most technically advanced facilities, equipment, and special-use spaces to be found anywhere are used to implement the educational and cultural mission of the college.

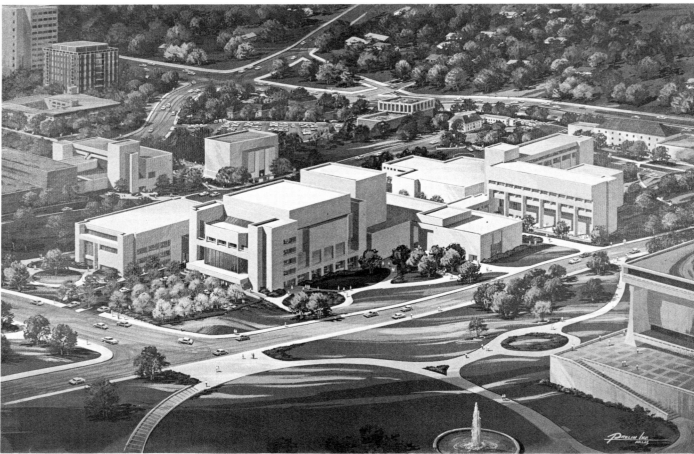

The Art Building (*top left*), opened in 1963 and enlarged in 1976, contains a 350-seat auditorium, classrooms, and the Archer M. Huntington Gallery, a large exhibition gallery. The building is functional, with vast clear wall spaces for display, flexible gallery areas, and natural lighting for studio work.

Loren Winship looks on as students work in the scenery shop of the Drama Building.

The Drama Building was completed in 1962, but the B. Iden Payne Theater and a new façade were added in 1976. Used for drama classes and productions, the building contains mirrored rehearsal rooms, practice stages, workrooms for building props, and a wardrobe collection.

In 1900, all lecture rooms in the Old Main Building were furnished with a teacher's desk of solid cherry, a heavy carved oak screw-spring teacher's armchair, and individual solid cherry desks and chairs, screwed to the floor, for the students.

In contrast, the Academic Center Auditorium in 1980 is representative of lecture halls and classrooms in new campus buildings. This particular octagonal-shaped lecture hall, seating 296, has a closed-circuit television system, tapes, films, simultaneous translation facilities, lighting controls, rear-screen projectors, a public address system, and ultraviolet and fluorescent lighting.

The Undergraduate Library and Academic Center has a large open-shelf collection of 140,000 books, an audio library, private study rooms, and rooms for junior fellows. It also houses various special collections and has spacious exhibit areas. Harry Ransom stood firm in his insistence that the building, originally dubbed "Harry's Place," would be the most practical addition to the inner campus.

The Lyndon Baines Johnson Presidential Library (1971) contains the greatest collection of presidential papers anywhere and is currently the only presidential library on a university campus. The University of Texas built it and then deeded 250,000 square feet of space to the National Archives and Records Service, under the aegis of the General Services Administration. Its papers give the University a prime research center, which has become a crossroads for scholars, speakers, and writers of national and international importance.

The Harry Ransom Center (HRC) was completed in 1972. Located on the southwest corner of the original Forty Acres, HRC is a complex of rare-book libraries and special collections in the humanities, social sci- ences, and history of science—altogether 800,000 volumes and 3 million manuscripts. Here, too, is housed and displayed the James A. Michener Collection of twentieth-century American painting, along with other collections of art and the recently acquired Gutenberg Bible.

The College of Education Building was completed in August 1975. The five-level structure with 252,000 gross square feet of floor space has non-load-bearing walls that can be taken out and restructured to fit changing needs. Designs and plans for the building received a special citation from the National School Boards Association/American Institute of Architects Jury. This photograph was taken before the Perry-Castañeda Library was built.

The old against the new . . . known as Radio House when it was home for KUT, the Littlefield Carriage House (1893) on the grounds of the Littlefield Home provides an interesting contrast with the new Communication Building (1973).

The George W. Littlefield Home (1893–94) was praised as "one of the handsomest and costliest residences in the state, and a credit to Austin," when it was opened with an "at home" on December 18, 1894. Although it has never been utilized as a president's home, as had been intended when it was given to the University, it has been used in various other ways and was completely renovated in 1967. The University Development Board office is on the second floor. The first floor is open to visitors and is also used for small official University functions, such as receptions and luncheons.

The home's interior, ornately Victorian, is filled with a variety of designs, patterns, and motifs. Bird's-eye ma-

ple, curly walnut, and vertical and curly pines are among the fifteen different patterned woods used.

Mrs. Littlefield's front parlor reflects the personality of the Southern lady. Gold trim outlines the fine woodwork in the white walls and doors. The large mirror adds light and a cheerful mood to the room. At the north end of the parlor (not visible in this photograph) is a white marble fireplace, one of the many the Littlefields acquired during their trips to Europe.

B. Hall and the Woman's Building were the only University-owned residence halls until Littlefield Dormitory was built in 1927. Among the privately owned and operated halls for women were Newman Hall (*top*), opened in 1917 by the Dominican Sisters, and Scottish Rite Dormitory (*center*), housing 318 women and constructed in 1923 by the Scottish Rite Masons of Texas.

The University currently owns and operates five residence halls that accommodate a total of 1,500 women. They are Littlefield (*bottom*), a freshman dormitory donated by Major George W. Littlefield in honor of his wife; Andrews; Carothers; Blanton; and Kinsolving (*top left, opposite page*), completed in 1956.

In addition to Brackenridge Hall for men (p. 71), other men's halls include Moore-Hill, Prather, Roberts, and Simkins, accommodating a total of 1,000 residents.

Twelve cooperative houses for women accommodate 218 undergraduate students. The first six permanent units were opened in 1952 (*top right*); six additional units were opened in 1969.

The Beauford H. Jester Center, named for a former chairman of the Board of Regents and two-term governor of Texas, accommodates 3,000 men and women residents and represents a world in itself. Completed in 1969 at a cost of approximately $19 million, the Center also has classrooms, an auditorium, departmental offices, service centers, and a store. It was the University's first experiment in coeducational living.

For student families, the University maintains apartments on the Brackenridge Tract near Town Lake. The Brackenridge, Deep Eddy, Colorado, and Gateway Apartments provide a total of 969 units. Students may use the shuttle bus to ride the four miles to the campus. The Brackenridge and Deep Eddy Apartments are scheduled for demolition and are to be replaced with new housing for families.

University presidents have lived in houses that reflect a variety of architectural designs.

Leslie Waggener, president ad interim (1895–96), lived in the house with a picket fence. David F. Houston, president from 1905 to 1908, lived in the house with the gingerbread trim around the top of the bottom porch. Robert E. Vinson's house was a two-story stucco. The house at 2101 Meadowbrook was acquired first when Logan Wilson was president but was later sold. It was purchased again in 1968 to serve as the president's home. President and Mrs. Norman Hackerman, standing at the front door, were residents until 1970.

4. University Regents

Authority. *The Legislature, which is given the duty and authority to provide for the maintenance, support, and direction of The University of Texas by Article VII, Section 10, of the Texas Constitution, has delegated the power and authority to administer The University of Texas System to the Board of Regents in broad terms. . . . Texas cases construing these statutes have held that the Board of Regents has wide discretion in exercising its power and authority and that the rules adopted by the Board of Regents have the same force as statutes. . . . The System's lands and buildings are state property subject to the control of the Board of Regents as the state's agent.*

—Rules and Regulations
of the Board of Regents
of The University of Texas System,
PART ONE, CHAPTER I, SECTION I (1979)

The act establishing the University, passed in 1881, was the original legislation giving authority to a Board of Regents, but since that time the authority has been more clearly defined. The Board is composed of nine members (originally eight) appointed by the governor, with the advice and consent of the Senate, for staggered terms of six years each, the term of three members expiring on January 10 of odd-numbered years. The Board elects its own chair, who serves at the pleasure of the Board and is responsible to the Board. Six standing committees consider policies for the government of all major areas: Committee of the Whole, System Administration, Health Affairs Committee, Building and Grounds Committee, and Land and Investment Committee. Meetings of the Board are open to the press and the public, unless otherwise determined by the Board, in accordance with the law.

Regular meetings of the Board are held at such times and places as the Board shall designate. In recent years, meetings have been held every six weeks to two months so that the Board meets an average of eight times each year. An attempt is made to hold a meeting on every System institution campus at least once every two years. Special meetings are held upon the call of the chair or upon the written request of three members of the Board.

From the 1950s until Ashbel Smith Hall was completed, this conference room on the second floor of the Main Building served as the meeting room of the Board of Regents when it met in Austin.

In its nearly one century of existence, the University has had approximately two hundred regents (see the Appendix for a complete list of regents). Taken as a group, they are universally white, generally male, Protestant, and Democrat. For years membership on the Board of Regents has been heavily weighted toward lawyers, though in the recent past more former politicians and financiers have been appointed. One rabbi was named in 1915, and in the 1960s Governor John Connally chose another. Forty years passed before the first woman was named in 1921, but since then the Board has nearly always had a woman among its members.

On April 1, 1881, the last day of the regular session of the Seventeenth Legislature, Governor Oran M. Roberts appointed the members of the first Board of Regents and submitted their names to the Senate: the Honorable T. J. Devine, Dr. Ashbel Smith, Governor James W. Throckmorton, Governor Richard B. Hubbard, Judge James H. Bell, Dr. James H. Starr, Mr. A. N. Edwards, and Professor Smith Ragsdale. Three of the original appointees resigned before the first meeting in Austin on November 15, 1881. Dr. Thomas D. Wooten succeeded Bell; Mr. J. L. Camp succeeded Throckmorton; and Mr. T. M. Harwood succeeded Starr. All were present at the first meeting except Camp.

Ashbel Smith, M.D., a Connecticut native and graduate of Yale, was the first president of the Board of Regents. After arriving in Texas in 1837, he became surgeon-general of the Republic of Texas Army. Classicist and teacher, physician and research scientist, soldier and writer, diplomat and legislator, he supported the cause of education at every level. He remained president of the Board from the time of his appointment until his death on January 21, 1886.

Since 1881, the regents have had twenty-seven chairmen, all of whom are pictured on the next several pages.

Following Dr. Smith, Thomas Dudley Wooten, M.D. (*top left*), member of the Board from November 14, 1881, until July 15, 1899, served as president from 1886 to 1895 and as chairman (when the title was changed) from 1895 to 1899. His tenure was one of the longer ones. He practiced medicine in Paris, Texas, before moving to Austin in the 1870s.

William Lambdin Prather (*top right*) was a member of the Board from February 7, 1887, until November 8, 1899. He was chairman of the Board and acting president of the University in 1899 and was president of the University from 1900 until his death in 1905.

Thomas S. Henderson (*bottom left*) was a member of the Board from January 21, 1895, until January 1911, serving as chairman from February 1900 to February 1903 and from June 1904 until January 1911. A former U.T. student, he was the first Board chairman born in Texas.

George Washington Brackenridge (*bottom right*) became a regent on November 27, 1886, and was chairman from February 1903 until June 1904. He served again from August 28, 1917, until January 14, 1919, and from November 15, 1920, until December 28, 1920. His tenure as regent totaled almost twenty-seven years. Born in Indiana, he was a Union sympathizer during the Civil War.

Clarence Ousley (*top left*), a member of the Board from January 19, 1911, to August 15, 1914, was chairman from 1911 to 1914. He was a prominent journalist and also served as assistant secretary of agriculture under President Woodrow Wilson.

Wilbur P. Allen (*top center*), an appointee of Governor James Ferguson, served on the Board from January 26, 1917, until October 11 of that year. He was chairman for a brief time from April until October.

Fred W. Cook (*top right*), a member of the Board from January 19, 1911, until he died on September 3, 1923, served as chairman from 1914 to 1917 and again, after a short interim, from 1917 to January 1, 1921.

H. J. Lutcher Stark (*center*) was another long-time re-

gent, serving almost twenty-four years, from May 28, 1919, to January 1931 and again from January 1933 until February 1945. He was chairman for eleven years, from January 1921 to January 1930 and from March 1935 to January 1937. A graduate of the University, he and his family rank among the University's outstanding benefactors.

In the summer of 1923, members of the Board met in the president's office on the campus (*bottom*). Present were (*left to right*) President ad Interim William S. Sutton, Marshall Hicks, Frank C. Jones, Cliff M. Caldwell, H. A. Wroe, Joe S. Wooten, Mary McClellan O'Hair, E. J. Mathews (secretary), Sam P. Cochran, and H. J. Lutcher Stark (chairman).

Robert Lynn Batts (*top left*), a member of the Board from January 1927 to January 1933, was chairman from January 20, 1930, until January 1933. Born in Bastrop and graduated from the U.T. Law School (1886), he was a law professor at the University from 1893 until he returned to private practice in 1901.

Beauford Halbert Jester (*top center*), Board member from June 27, 1929, until March 1935, was chairman from January 1933 until March 1935. A U.T. graduate, he was governor of Texas from 1946 until he died in July 1949.

Edward Randall, Sr., M.D. (*top right*), Board member from April 22, 1929, until January 1940, served as chairman from January 1937 until January 1939. He had been a member of the faculty of Texas Medical Department, which became the U.T. Medical Branch, from 1888 until he retired in 1928.

Members of the Board in 1927 included (*bottom, left to right*) R. L. Batts, M. E. Foster, Mary McClellan O'Hair, H. J. Lutcher Stark (chairman), Sam Neathery, Ed Howard, W. M. W. Splawn (University president), and (*standing*) C. D. Simmons (secretary), R. L. Holliday, and R. G. Storey.

J. R. Parten (*top left*), a U.T. Law School graduate, was a member of the Board of Regents from March 1935 until January 1941 and was chairman from January 1939 until January 1941.

Leslie Waggener, Jr. (*top right*), whose father was a member of the first U.T. faculty, was a Board member from January 1931, until March 1942 and was chairman from February 1941 until March 1942.

John H. Bickett, Jr. (*center left*), a Board member from March 1942 until November 1944, was chairman from January 1943 until November 1944, when he resigned during the Homer P. Rainey controversy.

Tom Sealy (*center right*) was a member of the Board from January 1951 until January 1957 and served as chairman from January 1953 until the end of his term.

Dudley K. Woodward, Jr. (*at head of table in bottom picture*), a regent from November 14, 1944, until January 1955, was appointed by Governor Coke Stevenson during the Rainey controversy. He served as chairman of the Board from November 1944 until December 31, 1952. With him at the Board meeting in 1948 are (*left to right*) James W. Rockwell, William E. Darden, E. E. Kirkpatrick, T. S. Painter (University president), David M. Warren, Margaret Batts Tobin, A. M. G. Swenson, and Edward B. Tucker.

J. Leroy Jeffers (*top left*), a member of the Board of Regents from January 1953 until January 1959, was chairman from February 9, 1957, until November 3, 1958.

J. R. (Bob) Sorrell (*top right*) served on the Board from January 1953 until January 1959 and was chairman from November 3, 1958, until January 1959.

Merton M. Minter, M.D. (*center left*), was a member of the Board from February 1955 until March 1961 and served as chairman from January 1959 until February 1961.

Thornton Hardie (*center right*), an El Paso lawyer, served as a member of the Board from January 1957 until January 1963 and was chairman from March 1961 until December 1962.

William Womack Heath was a member of the Board from January 1959 until he was appointed by President Lyndon B. Johnson in April 1967 to serve as ambassador to Sweden. Chairman of the Board from December 1962 until he resigned on December 1, 1966, his last official act as chairman was to disclose plans for the Lyndon Baines Johnson Library and related buildings, but he said his proudest achievement was that peaceful integration of the University had been accomplished during his tenure. In the bottom picture, Heath presides while Betty Ann Thedford, long-time secretary to the Board, listens.

Frank C. Erwin, Jr. (*top*), was a member of the Board from March 1963 until January 1975. A Phi Beta Kappa and outstanding graduate of U.T., he served as chairman from December 2, 1966, until March 12, 1971. His tenure was marked by the student protests of the late 1960s, the division of the College of Arts and Sciences, and a rapid increase in enrollment. Under his leadership, the University System was expanded and reorganized. In this picture, President Lyndon B. Johnson looks over Erwin's shoulder.

John Peace (*bottom left*) was a member of the Board from September 1967 until January 8, 1973. He was chairman from March 12, 1971, until the end of his term. When this picture was taken, the issue being discussed was the sale of alcoholic beverages in the Union.

A. G. McNeese, Jr. (*bottom right*), an attorney and banker from Houston, served on the Board from January 1959 until January 1965 and again from January 1971 until January 1977. He was chairman from January 1973 until December 1975.

Allan Shivers (*left*), former governor of Texas who holds the longest tenure as governor, served as regent from January 9, 1973, until January 1979. He was chairman from January 1975 until the end of his term. While at U.T. in the 1930s, he had been president of the student body and had helped plan the opening of the Texas Union in 1933.

Dan C. Williams (*right*) was appointed to the Board in January 1969 and was re-appointed in January 1975. He served as vice-chairman from January 1973 until March 1, 1979, when he was elected chairman. Former president and current chairman of the executive committee and director of the Southland Life Insurance Company in Dallas, he received a degree in petroleum engineering from the University.

Seven women have served as members of the University's Board of Regents.

Governor Pat M. Neff appointed the first woman, Mary McClellan (Mrs. H. J.) O'Hair (*top*), to the Board on May 11, 1921. At the end of her term, Governor Dan Moody asked her to serve another two years, until April 1929. Records identify her as a "housewife," but contemporary clippings show that she had interests in ranching and journalism.

Marguerite Shearer (Mrs. I. D.) Fairchild (*center left*), another "housewife" and the widow of a former senator, was appointed to the Board by Governor Miriam A. Ferguson in 1935. Serving for ten years, until February 1945, she cast the lone vote against firing Homer P. Rainey in 1944. She regarded her work in establishing the College of Fine Arts as her finest accomplishment as a regent.

Margaret Batts (Mrs. Edgar) Tobin (*center right*), daughter of former regent and law professor, Judge R. L. Batts, was appointed to the Board by Governor Beauford Jester in February 1947. The first woman regent to be a graduate of U.T., she served until January 1955.

Lyde Williford (Mrs. Charles K.) Devall (*bottom*) from Kilgore was a member of the Board from February 1955 until March 1961. In this photograph, she receives the oath of office from Associate Justice Ruel C. Walker of the Texas Supreme Court, a graduate of the University.

Ruth Carter (Mrs. J. Lee, III) Johnson, daughter of the late Amon G. Carter of Fort Worth and a graduate of Sarah Lawrence College, was a member of the Board from January 1963 until January 1969. At Board meetings she usually worked on a piece of needlework, a basket of yarn at her feet, but when plans for a new building were discussed, she set aside her needlework. Fellow regents recognized her as the "resident expert on art and architecture."

Claudia Alta Taylor (Lady Bird, Mrs. Lyndon B.) Johnson, a journalism graduate of U.T. and widow of the late president of the United States, became a member of the Board in January 1971. Known for her independent stands, she was popular among student groups with whom she met frequently. In this picture, former Mayor Roy Butler of Austin is helping her unveil a tablet paying tribute to her interest in beautification, an activity for which she is internationally acclaimed.

Jane Weinert (Mrs. Ronald K.) Blumberg, daughter of former Regent H. H. Weinert, was appointed to the Board in January 1977. A Phi Beta Kappa, she received her B.A. degree in English from the University and her M.A. from Northwestern University. Following her appointment, she said that one of her goals would be the removal of any antagonism between the Board and the University community.

105

H. H. Weinert (*top left*), a Seguin banker and U.T. graduate, was the father of Jane Blumberg, a current regent. Weinert served on the Board from 1933 until November 1944, when he resigned in the aftermath of the dismissal of President Homer P. Rainey.

Kenneth H. Aynesworth, M.D. (*top right*), of Waco, was a member of the Board from January 1933 until he died on October 30, 1944. He attended Baylor University and graduated from the U.T. Medical Department in Galveston in 1899.

H. Frank Connally, Jr., M.D. (*center left*), a former U.T. student, served on the Board from March 1961 until January 1967. From Waco, he is a collector of rare books and paintings.

Wales H. Madden (*center right*) from Amarillo was a member of the Board from January 1959 until January 1965. He was president of the Students' Association and has been president of the Ex-Students' Association.

Walter P. Brenan of San Antonio and W. H. Bauer of Port Lavaca, for whom the home of the chancellor is named, ponder the University's budget in 1966 (*bottom*). Brenan served on the Board from 1961 to 1967, and Bauer served from 1965 to 1971.

Jack. S. Josey (*top left*), a graduate of U.T., was a member of the Board from March 1965 until January 1971. He is a Houston oilman.

Frank N. Ikard (*top right*), a student leader in the 1930s, was a regent in the 1960s and 1970s. An oil executive and former congressman from Wichita Falls, he became president of the American Petroleum Institute in 1963.

Edward Clark (*bottom left*), ambassador to Australia during the administration of President Lyndon B. Johnson, was appointed to the Board on January 9, 1973, and served until January 1979. He is a graduate of U.T., a discerning book collector, and a prominent Austin attorney. He is shown here with his wife, Anne, in the performance of his duties as ambassador.

Rabbi Levi A. Olan of Dallas (*bottom right*) was a member of the Board from January 1963 until January 1969. During his tenure, he spent a considerable amount of time talking with faculty and students.

Board Chairman Allan Shivers is shown participating in a discussion with history professor Thomas L. Philpott in the mid-1970s.

A meeting of the Board in session in April 1971: seated at the end of the table is Chancellor Charles LeMaistre; regents Frank Ikard (*back to camera*), Frank Erwin, Jenkins Garrett, and Joe Kilgore—all U.T. student leaders in the late 1930s—are on his right.

Thos. H. Law, son of a long-time U.T. professor of Shakespearean literature, was appointed to the Board in January 1975. A Phi Beta Kappa and former student leader who was defeated by John Connally for student body president in the late 1930s, he is recognized by students as their advocate. Here, he sits with Bill Parrish, vice-president of the student body in 1975–1976.

Current members of the Board are (*seated, left to right*) Dr. Sterling Fly, Jr., Thos. H. Law, Dan C. Williams, Jane Blumberg, Walter Sterling, and (*standing, left to right*) James L. Powell, Howard Richards, Jess Hay, and Jon Newton.

Since Ashbel Smith Hall was completed in 1975, the Board of Regents have met in the new Board room in that building when they meet in Austin. This picture was made during the presidency of Dr. Lorene Rogers while Governor Allan Shivers was chairman of the Board.

109

Prior to September 1970, the administrative offices of The University of Texas System occupied office space on the U.T. Austin campus. Since that date, they have been housed largely in the Claudia Taylor Johnson Complex on Sixth Street, just west of Congress Avenue.

Claudia Taylor Johnson Hall (*top*), 210 West Sixth Street, was constructed during the period 1912–1914 and served as the post office until 1965, when it was given to The University of Texas System by the federal government. It was remodeled into administrative offices by the University in 1970 and named in honor of the wife of the thirty-sixth president of the United States.

O. Henry Hall (*bottom*), 601 Colorado Street, was built during the period 1877–1881 as a federal courthouse and post office. Following construction of the new post office, the building continued to be used as a courthouse and later for miscellaneous federal agencies until 1968. Given to The University of Texas System by the federal government, the building was restored by the University in 1971 and named after William Sydney Porter, the noted American short story writer whose embezzlement trial was held in the courthouse. The chancellor's office is located in this building.

Ashbel Smith Hall, the nine-story structure at 201 West Seventh Street, was completed in 1975 and named for the first president of the Board of Regents. The office of the secretary to the Board and the Board meeting room are in this building.

5. Faculty and Administration

The size of the faculty of the University has increased in proportion to other aspects of the University. Growth has been from only 8 faculty members and 1 nonteaching staff member in 1883 to almost 1,800 faculty members (full-time equivalents) and an additional staff of approximately 10,000 (full-time equivalents) almost a century later. Among the 10,000 are between 1,200 and 1,300 teaching assistants, assistant instructors, academic assistants, and research assistants, most of whom are graduate students.

By policy and tradition, the University employs relatively few part-time faculty members, mostly in a few professional fields. Such appointments often carry the titles of lecturer and adjunct professor or adjunct associate professor, which are nontenured and do not entail membership in the General Faculty.

Dr. Oscar Henry Cooper and Dr. Ashbel Smith, active leaders in the establishment of the University, urged the selection of a scholarly faculty without regard to geographic origin or creed. Nevertheless, the first faculty, composed of 8 men, was chiefly Southern. A resolution passed in the Texas Legislature in June 1897 requested the regents to exercise great care in selecting as members of the faculty only those who were known to be in sympathy with Southern political institutions. By 1933, the 287 faculty members in the College of Arts and Sciences held 619 degrees from 108 colleges and universities, 49 of which were Southern and 17 Texan. University administrators complained at that time that low salaries would not attract faculty from other parts of the country.

Analysis of today's faculty shows that it is highly educated, productive, and experienced with the diversity and balance needed for sound instruction and research programs. Salaries are more competitive and fringe benefits are more attractive, yet salaries and fringe benefits are still critical issues.

Initiative for recruiting faculty members lies with department chairs and budget councils, aided often by smaller personnel committees. Final appointments are made by the Board of Regents upon recommendation of the president.

The Board of Regents grants a major role in the governance of the University to the faculty in the areas of general academic policies and welfare, student life and activities, requirements for admission and graduation, honors and scholastic performance gener-

Serving as senior marshal, H. Malcolm Macdonald, government, leads a commencement procession.

ally, approval for degrees, and faculty rules of procedure. All actions taken by the faculty are subject to the authority of the Board of Regents and to the authority the Board vests in the various administrative officers of each institution. The General Faculty, on the other hand, delegates the detailed exercise of its powers to the University Council, a group consisting of administrators, elected faculty, and students.

To illustrate the University's faculty and the development of its colleges and schools and departments for a hundred years is a formidable task. Because of space limitations, numerous outstanding scholars who have spent their lives on this campus are not pictured, but those who are symbolize the entire roster of individuals whose diverse talents made this University.

The eight men shown in the top picture constituted the first faculty (1883) of the University. They were (*left to right, seated*) John William Mallet, professor of physics and chemistry and chairman of the faculty; Robert L. Dabney, professor of mental and moral philosophy and political science; Oran M. Roberts, professor of law; Milton Humphreys, professor of ancient languages; William LeRoy Broun, professor of mathematics; (*standing*) Leslie Waggener, professor of English language, history, and literature; Robert S. Gould, professor of law; and Henri Tallichet, professor of modern languages.

The second faculty (1884) included some associates and assistants. The seated teachers (*left to right*) are Gould; Humphreys; Waggener, chairman of the faculty; Roberts; and Dabney. Standing are I. F. Harrison, associate professor of physics; George Pierce Garrison, assistant instructor in English and history; E. Everhart, associate professor of chemistry; G. B. Halsted, professor of mathematics; Tallichet; G. F. Gompertz, assistant instructor in modern languages; A. V. Lane, assistant instructor in English and history; and E. E. Bramlette, assistant instructor in mathematics and ancient languages.

Captain James B. Clark was proctor from 1885, when he replaced Smith Ragsdale as the only nonteaching staff member, until he died in 1908. His work included duties that might have been performed by registrar, auditor, comptroller, dean of students, superintendent of buildings and grounds, librarian, and secretary to the regents. Old Clark Field and the current freshman field were named for him.

Helen Marr Kirby (*center*) was elected "lady assistant" in 1884 and retired as dean emerita in 1919 when she was 82 years of age. Her title was changed to "dean of women" in 1903. The influence of Mrs. Kirby on the campus culture is immeasurable. Stories of her activities as dean and of her influence on two generations of women at the University became a part of campus lore. A proper Victorian herself, she insisted that her "girls" should be ladies, wear hats and gloves, and never tolerate impropriety in dress or behavior.

By 1913, when the faculty gathered for an official portrait in front of the old Law Building, the University had slightly more than 2,200 students and approximately 200 faculty members.

A group picture of the University faculty in front of Gregory Gymnasium in 1936 indicates its growth. A picture of the entire faculty has not been made since that time.

After the declaration of World War I in April 1917, the faculty formed a military company and began drilling. One wag claimed that the activity was to prepare them to lose lives in defense of University Avenue. A portion of the company is shown below.

The University did not have a president for the first twelve years, but John William Mallet (*top left*) was the first chairman of the faculty and professor of physics and chemistry. He stayed at Texas only one year before returning to Virginia. He was succeeded by William LeRoy Broun, who served only a short period.

Leslie Waggener (*top right*), a native of Kentucky and a graduate of Bethel College and Harvard Law School, was a member of the first faculty and served as chairman of the faculty from 1884 until 1894. He was president ad interim for the school year 1895–1896 before he died on August 19, 1896.

Thomas Scott Miller (*center left*), a native of Louisiana and a graduate of Harvard Law School, became professor of law in 1893 and, in May 1894, chairman of the faculty and dean of the Law Department. After one year, he resigned to become general counsel for the Missouri, Kansas, and Texas Railroad.

George Tayloe Winston (*bottom left*), a native of North Carolina and a graduate of Cornell, was the first U.T. president (1896–1899). Unhappy over slowness in improvements, he resigned in 1899 to accept the presidency of the A.&M. College of North Carolina.

William Lambdin Prather (*bottom right*) was a member of the Board of Regents from 1887 until he was made president of the University when President Winston resigned in 1899. He served as president until he died on July 24, 1905.

David Franklin Houston (*top left*) came to U.T. in 1894 as adjunct professor of political science and became the first dean of the faculty in 1899. He left to become president of Texas A&M from 1902 to 1905 but returned after President Prather's death to serve as president of U.T. until 1908, when he resigned to become chancellor of Washington University in St. Louis.

Sidney Edward Mezes (*top right*), a native of California and graduate of Harvard, became adjunct professor of philosophy at Texas in 1894. He became dean of the Department of Literature, Science, and Arts in 1902 and president in 1908. In 1914, he was elected president of the City College of New York.

William James Battle (*bottom left*) served as presi-

dent ad interim of the University from 1914 until 1916. A professor of Greek, he was dean of the faculty under President Mezes.

Robert Ernest Vinson (*bottom right*) came to Texas from South Carolina in 1876. He received the B.D. degree from Union Theological Seminary in Virginia (1899). He was elected president of The University of Texas at a time of political crisis in its history and used his energy to arouse public sentiment for the right of a state university to withstand harmful political pressure. He resigned in 1923 to become president of Western Reserve University. William Seneca Sutton, dean of the School of Education (see p. 161), served as president ad interim, 1923–1924.

Walter Marshall William Splawn (*left*) was born in 1883 in Arlington, Texas. He was a graduate of Decatur Baptist College and Baylor University before attending Yale University and the University of Chicago. He joined The University of Texas faculty as an economics professor in 1919 but took leave to serve on the Texas Railroad Commission from March 1923 to August 1924. He left the commission to become president of the University in 1924 and served during the time that oil development of University lands was broadening the horizons of the University's future. He left the University in 1927 to become dean of the graduate school and director of political sciences at American University in Washington, D.C.

Harry Yandell Benedict, tenth president of the University, served from 1927 until his death on May 10, 1937. He graduated from U.T. with the B.S. degree in 1892 and later completed the Master's and Ph.D. degrees at Harvard. He joined the U.T. faculty in 1899 as a teacher of mathematics and astronomy, and he also served as director of extension, dean of men, and dean of the College of Arts and Sciences. Under his presidency, the University undertook a building program that added fifteen buildings to the campus. Even so, he held steadfastly to the doctrine "that men are more important than mortar, that learning is more precious than land, and that character is more essential than oil." This portrait was painted by Wayman Adams.

John William Calhoun (*top left*) served as president ad interim of the University from 1937 until 1939. A U.T. graduate in 1901, he came back to the University in 1909 as a mathematics instructor. In 1925 he became comptroller and supervised oil production, investment of funds, and erection of buildings.

Homer Price Rainey (*top right*) was president of the University from 1939 until 1944, when he was fired by the Board of Regents by a six-to-two vote during a dispute about academic freedom. Rainey, a native Texan, received the M.A. and Ph.D. degrees from the University of Chicago.

James Clay Dolley (*center right*), a native of Illinois, came to U.T. in 1928 after completing a Ph.D. degree in economics at the University of California, Berkeley. He served as acting president in 1952. In addition to being professor of banking and investments, he was vice-president for fiscal affairs, 1955–1960, and vice-chancellor for fiscal affairs, 1960–1966.

Theophilus Shickel Painter (*bottom*), a Virginian, received the Ph.D. degree from Yale in 1913. After postdoctoral work at the University of Würzburg, he was appointed adjunct professor of zoology in 1916 at U.T., where he remained for the next fifty years. In 1944 he was appointed acting president of the University, and from 1946 to 1952 he served as president. He resigned in 1952 but continued as professor of zoology until his retirement in 1966.

121

The University of Texas has had five chancellors. James Pinckney Hart (*right*), the first chancellor, occupied the position from the time it was created in 1950 until his resignation on December 31, 1953. On January 1, 1954, President Logan Wilson (*left*) became president and acting chancellor until September 30, 1954, at which time the chancellorship was abolished, and he remained as president of the Main University and System. In September 1960, the chancellorship was re-established, and President Wilson became chancellor. On the same date, the title of the chief executive officer of the Main University was changed to president, and Harry Huntt Ransom (*center*) was named to that position. On April 1, 1961, Wilson resigned as chancellor and Ransom became chancellor, continuing to serve as acting president until Joseph R. Smiley was named president. In 1963 the presidency was abolished and Ransom served in a dual position until 1967, when the presidency was re-established. Ransom resigned from the chancellorship on December 31, 1970, and became chancellor emeritus on January 1, 1971, a position he retained until his death in April 1976.

Joseph Royall Smiley (*top left*) was president from 1961 to 1963. He came to the University in 1960 as vice-president and provost. A native Texan, he received the Ph.D. degree from Columbia University.

Norman Hackerman (*top right*), a native of Maryland and a graduate of Johns Hopkins, came to the University as assistant professor of chemistry in 1945 and became a full professor in 1950. He served as vice-president and provost from 1961 to 1963, vice-chancellor for academic affairs from 1963 to 1967, and president from 1967 to 1970, when he resigned to become president of Rice University.

Bryce Jordan (*bottom*), who received his first degree from U.T., came back in 1965 as chairman of the Mu-

sic Department. He was the first vice-president for student affairs (1968–1970) and served as president ad interim in 1970–1971. He became the first president of The University of Texas at Dallas in 1971.

Stephen Hopkins Spurr (*top left*) was appointed president of The University of Texas at Austin in 1971 and was fired by Chancellor Charles LeMaistre and the Board of Regents in September 1974. He came to Texas from the University of Michigan, where he had been since 1952. His Ph.D. degree in forestry was from Yale University. He now teaches in the Lyndon B. Johnson School of Public Affairs.

Charles A. LeMaistre, M.D. (*top right*), has been affiliated with the U.T. System administration since 1966, when he was appointed vice-chancellor for health affairs. Subsequently, he served as executive vice-chancellor for health affairs, May 1968 to June 1969; deputy chancellor, June 1969 to July 1970; chancellor-elect, July 1970 to December 1970; and chancellor, January 1, 1971, to August 1, 1978. He left the chancellorship to become president of The University of Texas System Cancer Center in Houston.

Lorene Lane Rogers, a native Texan with a Ph.D. degree from U.T., came to the staff in 1950 as a research scientist with the Clayton Foundation Biochemical Institute. She was associate dean of the Graduate School from 1964 to 1971 and vice-president from 1971 to 1974. In September 1974, she was appointed president ad interim and in September 1975 became the first woman president of a major university. She retired from the presidency in August 1979.

Peter Tyrrell Flawn (*left*), an internationally known geologist who is a former president of U.T. San Antonio and a long-time member of the U.T. Austin faculty, became president on September 1, 1979. With a B.A. degree from Oberlin and a Ph.D. degree from Yale, Flawn began his administration with vigor, pledging a "War on Mediocrity."

Everitt Donald Walker (*right*) joined the U.T. System administration in 1965. He has served as director of facilities planning and construction, vice-chancellor for business affairs, executive vice-chancellor for business affairs, executive vice-chancellor for fiscal affairs, deputy chancellor for administration, and deputy chancellor. In July 1977, he was named the first president of the U.T. System, and, after LeMaistre left the chancellorship, Walker became acting chancellor and also retained the title of president until April 7, 1978, when he became chancellor and the position of president of the System was abolished.

The Faculty Council was organized in 1945. Members of that first council (*top*) included (*left to right, bottom row*) W. F. Gidley, C. M. Rosenquist, H. T. Parlin, T. S. Painter, M. R. Gutsch, Donald Coney, and C. D. Simmons; (*middle section*) T. H. Shelby, R. J. Williams, C. A. Smith, C. R. Granberry, Byron Short, W. P. Webb, J. W. Calhoun, Roy Bedichek, W. R. Woolrich (*above*), M. Y. Colby (*below*), E. J. Mathews, C. T. McCormick, Loren Mozley, Fredrick Duncalf, H. A. Calkins, C. E. Ayres, and J. G. Umstattd; (*top row*) P. M. Ferguson, A. P. Brogan, H. N. Smith, J. J. Jones, Philip Graham, and J. N. Thompson. Absent were J. Alton Burdine, E. W. Doty, H. J. Ettlinger, W. A. Felsing, J. A. Fitzgerald, B. F. Pittenger, and R. C. Stephenson.

Members of the 1979–1980 University Council are shown in the bottom picture. The University Council, formed in 1969, consists of twenty-five administrative members ex officio with vote and two without vote; fifty-three voting members of the General Faculty; and six students with vote. The president presides at council meetings, and the secretary of the General Faculty serves as ex officio secretary of the council. The University Council initiates legislation, acts on recommendations presented to it, and may conduct studies and investigations. The faculty members of the council form the Faculty Senate, a "separate forum for free discussion and decision regarding a broad range of matters of importance to the University . . ."

Until the College of Arts and Sciences was divided in 1970, it was always the largest college in the University in numbers of students and faculty. It grew out of the Academic Department (1883–1891); the Department of Literature, Science, and Arts (1891–1906); and the College of Arts (1906–1921). Some of its faculty in 1930 included (*left to right, bottom row*) D. B. Casteel, Paul M. Batchelder, W. J. Battle, E. R. Sims, Milton R. Gutsch, H. R. Henze, and Fred M. Bullard; (*top row*) E. M. Clard, L. M. Hollander, J. E. Pearce, E. T. Mitchell, F. A. C. Perrin, and Roger J. Williams.

Hanson Tufts Parlin came to U.T. in 1908 as an instructor in English after taking the Ph.D. degree at the University of Pennsylvania. For twenty-one years (1929–1950) he was dean of the College of Arts and Sciences.

127

Charles Paul Boner (*top left*), who did his undergraduate work at U.T. and earned a Ph.D. degree at Harvard, came to the University as a physics tutor in 1920. He served as dean of the College of Arts and Sciences, 1949–1954; dean of the University, 1953–1954; and vice-president for academic affairs, 1954–1957. An acoustics expert, he was famed as a maker of pipe organs and as an organist.

John Alton Burdine (*top right*) was dean of the College of Arts and Sciences from 1957 to 1966 after having been vice-president during the Rainey years. He succeeded Harry H. Ransom, who was dean from 1954 to 1957 and who then served as vice-president and provost from 1957 to 1960, when he became president (see p. 122).

John R. Silber is shown here addressing faculty members in the College of Arts and Sciences in 1970 shortly before he was fired as dean, a position he held from 1967 to 1970. A music major who turned philosopher, he held graduate degrees from Yale and came to Texas as a young professor in 1955. Brilliant, impatient, and extremely noticeable from the outset, he had no time for mediocrity, and his classroom performances won him several teaching awards.

The College of Arts and Sciences was divided in 1970 into three colleges and a division. Stanley R. Ross (*top left*), who came to U.T. in 1968 as professor of history and director of the Institute of Latin American Studies, was appointed provost for the arts and sciences. He was vice-president and provost from 1973 to 1976 and served as chairman of the University's bicentennial committee in 1976.

The first deans of the divided College of Arts and Sciences (*bottom*) were Samuel P. Ellison, Jr., geology (*left*), College of Natural Sciences; James W. McKie, economics (*center*), College of Social and Behavioral Sciences; Stanley N. Werbow, Germanic languages (*right*), College of Humanities; and James R. Roach, government (shown on p. 146), Division of General and Comparative Studies.

In April 1978, the Board of Regents voted unanimously to reunite the Colleges of Humanities and of Social and Behavioral Sciences and the Division of General and Comparative Studies. A new College of Liberal Arts became operational on January 1, 1979, with Robert D. King (*top right*) as dean. King, an internationally known scholar of historical linguistics who joined the faculty in 1965, had been dean of the College of Social and Behavioral Sciences since 1976.

The Academic Department, established in 1883, included the natural sciences. J. W. Mallet, first chairman of the faculty, was a chemistry professor. The faculty members presented on the next six pages are among those who, through the years, helped to develop the various departments in the natural sciences at the University. Unfortunately, space limits the inclusion of all who were of significance.

William Tyler Mather (*top left*) came to U.T. as an associate professor of physics in 1897 and was promoted to full professor in 1906.

John M. Kuehne (*top right*), professor of physics, held two degrees from U.T. and became a tutor in 1900. His Ph.D. degree was from the University of Chicago. He

was also noted for his work in photography, and some of his early photographs are used in this book.

Herman Joseph Muller (*bottom left*), professor of zoology who came to U.T. in 1920, is shown in his laboratory. He engaged in genetics research conducted by breeding experiments on the fruit fly Drosophila. He became a Nobel laureate after he left U.T. in 1936.

Osmond Philip Breland (*bottom right*), zoology, became an instructor in 1938. He is shown photographing mosquito chromosomes in his laboratory.

Mary Edna Gearing (*top left*) came to U.T. in 1912. She was professor of home economics and also served as the head of the Department of Home Welfare in the Division of Education. The home economics building is named for her.

Frederic William Simonds (*top center*) came to the University in 1890 as the only geology teacher on the faculty. He spent fifty years on the campus building the Geology Department into one of the finest in the nation.

Roy Bedichek (*top right*) was long-time head of the Texas Interscholastic League and a naturalist with a philosophic bent. Between his seventieth and eightieth birthdays, he wrote four books that assured him an in-

ternational reputation among nature lovers and philosophers of competition. He was the senior member of the triumvirate that included Walter Prescott Webb and J. Frank Dobie and that dominated Texas letters and thought in the middle twentieth century.

William Albert Noyes, Jr. (*bottom left*), was Ashbel Smith Professor of Chemistry from 1963 to 1973, when he retired.

Malcolm Young Colby (*bottom right*), professor of physics, came to U.T. in 1924.

Paul M. Bachelder (*top left*), a mathematician, served one stint as department chairman. An avid walker, Cosine Red, as students called him, was one of the most familiar sights around Austin in the 1930s and 1940s.

Robert L. Moore (*top right*) was another man with significant influence in building the Mathematics Department. He received the B.S. and M.A. degrees from The University of Texas and the Ph.D. degree from Chicago. He taught at U.T. from 1920 until his retirement in 1969. In 1931–1932, he was the first American mathematician chosen by the American Mathematical Society to be its visiting lecturer. The University named its new physics-mathematics-astronomy building in his honor in 1973.

Hyman Joseph Ettlinger (*bottom left*) taught mathematics from 1913 to 1969 when he semi-retired. Once an assistant football coach, he served in 1928–1930 as acting director of intercollegiate athletics. Now, more than sixty-five years since he joined the faculty, he still comes to his office.

Harry Schultz Vandiver (*bottom right*) taught at the University from 1924 until he retired in 1966. The author of more than 175 scholarly articles, he contributed to such fields as number theory, finite algebras, fields, rings, and groups. Throughout his career he received numerous research appointments and in 1931 won the prestigious Frank Cole Prize of the American Mathematical Society.

William R. Muehlberger (*top left*), geological sciences, is one of U.T.'s links with the astronauts. He served as principal investigator of the field geology investigations for the Apollo 16 and 17 lunar landing missions of the National Aeronautics and Space Administration. He has been on the faculty since February 1954 and served as chairman of the Geology Department from 1966 until 1971.

Robert Todd Gregory (*left*), professor of computer science and mathematics, and David M. Young, Jr. (*right*), director of the computation center, were discussing their work in 1961.

Fred M. Bullard (*bottom left*), one of the world's leading experts on volcanoes, was professor of geological sciences from 1924 to 1971, when he became emeritus.

S. Leroy Brown (*bottom right*), physics, was working in his laboratory in 1940 when this picture was taken. He became a member of the faculty in 1911.

133

Alfred Schild (*top left*), professor of mathematics and physics (1957–1977), was Ashbel Smith Professor of Physics at the time of his death. A series of lectures has been dedicated to him.

Walter K. Long (*top right*), an Austin physician, has been a lecturer in zoology since 1964.

Roger J. Williams (*center left*), professor of chemistry since 1939 and director of the Clayton Foundation Biochemical Institute from 1941 to 1963, discovered pantothenic acid, an important member of the vitamin B family. He also concentrated and christened folic acid, another B vitamin, in his pioneering studies of vitamins and nutrition. While he was director of the Biochemical Institute, more vitamins and their vari-

ants were developed there than in any laboratory in the world. His books continue to sell throughout the world.

Robert E. Greenwood (*center right*) has taught mathematics at the University since 1938, except for leaves of absence during World War II and the Korean War. He is noted for his unique classroom presentations.

Margaret Eppright (*bottom left*), home economics and education, was chairman of the Home Economics Department from 1961 to 1971.

Lucy Rathbone (*bottom right*) was professor of home economics, 1922–1961.

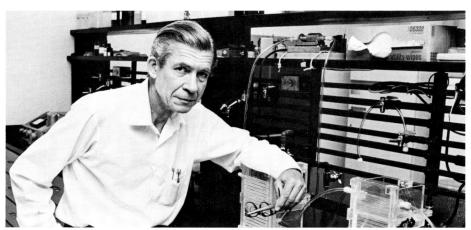

William Shive (*top left*), chemistry, came to U.T. in 1937. He was department chairman, 1965–1967.

A. Raymond Schrank (*top center*), zoology, has been a member of the faculty since 1939. He was acting dean of the College of Natural Sciences from 1972 until 1974 and again in 1976. He served as dean from 1977 until 1980.

Gerard F. Moseley (*top right*), an astronomer, was assistant dean of the College of Natural Sciences from 1972 until 1978. He was active in helping to develop the role of student dean in the colleges.

William T. Guy, Jr. (*bottom left*), mathematics and education, came to the University in 1945.

Gerhard J. Fonken (*bottom right*), professor of chemistry, has been at U.T. since 1959. He has served the University in many ways—as chairman of important committees, as associate provost, as acting vice-president for academic affairs, as executive assistant to the president, and currently as vice-president for academic affairs and research.

The original Academic Department included the humanities—rhetoric and English literature, Greek, Latin, modern languages, and philosophy. Prominent professors in the humanities have contributed to the greatness of the University; only a few can be shown here.

Lee Hollander (*top left*), professor of Germanic languages and a translator of Norse sagas, came to the University in 1921 to remain for a half-century.

Jessie Andrews (*top right*) was the first woman to matriculate in the University, the first woman to graduate, and the first woman to be employed as a teacher. She remained an active member of the School (later Department) of Germanic Languages until 1918.

W. E. Metzenthin (*bottom left*), a German scholar, came to the University in 1906. He once served as an assistant coach.

Morgan Callaway, Jr. (*bottom right*), began teaching English at U.T. in 1890 and rose to be senior professor and actual, if not titular, head of the English Department.

Lilia Mary Casis (*top left*), professor of romance languages, came to the University in 1895. She served as dean of women from 1919 until 1921. One of the state's best elementary schools, located in Austin, is named for Miss Casis and her sister.

Two other professors of romance languages who served long tenure were Aaron Schaffer (*top right*), who came to the University in 1920, and Carl Alvin Swanson (*top center*), who came in 1924.

Reginald Harvey Griffith (*bottom left*) was a world-acclaimed scholar in the literature of Alexander Pope and his circle. Associated with The University of Texas from 1902 until his retirement in 1951, he was an outstanding scholar and teacher. His enthusiasm and inspiration were largely responsible for the founding of the Rare Books Collections, which later formed the nucleus of the Humanities Research Center. His interest and encouragement were major factors in the establishment of the University of Texas Press.

Killis Campbell (*bottom right*) taught at the University from the turn of the century until he died in 1937. His first love as a scholar lay in the literature of the Middle Ages, but in the classroom he was drawn to the study of American literature, with a special interest in Edgar Allan Poe.

Katherine Wheatley (*top left*), professor of French and Italian from 1917 to 1963, wrote the standard work on French tragic dramatist Racine.

L. L. Click (*top right*), professor of English, served as assistant dean of the College of Arts and Sciences from 1928 until 1954, when he became dean of the student division of the college for one year before he retired from that position. He taught English from 1919 until 1960, when he became professor emeritus.

Rudolph Willard (*center*) was professor of English from 1937 to 1964.

T. V. Smith (*bottom left*), who held two degrees from the University, taught philosophy from 1919 to 1921 and then went to the University of Chicago where he later was instrumental in organizing and producing, and moderated, a famed and influential program in educational radio, the "University of Chicago Round Table," the oldest educational program continuously broadcast.

Edgar C. Polomé (*bottom right*) has been a professor of Oriental and African languages since 1960 and has taught in the University's distinguished Department of Linguistics.

J. Frank Dobie, a U.T. legend and sometimes cause, was an excellent storyteller, folklorist, and artist. His firing by the regents in 1947 after his return from a visiting lectureship at Cambridge University provoked a University crisis and made him a student hero. A prolific writer with more than a score of books still in print, Dobie left his beloved Paisano Ranch to the University.

James B. Wharey (*top right*), specialist in John Bunyan, came to the University in 1912 and rose through various ranks to a graduate professorship and the chairmanship of the English Department.

Robert Adger Law (*bottom right*), father of a future regent, came to the University as a young Harvard graduate in 1906. His numerous publications in the field of Elizabethan literature and his eminence in national and regional modern language societies served to identify him with the best traditions of American scholarship. His popularity as a professor was manifested by the large enrollment in his classes on Shakespeare.

Harry Joshua Leon (*top left*), classical languages, became an instructor at U.T. in 1923 and retired as professor emeritus in 1967. He was department chairman for twenty years.

Wolfgang Michael (*top center*), Germanic languages, came to U.T. in 1946. The Goethe Medallion in Gold was awarded to him in 1973 for his outstanding contributions to the study of the German language, literature, and culture.

Pablo Max Ynsfran (*top right*), former minister from Paraguay to the United States, became visiting lecturer in the Department of Romance Languages in 1942 and continued teaching until his retirement in 1963. He served as a member of the Executive Committee of the

Institute of Latin American Studies for many years after the institute was organized in 1942.

Eugene D. Pendergraft (*left*) and Winfred P. Lehmann (*right*), in the bottom photograph, represent two of the reasons why the University's Department of Linguistics is rated among the best. Here, the two men are standing before a linguistics computer in 1964.

Theodore Andersson (*top left*), Spanish-Portuguese and education, came to the University in 1957 and revolutionized the teaching of Spanish in the public schools.

Ramón Martínez-López (*top center*), professor of Spanish and Portuguese from 1940 to 1971, was a native of Spain with all the charm and courtliness of a Spanish grandee.

Rajo Rao (*top right*), a distinguished Indian novelist and philosopher, came to U.T. in 1966 as a lecturer in philosophy. He is now a full professor. His most noted publication is *The Serpent and the Rope*, a philosophical, symbolic work which in 1964 won the Indian Academy of Letter's Sahitya Akademi Award for Literature. In 1972 he was selected as a Fellow of the Woodrow Wilson International Center for Scholars in Washington, D.C.

Douglas Morgan (*bottom*), professor of philosophy, coached the University's entry that won the national championship in TV's College Bowl competition for superior students. The Tower turned orange for their academic victory. Although he died prematurely, Morgan's impact on the University has lasted.

Edwin Bowden (*top left*), a member of the English Department since 1956, examines detective books, his specialty, at the Humanities Research Center.

David L. Miller (*top right*), professor of philosophy, came to U.T. in 1934. He served as chairman of the department from 1952 to 1959. His publications include a book about A. N. Whitehead and another on the theory of value and valuation.

Frederick H. Ginascol (*center left*), professor of philosophy, became a member of the faculty in the summer of 1952 as a half-time instructor and retired in 1973 as professor emeritus. An excellent classroom teacher, he expressed "real concern for the dignity and the needs of the students as individuals who cannot and must not be reduced to 'classes.'"

William A. Arrowsmith (*bottom left*), university professor in arts and letters and chairman of the Classics Department during the 1960s, received national recognition for his translation of Greek drama.

Willis Pratt (*bottom right*) joined the faculty in 1935. A professor of English, he published several books and monographs and many articles on the English Romantic poets.

History was the only department of the former College of Social and Behavioral Sciences (now part of the College of Liberal Arts) included in the original Academic Department. Political science was added in the early 1890s, and the behavioral sciences came later. The Department of History—the "old department," as it is generally dubbed—set a record for continuity. A majority of its members who joined the department between 1900 and 1918 remained into the 1950s and 1960s. They included (*left to right, first row*) Rudolph L. Biesele, Thad Weed Riker, Eugene C. Barker (department head), and Frederic Duncalf; (*second row*) Charles W. Ramsdell, Charles W. Hackett, Milton R. Gutsch, Walter Prescott Webb, and Frank Burr Marsh.

At the top are three early professors in the department, Leslie Waggener, George Pierce Garrison (for whom Garrison Hall is named), and Lester G. Bugbee, the first man to make a systematic study of Texas history.

Joe B. Frantz, first occupant of the Walter Prescott Webb Chair in History, was visiting in 1964 with Arthur Schlesinger, Jr., a guest speaker on the campus.

143

Milton R. Gutsch (*top left*) began his career at the University in 1912 as an instructor in British history. Noted for his ability as a teacher, in 1927 he became chairman of the Department of History; in 1928 he was made secretary of the General Faculty; and in 1944 he became secretary of the first Faculty Council. He held these administrative positions until he retired in 1951.

Robert H. Montgomery (*top right*), professor of economics, came to the University in 1922. He was perhaps the sharpest debater in the University's history, and accounts of his jousts with legislative investigating committees and University administrators are legend. Students adored him and flocked to his courses.

Arnold Toynbee (*bottom left*), a guest on the U.T. campus in the early 1960s, talks with one of U.T.'s greatest, Walter Prescott Webb—scholar, writer, philosopher, renowned historian.

From the 1930s to the 1960s, Ione Spears taught history of Western civilization for freshmen. Her strict requirement that each student keep a notebook and her lectures on manners and morals made her unforgettable. She talks here with Walter Long, known for many years as "Mr. Austin."

144

Caleb Perry Patterson (*top left*), colorful, outspoken professor of government whose trademarks were an ever-present cigar, a beaver hat (in the winter), and a booming voice, came to the University in 1919. Possessor of thirteen academic degrees, Dr. Pat was a lifetime Jeffersonian student and a prolific writer. He is shown here at a retirement party with Dr. H. Frank Connally, Jr., U.T. regent, and Mrs. Howard Calkins.

O. Douglas Weeks (*top right*), professor of government, first taught at the University in 1924–1925. After a year's interval, in 1926 he returned to Texas, where he taught until his retirement in 1966. He served as chairman of the department and conducted research on Mexicans in Texas politics and on Texas voting patterns.

Standish Meacham, history, and Frank Bash, astronomy, conduct a class session in 1975 (*bottom left*).

William H. Goetzmann (*bottom right*), Stiles Professor of American Studies and professor of history, won the Pulitzer award in 1967 for his book *Exploration and Empire*.

Dr. Henry Bullock (*top left*), history, was one of the first black professors at U.T. He was the 1969 recipient of Columbia University's Bancroft Prize, a $4,000 award, for the publication of *A History of Negro Education in the South*. By nature one of the gentlest of men, he was also one of the firmest in insisting on black recognition.

James R. Roach (*top right*), an expert on government in India, has been a member of the faculty and administrative staff since 1949. A professor of government since 1965, he has also been director of special programs (1965–1969), vice-provost and dean of interdisciplinary programs (1971–1972), and dean of general and comparative studies (1972–1974).

Walt Whitman Rostow, professor of economics and history, has been an adviser to presidents since the Eisenhower years. A graduate of Yale University and a Rhodes Scholar, he was perhaps best known as President Johnson's special assistant for national security affairs from 1966 to 1969; earlier he served in the Kennedy and Johnson administrations as chairman of the State Department's Policy Planning Council. He is the first Rex G. Baker Professor of Political Economy. His wife, Elspeth, currently dean of the Lyndon B. Johnson School of Public Affairs, is also an incisive teacher and administrator. Here the two teach a televised class in 1976 in problems of the American presidency.

Harry E. Moore (*top left*), distinguished professor of sociology, was a member of the faculty from 1937 until his death in 1966. The Research Collection for the Study of Human Response to Disaster is named for him because of his own significant contributions.

Emmette S. Redford (*top right*), Ashbel Smith Professor of Government and professor in the Lyndon B. Johnson School of Public Affairs, came to U.T. in 1928. He has periodically held positions in national government since the days of Franklin D. Roosevelt.

Clarence E. Ayres, professor of economics from 1930 to 1969, was on the national committee of the American Civil Liberties Union for twenty years. He was also director of the consumers' division of the U.S. Depart-

ment of Labor in 1936 and, in 1950–1953, a member of the Commission of Southwest Economy for the President's Council of Economic Advisers.

William S. Livingston (*bottom left*) came to U.T. in 1949 as assistant professor of government. He became chairman of the department in 1965 and then served as vice-chancellor for academic programs from 1969 to 1970. After serving as chairman of comparative studies and chairman of the Faculty Senate, he became vice-president and dean of graduate studies.

Clifton Grubbs (*bottom right*), the Sue Killam Professor in the Foundation of Economics, came to U.T. in 1965.

Américo Paredes (*top left*), a University graduate, has been a member of the faculty since 1957. Professor of anthropology and English, he was director of the Center for Intercultural Studies in Folklore, 1967–1970, and editor of the *Journal of American Folklore*, 1968–1973.

J. Gilbert McAllister (*top right*), anthropology, came to the University in 1935 and became professor emeritus in 1969.

Michael G. Hall (*center left*), currently serving as chairman of the History Department, has been at U.T. since 1959.

Janet Taylor Spence (*center right*), professor of psychology at U.T. since 1967, served as chairperson of the department in 1971–1972. Spence and Robert Helmreich, also professor of psychology, have conducted extensive research on masculinity and femininity.

Karl M. Dallenbach (*bottom left*), psychology, taught at U.T. for twenty-one years. He was former editor-owner of the *American Journal of Psychology*, the oldest existing psychology journal.

Ira Iscoe, 1951–present, professor of psychology and education and director of the Counseling Psychological Services Center from 1968 to 1978; John Silber; and Richard Blair, music, were attending a Faculty Council meeting in 1966.

In 1894, the Department (later College) of Engineering was inaugurated. Prior to that date, students studying engineering did so in the Academic Department. Twelve students graduated as engineers between 1888 and 1893. T. U. Taylor (*top center*) became the first dean of engineering and served until he retired in 1936. He is shown with the first engineering graduate (H. P. Hunnicutt, B.S., 1888) and the thousandth (Robert Lee Lowry, Jr., B.S. in C.E., 1929).

The College of Engineering faculty in 1931 included (*left to right, bottom row*) H. E. Degler, E. C. H. Bantel, R. Everett, T. U. Taylor (dean), Goldwin Goldsmith, and J. A. Correll; (*second row*) R. L. White, W. T. Rolfe, P. M. Ferguson, J. W. Ramsey, J. A. Focht, and W. H. McNeill; (*third row*) M. S. Bowen, S. P. Finch, L. Barclay, B. N. Gafford, Read Granberry, and H. L. McMath; (*top row*) J. D. McFarland, M. B. Reed, Banks McLaurin, M. A. Thomas, J. L. Bruns, and Carl J. Eckhardt.

Willis R. Woolrich (*top left*) was the second dean of the College of Engineering, serving from 1937 until he retired in 1958 as dean emeritus. His most important contribution was obtaining accreditation for the College of Engineering. Graduate programs in engineering were improved, and the first Ph.D. in Engineering degree was awarded.

Ervin S. Perry (*top right*) was the first black professor employed by the University (1964). His premature death in 1970 cut short a promising career in the College of Engineering. Named to receive posthumously the first Young Engineer of the Year award of the National Society of Professional Engineers, he is the Perry for whom the Perry-Castañeda Library is named.

Stanley P. Finch (*bottom, right*), professor of civil engineering, was presented an award when he retired in 1952 after a forty-seven–year career at the University. He served as departmental chairman from 1937 to 1943 and was one of the first two engineering faculty named to the Graduate Faculty.

Earnest F. Gloyna (*top left*), environmental health engineering professor, has been dean of the College of Engineering since 1970. He came to the University as an instructor in 1947 but left in 1950 to complete a doctorate. He returned to U.T. in 1952 and applied his energies to development of a program in environmental health engineering. A member of the National Academy of Engineering, he has also served as director of the Environmental Health Engineering Research Laboratories at the Balcones Research Center and of the Center for Research in Water Resources.

John McKetta (*top right*), another member of the National Academy of Engineering, was dean of the College of Engineering from 1963 to 1969. He served as vice-chancellor for academic affairs for the U.T. System in 1969–1970, and, since 1970, he has been E. P. Schoch Professor of Chemical Engineering. Billy Amstead (*left*) was acting dean of the College of Engineering in 1969–1970. William Walsh Hagerty (*center*) was dean of the college from 1959 until 1963. Most of his last year on the campus was spent raising research funds, reorganizing research along interdisciplinary lines, recruiting new faculty, and strengthening the graduate program.

Alexander Fredericke Claire (*bottom, center*), patron saint of U.T. engineers, toasts a group of his admirers. The original Alex was "borrowed" from Jacoby's Beer Garden on Lavaca Street in 1908 by a group of students.

M. J. Thompson (*top left*), aeronautical engineering, checks the supersonic wind tunnel after a simulated flight before men made space flights. A professor at the University since 1941, he helped develop the Department of Aeronautical Engineering and the Department of Engineering Mechanics and has served as chairman of both.

E. P. Schoch (*right*) is considered to be the father of chemical engineering for the entire South, as well as a pioneer in bringing the chemical industry to the South. In 1896, he began teaching at the University, continuing until his retirement fifty-seven years later. Schoch organized the first Longhorn Band, supplied its instruments, and was its first director. William A. Cun-

ningham (*left*) taught chemical engineering from 1929 until 1974 and served on numerous faculty-student committees.

Kenneth Jehn (*center left*), professor of meteorology, studies a weather map in 1965. He became an instructor in 1946.

James E. Stice (*bottom left*), who came to U.T. in 1968, is professor of engineering education and director of the University's Center for Teaching Effectiveness.

The Law Department (called School after 1920) was organized at the same time the Academic Department was inaugurated in September 1883. Oran M. Roberts (see p. 115) and Robert S. Gould (not pictured) were the first two law professors.

William Stewart Simkins (*top left*), a colonel in the Confederate Army, joined the law faculty in 1899 and began a thirty-year tenure as the Law School's most colorful character. Simkins' long white hair, his love of applause, his traditional lecture on the Ku Klux Klan, his encounter with Carry Nation on the campus in 1903, and his tobacco became part of University folklore. He became professor emeritus in 1923 but continued to lecture once a week until his death in 1929.

John Charles Townes (*top right*) was appointed professor of law in 1896 and was made the first dean of the Law Department in 1902. After a year, he resigned to give full time to teaching. In 1907, he was reappointed dean and held that position until August 1923, when he again resigned. Townes Hall is named for him.

Charles T. McCormick (*bottom left*) became a professor of law in 1922 and was dean 1941–1950.

Ira Polk Hildebrand (*bottom right*) became professor of law at U.T. in 1907. Made dean of the Law School in 1924, he substituted the case method of teaching for the textbook method, supervised the enlarging of the curriculum, and established a Legal Aid Clinic.

Members of the Law School faculty in 1930 included (*left to right, bottom row*) A. W. Walker, Lucy Moore, Dean Ira Hildebrand, Helen Hargrave, Mattie Dodson, and Robert W. Stayton; (*top row*) Joseph A. Wickes, Bryant Smith, John E. Hallen, George W. Stumberg, D. F. Bobbitt, and Sol Goodell.

Robert Weldon Stayton (*top right*), a U.T. graduate in 1907, became professor of law in 1925 and, through his students, did much to influence changes in judicial procedure in Texas.

W. Page Keeton (*bottom left*), a U.T. graduate, became a member of the Law School faculty in 1932. He served as dean from 1950 until he retired in 1975. The first professorship to honor an active faculty member

was named for him. A specialist in torts, he was selected as a Fellow of the American Bar Foundation in 1961, and he has been honored by students on numerous occasions.

Ernest E. Smith III (*center right*), who came to U.T. as assistant professor in 1963, served as dean of the Law School from 1975 to 1979.

John F. Sutton, Jr. (*bottom right*), was made professor of law in 1957 and became dean in 1979. Sutton, who holds the endowed Joseph C. Hutcheson Professorship of Law, is a specialist in evidence, legal ethics, and torts.

Members of the Law School faculty in 1955 included (*left to right, front row*) Corwin W. Johnson, Leon Green, Edward W. Bailey, Leo G. Blackstock, W. Page Keeton (dean), Gus M. Hodges, Marion K. Woodward, Helen Hargrave, Charles T. McCormick, Earl K. Adams, Joseph P. Witherspoon, F. Lanier Cox, Robert W. Stayton, and George W. Stumberg; (*back row*) Julius F. Franki, Millard H. Ruud, Warner A. Hancock, Keith E. Morrison, Jack Proctor, Gaynor Kendall, Jerre S. Williams, William F. Young, William F. Fritz, Hubert W. Smith, Woodrow W. Patterson, Joseph T. Sneed, Gray Thoron, and William O. Huie.

Parker C. Fielder (*center left*), a former *Cactus* outstanding student at The University of Texas, is the

W. H. Francis, Jr., Professor of Law. He first became a member of the faculty in 1948, left to practice law, and returned to teach in 1961.

A. Wilson Walker (*bottom left*), a U.T. graduate, began teaching in the Law School in 1925. He was a specialist in oil and gas law.

Charles Alan Wright (*bottom right*), a member of the U.T. law faculty since 1955, is recognized as one of the foremost constitutional lawyers in the United States. When President Richard Nixon's problems with the Watergate tapes impended, the White House sent for Wright as the one man most likely to understand the constitutional problems involved. Wright was chairman of the Faculty Senate from 1969 to 1973.

For a number of years, Charles Alan Wright has coached an intramural football team composed of law students. In this picture, he and his team forget the courtroom and the classroom for a pleasant fall afternoon of play.

Dean Page Keeton (*seated, second from right*) and Associate Dean T. J. Gibson (*standing, right*) are shown in 1962 with some prominent members of the Law School Foundation: (*left to right, seated*) Robert Hanger, Robert Hardwicke, and Hines H. Baker; (*standing*) Gene Woodfin, St. John Garwood, Sylvan Lang, Jack Proctor, and Elton Hyder.

Leon Green (*top left*), a U.T. graduate, taught intermittently at the University from 1911 into the 1970s. His reputation in the field of torts made him one of the most distinguished professors on the faculty.

Gus M. Hodges (*top center*), a graduate of U.T., began teaching in 1940 and retired from full service in 1976. A unique and colorful character, he became a legend to law students. He is a specialist in court procedure.

Helen Hargrave (*top right*), who began at U.T. as a publications secretary in 1928, later became law librarian and taught legal bibliography. Sitting with her (*right*) is Madge Keeton.

Leon Lebowitz (*bottom left*) has been professor of law at U.T. since 1954.

Jerre Stockton Williams (*bottom center*) joined U.T. in 1946. From 1967 to 1970, he was on leave to be the first chairman of the Administrative Conference of the United States. As president of the Association of American Law Schools, he is the fourth from U.T. to hold this position. Others were John Townes, Charles T. McCormick, and Page Keeton. In 1980, Williams was appointed to the U.S. Fifth Circuit Court of Appeals.

Byron Fullerton (*center right*) joined the Law School faculty in 1963 and is currently serving as associate dean for continuing legal education for the Law School.

Roy Mersky (*bottom right*) came to U.T. in 1965. Currently law librarian, he has also been a consultant to the Israelis.

Architectural education at U.T. was started in 1910 when Dean T. U. Taylor of the Engineering Department asked Hugo F. Kuehne to start a School of Architecture. Kuehne was made adjunct professor and was the only teacher in the school, which consisted of fifteen students in a drafting room in the west wing of the second floor of the old Engineering Building (now Student Services Building).

In 1912, F. E. Giesecke (*top left*) was appointed chairman of the school, and the following year the first degree in architecture was granted to his son, Bertram.

By 1927, enrollment was so large that new quarters were needed, and the department (changed from school after 1920) was moved to B. Hall. In 1928, Goldwin Goldsmith (*top right*), for whom the architecture building is named, assumed duties as chairman.

The architecture faculty gathered for a photograph in 1955.

Goldsmith resigned as chairman in 1935 and was succeeded by Walter T. Rolfe (*bottom left*), who served as chairman until spring 1946, when he resigned to enter practice in Houston.

Hugh L. McMath (*bottom right*), who came in 1929, was named chairman after Rolfe resigned and was appointed director of the School of Architecture when it was established in February 1948 as a division of the College of Engineering. He also served as acting director of the school in 1955–1956.

J. Robert Buffler discusses an architectural design problem in the early 1940s with Samuel E. Gideon, while a group of students observe.

Harwell H. Harris (*bottom left*) served as director of the School of Architecture from 1951, when the school became autonomous, until 1955.

Werner W. Dornberger (*bottom right*), architectural engineering professor, helped guide the University through one of its most ambitious building programs. He was architect and chief engineer for the original buildings at McDonald Observatory and helped with the construction of the Texas Union, Hogg Memorial Auditorium, Texas Memorial Museum, and John Sealy Hospital at the Medical Branch in Galveston.

Philip Douglas Creer (*top left*) was director of the School of Architecture from 1956 to 1969.

Charles Burnette (*top center*) was dean from 1973 to 1976.

Reynelle M. Parkins (*top right*)—environmentalist, architect, and theologian—was a member of the faculty from 1968 until 1975.

Alan Y. Taniguchi (*bottom left*) was dean of the School of Architecture from 1969 to 1972, when he moved to Rice University. Sinclair Black then served briefly as acting dean.

J. Harold Box (*bottom right*) became dean of the school in 1976. John E. Gallery served as acting dean for a short period prior to Box's appointment.

The College of Education had its origin as a Department of Pedagogy in the Department of Literature, Science, and Arts in 1891. Joseph Baldwin was the first professor. In 1905 the Department of Pedagogy became the School (later to become College) of Education.

William Seneca Sutton and A. Caswell Ellis succeeded Baldwin in 1897. Sutton (*top left*) was president ad interim of the University in 1923–1924. A graduate of the University of Arkansas, he came to U.T. as an instructor. He was made dean of the School of Education in 1909.

A. Caswell Ellis (*top right*) served as professor of philosophy and psychology of education at the University for thirty-seven years before he went to Western Re-serve University. He returned in 1941 as a part-time staff member.

School of Education professors gathered for a photograph in 1931.

Benjamin Floyd Pittenger (*bottom left*) was dean from 1926 until 1947, when he retired. He also served as dean of student life in 1926–1927.

Laurence Defee Haskew (*bottom right*) came to U.T. in 1947 as dean of the College of Education, a title he retained until 1962. He also served as vice-president of the University, 1954–1960, and vice-chancellor of the University System, 1961–1967, after which he was professor of educational administration. He is now professor emeritus.

Clyde C. Colvert (*top left*) came to U.T. as professor of junior college education in 1944. He served as professor and chairman of the Department of Educational Administration from 1946 to 1957 and was dean of the College of Education, 1962–1964. He is widely known as "Mr. Junior College."

Lorrin B. Kennamer, Jr. (*top center*), first came to U.T. in 1956 as professor of geography. He was associate dean of the College of Arts and Sciences from 1961 to 1967, when he left U.T. He returned in 1970 as dean of the College of Education.

Joseph Lindsey Henderson (*top right*) came to the University in 1906 as a "Visitor of Schools." He became full professor in 1912 after he received a Ph.D. degree from Columbia University.

Charles Flinn Arrowood (*bottom left*), an ordained Presbyterian minister, became professor of history and philosophy of education in 1928.

Two U.T. greats, D. A. Penick (*left*) and Frederick Eby (*right*). Penick, professor of Greek, coached the tennis team for more than fifty-five years. Eby, regarded as the father of the Texas junior college movement, was professor of history and philosophy of education. He joined the U.T. faculty in 1909 and was associated with the University almost sixty years.

Cora M. Martin (*top left*), professor of elementary education, taught at U.T. from 1927 to 1953.

Lynn W. McCraw (*top right*), professor of health, physical education, and recreation, served as head of the department before it was reorganized and renamed the Department of Physical and Health Education.

George I. Sánchez (*center left*) began teaching at U.T. in 1940 as professor of Latin American education. When he died in 1971, he was a professor in the Department of Cultural Foundations of Education.

Hob Gray (*bottom left*), whose Ph.D. degree was from U.T., became a member of the staff in 1933. For many years he was the placement officer for the College of Education.

H. Paul Kelley (*bottom right*), professor of educational psychology and a graduate of Princeton, is director of the Measurement and Evaluation Center. He came to the University as a freshman in 1946.

William G. Wolfe (*top left*) came to U.T. in 1961 as professor of educational psychology and director of the program of special education. He was chairman of the Educational Psychology Department, 1961–1965, and chairman of the Department of Special Education until 1969. Since 1969, he has continued to serve as professor of special education.

Anna Hiss (*top center*), for whom Anna Hiss Gymnasium is named, became instructor of physical training for women in 1919. She resigned in 1957 but was made professor emeritus in 1969.

Shiela O'Gara (*top right*), director of the Department of Physical Training for Women and director of women's intramural sports until her death in 1968, came to the University in 1932.

Arthur Henry Moehlman (*bottom*) came to U.T. in 1954 as professor of history and philosophy of education. A specialist in comparative education systems, he was director of the History of Education Center from 1966 until 1978.

The College of Business Administration was first created as a department of the College of Arts in 1912. In 1922 it became a separate school, and in 1945 it was reorganized as a college. The degree of Bachelor of Business Administration was first offered in 1916–1917. The Business Administration–Economics Building, completed in 1962, houses the College of Business Administration; the Graduate School of Business Building, located on the site of the old Law School, was completed in 1976.

Spurgeon Bell (*top left*) was the first dean of the School of Business Administration, from 1922 to 1925.

J. Anderson Fitzgerald (*top center*) served as dean of the school from 1926 to 1945, when the school became a college. He continued as dean until 1950.

William R. Spriegel (*top right*), dean from 1950 to 1959, came to the University from Northwestern University and from private industry.

Faculty members in the school in 1925 included (*left to right, bottom row*) Ralph J. Watkins, Florence Stullken, Spurgeon Bell, Mattie Fraser, and H. G. Guthman; (*top row*) E. Karl McGinnis, C. Aubrey Smith, A. H. Ribbink, B. M. Woodbridge, P. P. Winston, and A. F. Hughes.

John Arch White (*top left*) was acting dean of the College of Business Administration, 1959–1961, and was dean from 1961 until he retired in 1967.

George Kozmetsky (*top right*), dean of the College of Business Administration since 1967, saw the enrollment of the college grow from 3,577 in the fall of 1967 to 10,549 in the fall of 1979. Founder of the Teledyne Corporation, he has led the college forward, especially in the fields of graduate work and computer application.

Erich W. Zimmermann (*center left*), who became distinguished professor of economics in 1942, had a worldwide reputation for his knowledge of resources.

Jack Greer Taylor (*center right*), an honor graduate,

came to the staff in 1940 as an investment analyst. He was business manager of the University in 1951 and then served as associate professor in business administration.

E. Karl McGinnis (*bottom left*) came to U.T. as an adjunct professor in the Department of Business Services in 1918. He remained at U.T. until his retirement.

F. Lanier Cox (*bottom right*), now professor of general business and education, came to U.T. as a student in 1932. He began teaching in 1937 and served for eleven years in U.T. administration under Chancellors Wilson, Ransom, and LeMaistre. For years, he represented U.T. interests before the state legislature.

John R. Stockton (*top left*), a member of the Department of General Business, was director of the Bureau of Business Research from 1949 to 1969.

Rueben R. McDaniel, Jr. (*top right*), came to U.T. in 1970 as associate dean of students. He later served as associate dean of the College of Business Administration and currently is associate professor of management.

Charles T. Zlatkovich (*bottom left*), C. Aubrey Smith Professor in Accounting, projects a proposed University calendar before the Faculty Council in 1966. He first became an instructor at the University in 1940.

Eugene W. Nelson (*center right*), professor of general business, has been a member of the faculty since 1940. For a number of years he served as secretary of the General Faculty.

William P. Boyd (*bottom right*), an assistant in the president's office in 1925–1926, was a full professor in the College of Business Administration from 1950 to 1972.

Elizabeth Lanham (*top left*) was the first woman head of a department in a hitherto man's world—business—when she became chairman of the Department of Management in 1973. She has also been a member of the Athletic Council.

Stanley Arbingast (*top center*) retired in 1976 as director of the Bureau of Business Research, which was established in 1926. He is professor of marketing administration and geography.

Charles T. Clark (*top right*) came to U.T. in 1945 as assistant to the dean of men. He has also served as director of the student employment bureau and as director of nonacademic personnel. He is professor of general business and has been the recipient of numerous teaching awards.

Members of the Accounting Department in 1956 included (*left to right*) William Eugene Wright, Harry H. Wade, Charles T. Zlatkovich, George Hillis Newlove, C. Aubrey Smith, Glenn Albert Welsch, John Arch White, Jim G. Ashburne, Robert E. Linde, and Robert E. Seiler.

The School of Communication was organized in 1966, bringing together four related departments—speech, journalism, advertising, and radio-television-film. A Department (called School at the time) of Journalism in the College of Arts was organized in 1914. Will H. Mayes (*top, left*), editor of the *Brownwood Bulletin* for twenty years, became the first professor of journalism. Other faculty in the new department soon after it was organized included (*left to right*) B. O. Brown, Vaughan Bryant, and B. W. Collins.

Thomas A. Rousse (*bottom left*) became an instructor of speech in 1928 when he completed the B.B.A. degree. He trained a legion of debaters.

Olin E. Hinkle (*bottom center*) became associate professor of journalism in 1946 and retired as professor in 1972.

Granville Price (*bottom right*), editor of the *Daily Texan* in 1927 and former city editor of the *New York Herald-Tribune*, became adjunct professor of journalism at the University in 1933.

DeWitt C. Reddick received his bachelor's degree from U.T. in 1925 and taught journalism, especially feature writing, for nearly a half-century. He became the first dean of the School of Communication in 1967. Here, he is presenting a portrait of Paul J. Thompson, director of the School of Journalism for three decades from 1919. With Reddick is Jo Meyer, executive assistant in communications.

Wayne Danielson (*bottom left*) succeeded DeWitt Reddick as dean of the School of Communication in 1969. He resigned as dean in 1978 but has continued to teach.

Robert C. Jeffrey (*bottom right*) joined the U.T. faculty in 1968 and became dean of the School of Communication in 1978 after Danielson resigned.

The Speech faculty gathered for a photograph in 1970.

Stanley T. Donner (*center left*) came to U.T. in 1965 as professor of radio-television-film and education. He retired in 1976.

Ernest Alonzo Sharpe (*bottom left*), who began teaching journalism at U.T. in 1946, holds the Jesse H. Jones Professorship in Journalism, the first endowed chair in the School of Communication.

Norris G. Davis (*bottom center*), professor of journalism, is a specialist in libel law.

A specialist in conflict management and organizational communication, Donald W. Zacharias (*bottom right*) became a member of the faculty in 1969, served for three years (1973–1976) as assistant to the president, and was executive assistant to the chancellor (1978–1979) before leaving to become president of another university.

The School of Pharmacy was first established at the Medical Branch in Galveston in 1893, with James Kennedy, M.D., from San Antonio as the first professor of pharmacy. The school was moved from Galveston to the Main University campus in 1927, and its name was changed to the College of Pharmacy. W. F. Gidley (*top left*) was named the first dean of the college.

In 1947, Henry M. Burlage (*top right*) succeeded Gidley in the deanship and served the college in this capacity until 1962. During his administration, graduate programs were added.

Faculty members who taught in the college in 1930 included (*left to right, bottom row*) H. R. Henze, Alice Conklin, W. F. Gidley, and C. C. Albers; (*top row*) W. R. Neville, L. W. Schleuse, and J. Bliss Norton.

Lee F. Worrell (*bottom left*) served as dean from 1962 to 1966.

Carl C. Albers (*bottom right*) was dean from 1966 to 1967.

Joseph B. Sprowls (*top left*) was dean of the College of Pharmacy from 1967 to 1971. The undergraduate curriculum was revised significantly during both Dean Worrell's and Dean Sprowls' administrations. Clinical training was first made available to students on an elective basis in the summer of 1970.

Victor A. Yanchick (*top center*), associate professor of pharmacy and assistant dean, became a member of the faculty in 1968.

James T. Doluisio (*top right*) became dean in 1973.

In 1970, the following faculty members taught in the College of Pharmacy: (*left to right, bottom row*) Victor Yanchick, Lee Worrell, John Davis, Charles Walker, and Herbert Schwartz; (*second row*) E. Wood Hall, Henry Burlage, William Haney, Frederick Lofgren, and John Biesele; (*third row*) Charles T. Clark, Jaime Delgado, Karl-Heinz Rosler, Jean Scholler, Jay Nematollahi, and Dean Joseph Sprowls; (*fourth row*) Ronald Garrett, Gerald Sullivan, Wallace Guess, Billy Wylie, William Sheffield, and Gordon Jensen.

E. William Doty (*top left*) was the only dean the College of Fine Arts knew from its founding in the fall of 1938 until his retirement in 1971. Composed of the Departments of Art, Drama, and Music, its first faculty numbered ten members—four each in music and drama and two in art. They taught the 140 fine arts students in the Old Library Building (now Battle Hall). Doty built a remarkable faculty of performing and teaching artists during his tenure.

Ellsworth P. Conkle (*top right*), at U.T. since 1939, wrote prize-winning plays, some of which also proved commercial successes on Broadway.

Dalies E. Frantz (*center left*) had a notable career as a concert pianist and motion picture actor when he re-tired from the road to teach at the University from 1943 until his death. A demanding mentor, he produced students who won numerous national and international competitions.

Loren Winship (*center right*), who became director of drama in the Division of Extension in 1938 and later chairman of the Drama Department in the College of Fine Arts, is shown here with one of his famous students, Pat Hingle.

Francis R. Hodge (*at desk*), professor of drama, has been a member of the Drama Department faculty since 1949. His teaching specialties are directing, theater history, and criticism. Here, he works with four students in 1966.

J. Ward Lockwood (*top left*) came to U.T. in 1938 as professor of art. Loren Mozley (*in bow tie*) arrived the same year.

Lucy Barton came to the University to be costumer for the Drama Department in 1947. She remained until her retirement in 1961 as the department's first professor emeritus. During those fourteen years, she costumed at least four productions a year, but often did as many as six or seven.

B. Iden Payne (*bottom left*) made the University's Shakespeare productions nationally famous. He came to the University in 1946, serving that year and again in 1951–1952 as chairman of the Department of Drama. He retired in 1973 as professor emeritus after directing twenty-nine plays at U.T., of which twenty-four were by Shakespeare.

Morris J. Beachy (*bottom right*), professor of music, came to the faculty in 1957. An experienced soloist in opera, oratorio, and lieder, he has served as director of U.T. choral organizations. Since their formation in 1958, his Chamber Singers (known first as Madrigal Singers) have toured the Middle East and Europe for the State Department, were one of six college choirs chosen to record an album of Christmas music for the Book-of-the-Month Club, and won first prize in the Villa-Lobos Festival's First International Competition for Mixed Chorus in Rio de Janeiro.

Michael G. Frary, professor of art, is discussing one of his paintings with Congressman J. J. Pickle, former student body president in the late 1930s.

When the Art Building was dedicated in 1963, the U.T. art faculty was photographed.

Walter E. Ducloux *(top)*, born in Switzerland, came to the University in 1968. He directed the University symphony and produced opera in the grand style.

William C. Race *(bottom left)*, piano professor, came to U.T. in 1967.

Charles Umlauf *(bottom center)*, sculptor and professor of art since 1941, teaches an advanced sculpturing class. A number of his statues may be seen on the campus; in front of the Academic Center is *Torchbearers* and in front of the Graduate School of Business Building is *Family*.

Marian B. Davis, now professor emertius of art, is visiting with students Judy Gillespie and Jessica Darling, 1963–1964 U.T. sweetheart and cheerleader.

Peter Garvie (*top left*), who came to U.T. from Canada, succeeded E. W. Doty as dean in 1971 and served until 1978.

Dr. Oscar Brockett (*top right*), a distinguished theater historian and former president of the American Theater Association, was dean of the College of Fine Arts from 1978 to 1980.

Charlotte DuBois, Nelson Patrick, and Janet McGaughey have long served the Music Department in various capacities. Patrick served as acting dean of fine arts for a while after Dean Garvie resigned.

The University of Texas awarded its first master's degree in 1886; it has now awarded more than 25,000. The first Ph.D. degree was awarded in 1915; the total has now passed 9,000. Becoming the twenty-ninth member of the Association of American Universities in 1929, the University can cite a distinguished history of graduate studies. During the past seventeen years, the graduate program has experienced rapid and large growth, with enrollment increasing from 2,598 in 1963–1964 to 7,959 in the fall of 1979.

Henry Winston Harper (*top left*) was chairman of the Council of the Graduate Department from 1910 to 1920, when he became the first dean of the Graduate School, serving until 1937. Dean Harper was always known by his bright red ties that celebrities the nation over vied to supply him.

Albert P. Brogan (*top right*), professor of philosophy, was dean of the Graduate School from 1937 until 1958.

W. Gordon Whaley (*bottom left*), Ashbel Smith Professor of Cellular Biology and an expert on grasses, was dean from 1958 through 1971. He is shown here hooding a new doctoral student (John Burnham).

Gardner Lindzey (*bottom right*), psychologist, was vice-president and dean of graduate studies from 1973 to 1975.

Robert Raymond Douglass (*top left*) was the first director of the Graduate School of Library Science, serving from 1948 to 1969.

Claud Glenn Sparks (*top right*) was acting dean of library science in 1972–1973 and then became dean.

Lora Lee Pederson (*middle left*) served as director of the Graduate School of Social Work from its beginning in 1950 until 1964.

Jack Otis (*middle right*) served as director of social work in 1964–1965 and then returned as dean in 1972, from which position he resigned in 1978.

Billye Brown was dean of the School of Nursing when it became a part of U.T. Austin in 1976. Originally an integral part of the Medical Branch at Galveston, a System-wide School of Nursing was established in 1967 with Marilyn D. Willman as president. The school had six branches, including one at Austin. In 1976, the System organization was dissolved, and the Austin branch became a part of U.T. Austin.

DR. BILLYE J. BROWN

The Lyndon B. Johnson School of Public Affairs admitted its first students in 1970. The first dean was John A. Gronouski (*top left*), former postmaster general of the United States (1963–1965) and ambassador to Poland (1965–1968). He served as dean from 1970 until 1973.

Elspeth D. Rostow (*top right*) has been dean of the school since 1977. Professor of American government and American studies and former dean of the Division of General and Comparative Studies, she succeeded Alan K. Campbell, who resigned the deanship to become chairman of the U.S. Civil Service Commission. Her principal scholarly interest is the institutional analysis of American government.

Alexander P. Clark (*bottom left*), a sociologist, was acting dean of the school from 1973 to 1975.

Barbara Jordan (*bottom right*) became the Lyndon B. Johnson Public Service Professor in the School of Public Affairs in January 1979. Serving in the Texas Senate (1966–1972) and the U.S. House of Representatives (1972–1978), she became recognized as one of the most influential women in American public life. She is the recipient of twenty-five honorary degrees.

Edwin DuBois Shurter (*top left*) was director of the Department of Extension from 1916 to 1920. Extension was a department from the time it was organized in 1909 until 1920, when it became a bureau. It became a division in 1924 and, finally, after a considerable amount of reorganization, the College of Continuing Education in 1976.

Thomas Hall Shelby (*top center*) was director of the Bureau of Extension from 1920 until 1925, when he became dean of the division. He retired from the deanship in 1951.

James R. D. Eddy (*center left*) was dean of the division from 1951 to 1967.

Norris Andrews Hiett (*center right*) was dean of the division from 1967 until his death in 1970.

Staff members in the Division of Extension in 1967 included (*left to right*) Francis A. Flynn, Rodney James Kidd, Ernest Fred Tiemann, William E. Barron (who became dean ad interim in 1970 and then dean, serving until 1976), and John W. Woodruff.

Thomas M. Hatfield (*top right*) assumed duties as dean of the Division of Continuing Education in February 1977. The Division of Extension was abolished, and some of its components were assigned to the new organization.

Only a few of the numerous administrative personnel and classified staff can be included here as representative of the numerous individuals who have helped shape the University since it was established.

In 1930, these men held important administrative positions at U.T.: (*left to right*) W. R. Long was in charge of the auditor's office; E. J. Mathews was registrar; E. W. Winkler was director of University libraries; and John W. Calhoun was comptroller and later president.

Carroll D. Simmons (*left*), professor of business administration, became a member of the staff in 1924 as an editorial assistant. From 1948 to 1951, he was vice-president and comptroller; from 1951 to 1953, he was vice-chancellor for business and finance, after which he moved to Houston as a bank executive.

Charles H. Sparenberg (*center right*), a U.T. student from 1922 to 1926, became auditor for the University in 1931. He served as comptroller of The University of Texas System from 1953 until 1967, when he was made consultant to the vice-chancellor for business affairs.

James H. Colvin (*bottom right*), currently senior vice-president for business affairs, came to U.T. in 1961 as business manager.

Victor I. Moore (*top left*), who was assistant dean of student life in 1925, became dean of men in 1926. In 1927, he was appointed dean of student life and dean of men. He served in this position until his death in 1943.

Ruby R. Terrill (*center left*), a U.T. graduate, became dean of women in 1925 after Lucy Newton resigned. She held the position until 1936, soon after her marriage to John A. Lomax. She was also associate professor of classical languages.

Dorothy Gebauer (*top right*), elected assistant dean of women in 1927, became dean of women in 1936, when Ruby Terrill Lomax resigned, and remained in that position until 1960, after which she served as consultant to the dean for a few years. She was a major force in organizing the women's cooperative houses, establishing a program of peer advising in women's housing, and working for integration of student housing.

Margaret Peck (*bottom left*) came to U.T. in 1930 as student life secretary of the University YWCA. In 1937, she became social director of Littlefield Dormitory. Later, she moved to the office of the dean of women, where she served as adviser to sororities for a number of years. In 1960, she was appointed dean of women and was the last to hold that position. During the year 1968–1969, she was dean of students ad interim.

Dorothy Dean (*left*) and Helen Flinn, members of the dean of women's staff, are shown in this 1956 photograph.

The student life office has been staffed by numerous specialists who have worked with individuals and groups since the office was organized. Only a few can be included here as representative of those who have served.

If U.T. had an official greeter, it would have to be Arno Nowotny, shown here with La Verne, his wife. For more than fifty years, he has represented continuity, stability. A former cheerleader, Shorty became assistant dean of men in 1927. In 1943, he was named dean of men and in 1946 became dean of student life. He helped organize the Cowboys, Phi Eta Sigma, and Alpha Phi Omega and has long been adviser to the Friar Society and other student service groups and honor societies.

Members of the staff of the student life office were photographed in 1959: (*left to right*) Carl Bredt, Arno Nowotny (dean), Edwin Booth Price, Jack Holland, Carthy Ronway Ryals, William J. Hall, and Rollin A. Sininger.

Jack Holland (*top left*) was dean of men from 1948 to 1960 and dean of students from 1964 to 1968, when he became assistant vice-chancellor for student affairs.

Lawrence Turner Franks (*top center*) was dean of men from 1965 to 1970 and associate dean of students from 1970 to 1977.

Ronald M. Brown (*top right*) was vice-president for student affairs from 1971 to 1976. For the next three years, he served as vice-president for administrative services, but in September 1979 he again assumed the position of vice-president for student affairs.

As student enrollment increased during the 1970s, so did the size of the staff of the dean of students office. In 1973, members of the staff included (*left to right*) Rudy Garza, David McClintock, Lawrence Franks, Ruth Smith, Edward Nall, Almetris Duren, Geoffrey Grant, Dorothy Dean, Edwin B. Price, Carolyn Hewatt, Margaret Barr, James P. Duncan, and Robert P. Cooke.

William W. Stewart (*top left*), senior trust officer in the U.T. System, has been providing expertise in financial affairs since 1955.

Burnell Waldrep (*top center*), associate general counsel for the U.T. System when he retired in 1977, first came to the University's legal staff in 1956.

W. Byron Shipp (*top right*) began working for the University as a student in 1926 and retired in 1972 as registrar and director of admissions.

Robert F. Schenkkan, director of the Communication Center and professor of radio-TV-film from 1955 until 1977 and president and general manager of KLRN-TV from 1964 until 1977, holds numerous honors relating to the television industry. Here, he is conferring with crew members of "Carrascolendas," a bilingual show which won national awards.

Frances Hudspeth, executive assistant to Harry Ransom, is escorted from the Main Building by Chief Allen R. Hamilton during the 1965 Tower fire. Hudspeth joined the staff in 1940 and carried numerous heavy responsibilities. Hamilton was chief of U.T. police from 1947 to 1970, when he joined the System as assistant director of police-auxiliary services.

Dr. Joe Thorne Gilbert (*top left*), a Galveston physician and surgeon, was employed by President Sidney E. Mezes in 1909 because of the high mortality rate among students. Health services were first provided in Old Main by Gilbert and his assistant, George M. Decherd. Gilbert resigned in 1920 but was rehired in 1930 and served until 1947.

Dr. Margaret Roberta Holliday (*top center*) was employed in 1909 as the first woman physician with the Health Service.

Dr. Caroline Crowell (*top right*) joined the Health Service staff in 1925.

Dr. Paul White (*bottom left*) was director of the University Health Center from 1951 until he retired in 1968. He had been employed in 1937 as director of the mental hygiene clinic.

Dr. Paul C. Trickett (*bottom right*) became director of the Student Health Center in 1968. He is also director of athletic medicine for the Longhorns.

Charles N. Zivley (*top left*) became first director of the Texas Union when it opened in 1933.

C. C. (Jitter) Nolen (*top center*), a former cheerleader, was director of the Texas Union from 1951 to 1961, and Jack Steel (*top right*) was director from 1961 to 1973.

Shirley Bird and Elton "Bud" Mims were named Dads' Day outstanding students in 1957. Shirley (now Shirley B. Perry) was director of the Union for three years, 1973–1976, during its most recent renovation and became assistant to the president (for coordination of the centennial program activities) in 1979.

Eva Tiroff, director of the University Commons in 1953, is looking at a portrait of Anna Janzen, who began supervising the old Commons (or Caf) in 1922 and continued until her retirement in 1951.

Harry Eldon Sutton (*top left*), professor of zoology and education, was vice-president for research from 1975 to 1979. He is also a superior organist.

Block Smith (*top right*) was the long-time, dearly loved director of the University "Y," an important adjunct to the University.

Donald L. Weismann (*center left*), University professor in the arts, teaches courses in comparative studies. Artist, poet, collector, photographer, raconteur without peer, he came to the University faculty in 1954 as head of the Department of Art.

Graves W. Landrum (*center right*), vice-chancellor emeritus (for operations) also served many years in an administrative capacity at the U.T. Austin campus.

F. C. McConnell (*bottom left*) was director of housing from 1950 until 1968. He served as assistant to the vice-president for business affairs in 1968–1969, after which he retired.

William (Bill) Blunk (*bottom right*), director of development for the U.T. System from 1965 to 1976, served earlier as assistant to the U.T. chancellor, assistant dean of student life, associate director for development, and executive director of the Development Board.

Frank Dobie talks with painter-novelist Tom Lea (*center*) of El Paso and the first director of the U.T. Press, Frank H. Wardlaw (*right*). The paintings in the background are by Lea. Wardlaw was succeeded by Philip D. Jones, 1974–1977, and John H. Kyle, in 1977. The conference room in the Press' new building was dedicated to Wardlaw in 1978.

W. D. Hornaday (*bottom left*) was appointed by President R. E. Vinson in 1917 to set up the University's first Office of Publicity. He was director of the office for twenty-one years.

Amy Jo Long (*bottom right*) has been director of the office (now called University News and Information Service) since 1969.

Established in 1939, the Hogg Foundation for Mental Health, made possible by the $2.5 million bequest of Will C. Hogg, was formally inaugurated with a three-day series of conferences on February 11, 12, and 13, 1941. On September 1, 1940, Robert L. Sutherland (*top left*) became the first director and remained as director and then president until 1970.

Wayne H. Holtzman (*top right*) joined the Hogg Foundation in 1955 as associate director, served as dean of the College of Education from 1964 to 1970, and has been president of the Hogg Foundation ever since.

Bernice Milburn Moore (*center right*), now a consultant to the Hogg Foundation, formerly served as executive associate. A sociologist, she is nationally rec-ognized for her research and preparation of programs and publications in the fields of mental health, family relationships, and personality development.

Joe W. Neal (*center left*), on the staff since 1946, has made the International Office one of the nation's most respected since he became director in 1950.

Harry Birk Beck (*bottom left*), creator of Beck's Pond, was the first director of old B. Hall. Later, he became superintendent of buildings and grounds.

In 1929, fourteen men, six of whom are pictured, worked under the leadership of Beck to keep the campus beautiful. The campus still had only forty acres.

Carl Eckhardt (*top left*), a graduate of the University in 1925, started serving the University as a student assistant in 1924 and worked his way to a professorship in mechanical engineering in 1936. From 1961 until 1973, he directed the physical plant, leaving his creative mark all over the campus. He is, for instance, one of the two men responsible for salvaging the University's discovery oil well, Santa Rita #1, and placing it intact on San Jacinto Street just south of Memorial Stadium.

Missy K. Doss, a staff member since 1923, was purchasing agent for the University from 1950 until she retired in 1970.

Bill Neans (*bottom left*) was the guardian at the main entrance to the University campus for a long generation. He made access difficult enough that the students labeled him St. Peter and his entrance St. Peter's Gate.

George Harold (Jack) Leonard (*bottom right*) was a member of the campus security staff from 1953 until retirement in 1974.

6. Students and Student Activities

Characteristic of many University students, independence of thought and action prompted this group of seniors to hold an antisenior picnic on April 11, 1896. Included here are Annie Jenkins, P. S. Hargrove, Loula Cooper, Claude Carter, Rosa Weathered, Edwin Sneed, Belle Cundiff, I. Y. Magee, Louise Willis, A. B. Staten, Georgia Jenkins, M. L. Hargrove, Leona Randal, D. M. Jones, Morton Adams, Hugh Prather, Lizzie Speight, G. W. McDaniel, Lallie Bryan, E. Ammons, Calla Little, J. H. Eastland, Bertha Lattimore, H. C. Smith, Mr. and Mrs. Lyman Bryan, and Bill (last name unknown).

The University of Texas has had more than 300,000 students. As enrollment grew from 221 in 1883 to over 44,000 in the fall of 1979, the spirit changed, but certain pervasive traditions, customs, and folkways influenced student behavior to an extent impossible to measure.

The campus culture is tied to the larger culture but becomes more complex in many respects because of diverse representation. It is influenced by the culture of the surrounding area, but it develops its own traditions, customs, and ways of life consistent with or opposed to the outside social forces.

A historical study of students and their activities is a study of a society in interaction and the outgrowth of that interaction, the product of which is its distinctive environment, or the campus culture. The past influences the thoughts and actions of individuals as they operate within the structure that is the heritage of the group. Organized or not, these activities reflect social change on the campus.

A Students' Association, born out of conflict, uncertainty, chaos, and even distrust, became a reality by the beginning of the 1902–1903 term. It gradually assumed responsibility for student activities, and even though University regulations brought charges that students had no power, student leaders and student groups, year after year, exerted a considerable amount of influence. In 1978, students voted to abolish their Students' Association, claiming that it was irrelevant and useless. Re-establishment of the Association was begun in the spring of 1980.

Early societal restraints on activities of students contrast sharply with the newly found freedoms resulting from the cultural changes of the late 1960s and early 1970s. Activities through the years indicate that society and fashions have changed far more than the people. The photographs in this chapter portray many of these activities, some of which have become traditions, examined in another chapter. Approximately 400 registered student organizations in 1980 indicate the diversity of student interests.

Student life has reflected the values and pressures of the Texas culture. Primarily rural in 1883, today Texas is 80 percent urban. Students from all fifty states and from more than seventy countries tend to reduce provincialism, once dominant and reflected in student mores and activities.

Student life on the campus during the first two decades of the University's existence was far from exciting; it was simple, slow-paced, and often boresome in the pastoral setting of the University. Buggy rides along trails later to become busy thoroughfares; conversations in beer gardens around the campus; afternoons spent along the banks of Waller Creek where the low branches of trees tangled the high coiffures of the girls and the tall grass swished against their long, full-gored skirts; and pecan hunts, hikes to Mount Bonnell, and class excursions to San Antonio, Marble Falls, and Barton's Creek provided social and educational experiences.

Croquet was popular.

This group is enjoying a picnic at Lost Creek in 1902.

A canoe ride down the Colorado River was a good way to spend an afternoon at the turn of the century. It still is today.

A geological excursion to Marble Falls during the 1896–1897 session was made by train.

A trolley party was fun and inexpensive. Students would meet at the popular Car Shed on the campus near Guadalupe and board a trolley for a ride around the city, stopping at Sixth and Congress to buy popcorn for refreshments.

Early advertisements in the *Cactus* and the *Texan* give us insights into student life.

The *University of Texas Magazine* was first published in 1885 by the Athenaeum and Rusk Literary Societies (subsequently joined by the Ashbel Literary Society). It was later published by the Students' Association. In 1896–1897, the staff included (*top, left to right*) Taylor Moore, Yancey W. Holmes, J. Henri Tallichet, John A. Lomax (editor, first term), Frank T. West, MaryLu Prather, Clara H. B. Neville, Francis M. Law (editor, second term), Wm. T. Boyd, A. Heath Freeman, F. C. Hume, Jr., and J. L. Lockett.

The *Cactus*, student yearbook, was first published in 1894. Members of the 1895 staff were (*left to right, front row*) James W. McClendon, Lilia Casis, Walter Stephens (editor-in-chief), Edith Lanier Clark, and J. Bouldin Rector; (*back row*) W. W. Hilbrant, J. Walter Cocke, Jr., Jesse Andrews, B. F. Louis, W. Steele Lemly, Jr., and Claud F. Johnson.

The Final Ball, first held at the conclusion of the 1884–1885 session, remained a favorite custom for many years. To be chosen president of the Final Ball was to be stamped with success. President of the 1896 Final Ball was James Wooten McClendon, later a judge and for a long time the oldest living ex-letterman. Others on the committee were (*left to right*) David Watt Bowser, Daniel Parker, William Wallace Ralston, Victor Cloud Moore, and E. Dick Slaughter.

The Brownies, a social club pictured in the 1895 *Cactus*, included (*left to right, first row*) Nettie Swancoat, Florence Smith, Alma Evans, Mille Gray Dumble, Mamie Allen, and Cheba Preston; (*second row*) Hattie Evans, Minnie Malcolm, Emma Patrick, Maude Blaine, and Agnes Brady.

Sororities were discouraged and did not have administrative approval. Helen Marr Kirby, lady assistant who became dean of women, actively opposed any attempts to charter a group. Without official University approval, Pi Beta Phi established its Texas Alpha chapter, the first sorority at U.T., on February 19, 1902. Shown here are the charter members of the chapter: Jamie Armstrong, Minnie Rose, Aline Harris, Flora Bartholomew, Ada Garrison, Anna Townes, Loula Rose, Vivian Brenizer, Elsie Garrett, and Attie McClendon.

Fraternities came to the campus the day the University opened, September 15, 1883. The Phi Delta Theta chapter received its charter on that date. Pictured here are the 1895 members, including those who were on the faculty: (*left to right, first row*) Dr. Morgan Callaway, E. L. Buchanan, Chas. Herndon, C. A. Wilcox and daughter, and Dr. David F. Houston; (*standing*) S. R. Robertson, R. S. Baker, R. B. Renfro, B. Y. Cummings, Tom J. Murphy, E. L. Bruce, and Emmett Ellis.

The Troubadours were a popular quartet in 1898. Members were (*left to right*) L. A. Abercrombie, first tenor; J. W. Hawkins, second tenor; Ewing Boyd, first bass; and Jack Jenkins, second bass.

In the fall of 1900, Dr. Eugene Schoch organized this University band under his direction. When it appeared for the first time at the Kansas City–Texas game, it was not yet labeled the "Show Band of the Southwest."

The University band members, shown here in their first uniforms, white smocks, have often led parades down Congress Avenue. In the spring of 1905, they led the University's first Varsity Circus parade. The circus was promoted by Maurice Wolf, who is riding in the cart, hat doffed. K. C. Miller is the first man in the middle row of the band.

First forerunner of the *Texan* was the *Alcalde*, founded in the winter of 1895–1896 by L. E. Hill and C. D. Oldright, joint owners, editors, and business managers. When Oldright died in the spring of 1896, Hill became sole owner. In the fall of 1897, Hill sold the *Alcalde* to John O. Phillips, who changed its name to the *Ranger*, which he published until June 1900. Its editors included John C. Palm (1897–1898), Edward R. Kleberg (1898–1899), and Wilbur P. Allen (1899–1900), later a regent.

The *Ranger* editorial board in 1897–1898 included (*top, not in order pictured*) John C. Palm, editor-in-chief; John O. Phillips, manager; E. W. Townes, assistant manager; E. R. Kleberg; Herbert Springall; Tom T. Connally; Charles Leavell; Olinthus Ellis; L. M. Kemp; and R. S. Terry.

In 1898–1899, a rival paper, the *Calendar*, appeared. When R. W. Wortham, its founder, moved on, the paper was taken over by H. Lee Borden and James H. Hart, father of the first chancellor of the University. E. E. Witt and L. L. Featherstone were its editors. Since the University couldn't support two newspapers, they merged, and in October 1900, the *Texan* first appeared, still a private enterprise. The Student's Association took over publication in 1905. Shown here is the 1901–1902 staff (*bottom*).

Fritz G. Lanham, son of a governor and later a congressman from the Fort Worth area, became the first editor-in-chief of the *Texan*. When, in January 1901, ill health forced Lanham from school, Frank T. West succeeded him. For over seventy-five years, the *Texan* has ranked among the best college newspapers. It was a weekly publication from 1900 to 1907, when it became a semiweekly. In the fall of 1913, it became the *Daily Texan*. In 1921, Texas Student Publications, Inc., was created and placed in charge of all student publications. When the corporation charter expired in 1971, a trust was formed. Student editors, generally noted for their independence and irreverence, have not always been on the best of terms with University administrators.

Banquets, luncheons, and club activities have enriched the extracurricular life of students. Early banquets given by the engineering, law, and medical students were stag affairs that lasted far into the night. One event was a University Hall Club banquet at the Medical Branch in Galveston in 1901 (*top left*).

B. Hall was a stronghold for nonfraternity men because most fraternity men lived in their chapter houses. The P.E.C.'s, the Rusty Cusses, and the GooRoos were organized by the men in B. Hall for fun and fellowship. The Rustic Order of the Rusty Cusses in 1904 (*top right*) included N. J. Marshall as landlord and D. A. Frank as overseer. Their motto was, "Down with all trusts; oppose all musts; avoid all busts."

The senior luncheon was a tradition in 1913. Hosted by the University YWCA, this particular one had Allene Howren as toastmistress. The program consisted of numerous toasts and group singing.

Around the turn of the century, the Ashbel Literary Society annually presented a play. *A Study in Shakespeare's Sources* was presented on May 17, 1904, with (*top, left to right*) Mary Stedman as Ophelia; Emma Greer as Desdemona; Julia Estill as Lady Macbeth; Virginia Rice as Katherine the Shrew; Grace Hill as Juliet; Fanny West Harris as Portia; Annie Joe Gardner as Rosalinda; and Emily Maverick as Viola.

The Curtain Club, the oldest dramatic organization at the University, was founded in 1909 by Stark Young, who remained its director until 1915. The club was strictly extracurricular. Men appeared in women's parts until women were finally admitted to membership in 1915. Shown here are the characters in one of the first productions.

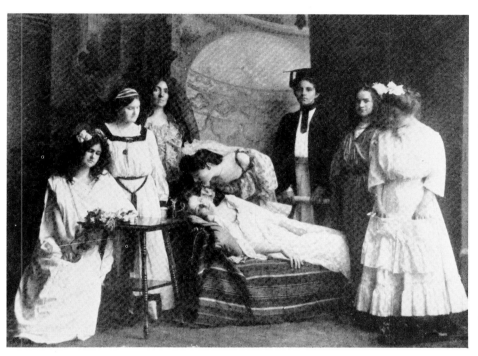

That the automobile was becoming a factor in student life was indicated by traffic regulations on campus announced as early as January 1914, although few students owned cars even then. Shown here is a student car in 1907.

The Texas Longhorns are escorted to the playing field, old Clark Field, in 1908 in automobiles. Old Main with its auditorium, the Engineering Building, and the water tank are in the background.

An out-of-town football game, a special event, always meant a train trip in the early years. The men went to the station en masse on November 1, 1916, to see the team off for Missouri.

The most popular form of entertainment between halves at football games was a snake dance. This one took place at the Wabash game in the fall of 1914.

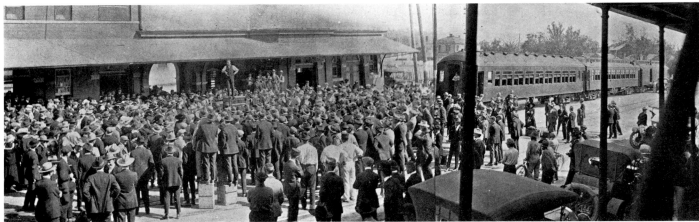

A football rally in the auditorium in 1911 was a formal occasion compared with those of later years. Note the attire—coats and ties. Note also that the women usually sat together during the early rallies, observing rather than participating.

Beginning in 1904 or 1905, nightshirt parades were popular before and after football games and other important events. After the notorious Texas-Aggie game in Houston in 1911, almost every nightshirt in school was out to celebrate the Texas upset. A big entourage had gone to Houston for the Monday game, but students who did not go were able to attend a football party at the New Theatre at Seventh and Congress for 25¢ and to hear telegraph reports of the game's highlights. Because of the built-up tension between students of the two schools due to the rough game and the threats made afterward, U.T. and A&M didn't play again until 1915.

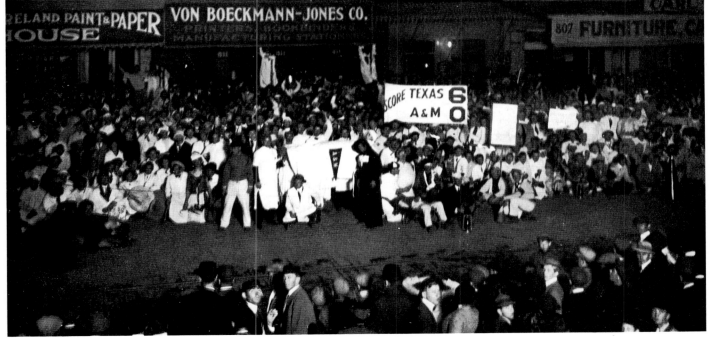

During Commencement Week each year until the 1920s, seniors in each college passed to the juniors the symbol representing their college. The law students presented Peregrinus; the "academs" presented the key of knowledge; the engineers presented the T-square; and the "pedoggies" from education presented the blue-back speller. Representatives of the 1917 seniors and juniors from the law and academ departments (*top*) are shown participating in the ceremony.

Even interdepartmental horseplay was different in 1912.

Two events held annually for many years were the junior-senior prom and the baby party. All-female events, both might raise eyebrows today, but they were wholesome, fun activities for the numerous women who attended them.

The junior-senior prom, sponsored by the junior class women, was given each spring during Junior Week. The junior women, dressed as men, escorted senior women in long formals to the dance in their honor. On the night of the prom, junior men usually had a smoker.

The baby party was held in the Women's Gymnasium. Women dressed as babies and carried dolls, entered baby contests, and enjoyed all-day suckers. This picture was made at the big party in 1916.

Some things through the years, such as student protests, often have a common theme: "University's future is threatened!" "Academic freedom is dead!" The earliest protest on record occurred when the first students had to attend classes in the old Temporary Capitol in the fall of 1883. They complained about the noise, the dust, and the overcrowded classrooms, and they cut classes to show disapproval. Another early protest occurred in the spring of 1896 when students met "in a quiet and dignified way" one day to adopt resolutions concerning the failure on the part of University regents to re-elect a physics professor. Pictures were not taken at these early protests.

Several memorable protests are featured on these two pages. In 1917, students organize a parade to protest the interference by Governor James E. Ferguson in University affairs (*top*).

In 1944, students march to the Capitol to request Governor Coke Stevenson's assistance when the regents fired President Homer Price Rainey (*bottom*).

Rapid social change in the late 1960s and early 1970s resulted in numerous demonstrations and protests. Among them were three shown here.

In 1968, students protest the termination of Larry Caroline's contract by the regents (*top left*).

In 1970, when President Richard Nixon announced that American troops would be sent to Cambodia, protests broke out on most of the nation's campuses. At Ohio's Kent State on May 4, four students were killed in a confrontation with the National Guard. The University Ad Hoc Strike Committee at U.T. called for a boycott of classes to protest U.S. involvement in Cambodia, the trial of Black Panther Bobby Seale, the city's

denial of a solicitation permit to the Community United Front, the arrest of ten anti-ROTC demonstrators, and the Kent State deaths. On May 8, a parade of approximately 20,000 march downtown in peaceful protest.

In 1975, students protest the firing of President Stephen H. Spurr by the regents by hanging a black wreath.

In the 1911 Varsity Circus parade, women students carry placards proclaiming, "No votes—no babies." Texas women were granted the right to vote in 1918, and more than three hundred University women attended a mass meeting to hear a state leader for women's rights explain the new privilege.

Life at the University during the 1918–1919 session, even before the war ended, took a still more serious turn when a worldwide epidemic of influenza gripped the community. Classes were dismissed for weeks. After they resumed, classrooms were aired ten minutes between classes, and students were ordered to take their temperature every morning (*top right*). One student at each rooming place made daily reports on the temperatures of residents.

During World War I, the School of Military Aeronautics, the Air School for Radio Operators, and the School of Auto Mechanics were established as subsidiaries of the University and operated until the armistice was signed. The total enrollment in the three schools was fourteen thousand men, and the total number of graduates was eight thousand.

Beauty pages in the 1918 *Cactus* were censored by Helen Marr Kirby, dean of women, who insisted that the pages be removed before the yearbooks were distributed. Below is one of the pages removed.

Shrieking whistles, ringing bells, pistol shots, enthusiastic yells, and cries of "Extra" ushered in "Glorious Monday"—November 11, 1918. The University of Texas had a big part in the parade that began at 3:00 P.M. Five thousand soldiers from the University's military schools, as well as students and faculty, were featured in the celebration.

On campus a ceremony was held: after the playing of taps, the Service Flag with 3,100 blue stars, representing alumni in the service, and 85 gold stars, representing alumni killed in action, was lowered.

The senior women have a banquet in 1921. They are entertained by a skit presented by some of their own members.

In 1921, Governor Pat Neff signed a bill appropriating a large sum of money to begin the expansion of the campus beyond its original Forty Acres. Approximately fifteen hundred students and faculty members marched to the Capitol to express appreciation to the governor for signing the University Expansion Bill.

The University celebrated its fortieth anniversary in 1923, and students joined the faculty in a parade to mark the occasion. Other events included the Varsity Circus with a pageant and the crowning of a queen, and a dinner honoring the students of 1883. The celebration was held during Commencement Week, May 10, 11, and 12.

After World War I, big student dances were popular. The Saturday night germans, started by the German Club and continued as all-University dances, were fun because of the large number of stags in attendance. The Thanksgiving dance was one of the special occasions of the year. Here, students enjoy the 1924 dance. Note the chaperon standing near the wall at the back.

The *Blunderbuss*, an unauthorized student publication, first appeared on campus on April 1, 1914. The first edition left most faculty members feeling indifferent, but Helen Marr Kirby seized 250 copies. After the appearance of this paper, the Faculty Discipline Committee suspended four prominent students for the remainder of the term; included were the editor and the managing editor of the *Daily Texan*. The counterpart of this publication in the 1960s was the *Rag*, another unofficial publication.

The *Texas Ranger* began publication as a student humor magazine in the fall of 1923. After a hectic existence and a number of national awards, it finally stopped publication in 1972. Shown here is Bob Burns, managing editor in 1966, selling the current issue.

Communications problems have always plagued students, even when the student population was small and the campus was limited to the original Forty Acres. Old Main had a rotunda at the center entrance that enabled students to stand around the banisters on the fourth floor and drop dodgers announcing the next play or dance or election. In the summer of 1912, the rotunda was closed, and students complained, "One more landmark, with its associations, has been effaced! One more tradition has been stifled!"

In contrast to this early method of distributing information is "the jungle" on the West Mall in 1951 when size and number of student election signs were not regulated as they are today. Student elections produced a new look on the campus for a few weeks, but student turnout on election day has never been sizable.

Hazing is not allowed around here! A photographer caught this group of young men requiring some freshmen to run a gauntlet back of old B. Hall on March 2 a few years before the hall was closed as a dormitory in 1926.

In the mid-1920s, playing poker was a popular pastime.

And a bull session in a student's room might be about girls, politics, classes . . .

Rooming houses were inexpensive and also crowded. During the days before air-conditioning, students moved their beds to the big "sleeping porches" for fresh air.

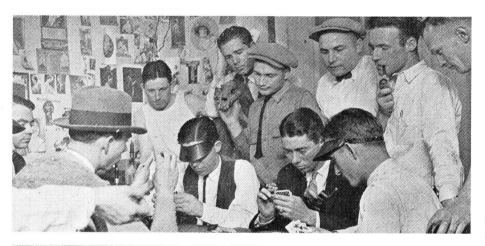

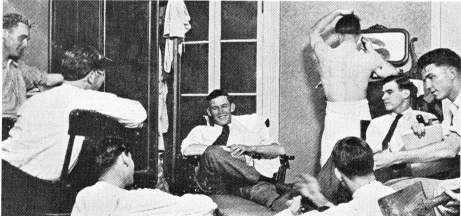

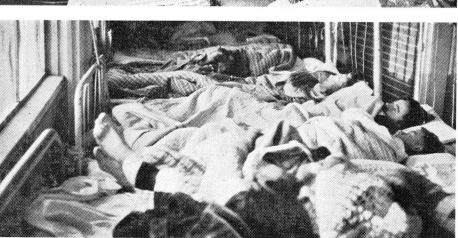

The Texas Cowboys, a men's honorary service organization, was formed in the fall of 1922 by Shorty Nowotny (*lying on ground*), head yell leader, and Bill McGill (*standing, extreme right*), the first foreman. They made their first public appearance in Dallas at the Texas-Vanderbilt game on October 21 before a crowd of eleven thousand.

For years, the Cowboys raised money for local charities with annual black-face minstrels. This one was dated 1950.

Some members of the Cowboys play with children in 1966 at a center their minstrels helped support.

Orange Jackets, organized in 1923 as a women's counterpart to the Cowboys, continues to hold a significant place on the campus. Its original purpose was "to represent the girls at rallies and games." Members (*standing*) wore their uniforms for the first time to the Texas-Oklahoma game in Austin on November 17 and were photographed with the Greenhorns (*seated*), a freshman group. Etelka Schmidt (Tek Lynn, a long-time staff member of the Hogg Foundation) was the first president of Orange Jackets.

The role of Orange Jackets has changed with the times. As members of the honorary service organization, they serve as campus hosts. In this picture, an Orange Jacket helps a freshman find a building.

Tapping in the fall and spring is always an emotion-filled experience. Here, Orange Jackets tap a new member in March 1964.

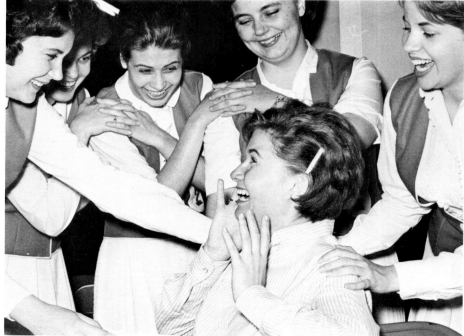

The Silver Spurs organized in November 1938. An honorary service group, the Spurs serve as custodians of Bevo. In this photograph, members escort Bevo in a 1941 torchlight parade down the Drag.

Bevo's birthday is celebrated each fall with a rodeo, proceeds from which go to charity. The Silver Spurs are sponsors.

After Pearl Harbor, December 7, 1941, campus activities assumed a new look. Several naval groups were established at the University. Shown here is part of the first graduating class at the Naval Flight Preparatory School, established in January 1943. This school enrolled several hundred aviation cadets in the first stage of their long course to Navy wings.

These Navy cadets are studying navigation.

Another Naval unit is parading in front of Carothers Dormitory on Whitis Street.

To prepare for their war-time assignment—whether in a factory, on a farm, or in civilian defense activities—U.T. women enrolled in a special war-conditioning course which met three times a week on campus to hurtle through, around, and over a city-block maze of obstacles scientifically designed to put all muscles of the body into play.

After World War II, ROTC units were established on the campus to continue training students to become officers in the military services. Personnel in the service were often honored at public ceremonies.

ROTC units parade between halves at a football game in 1952.

To learn the mountaineering technique of rapelling, Army ROTC cadets use Memorial Stadium walls as their "cliffs." From a rope attached to the top of the stadium, they can make a 130-foot drop to the ground.

Members of Angel Flight are presented in 1967.

Admirers surround the 1950 Varsity Carnival queen, Pola Ellis.

In the 1950s and early 1960s, the Texas Stars were a drill team that marched with the band.

The presentation of The University of Texas Sweetheart was the highlight of Round-Up from 1930 until the event was described as "irrelevant" in the late 1960s. Visiting representatives from other Southwest Conference schools served as members in the Sweetheart's court. Here, June Learned is overwhelmed by congratulations in 1937.

The Friar Society, founded in 1911, and Visor, shortly thereafter, were secret honor societies for senior men and women. Visor became part of the national Mortar Board in 1923, but the Friars remained local. Both groups were now co-ed. Some 1939 members of Mortar Board are shown here (*top right*).

Mortar Board honors fifteen new members in April 1962 (*top left*).

At Round-Up in 1950, the Friar Society had its annual initiation breakfast for six new members.

After Title IX of the 1972 Education Amendments went into effect, all single-sex organizations other than social groups had to become co-ed. John Craddock, Rick Potter, Mark Evans, and Alex Cranberg were the first four males elected to Mortar Board in 1976. Craddock (*bottom*) is visiting with (*left to right*) Anne Szablowski, Governor Allan Shivers, and Kathy Johnson at a Mortar Board and Omicron Delta Kappa reception.

Students participate in a Wednesday night vesper service in the Carothers Dormitory reception room in 1955.

In the 1950s, Religious Emphasis Week was a big all-University activity. Two members of the Freshman Council examine a poster with one of the fifty-one visiting speakers during a five-day period in 1956.

For years, students decorated a big tree that stood in the foyer of the Texas Union each Christmas season. They also attended a Christmas carol service in front of the Main Building during the week before Christmas.

Alpha Phi Omega members prepare to "run the Texas flag" at the Thanksgiving football game in 1962 following the acquisition of the flag from the University of Mississippi at the Cotton Bowl game on January 1 of that year.

Pancho, the Baylor Bear, was kidnapped by U.T. pranksters shortly before the Baylor game in 1955. The clown in the picture is a U.T. student dressed for a Campus Chest Drive stunt. On another occasion, in 1964, a Baylor Bear was accidentally killed when some U.T. students kidnapped it. The students made restitution by paying Baylor a sum equal to the cost of the bear; they were also suspended for one semester.

Littlefield Fountain has been host to many pinning parties and pledge dunkings, and numerous strange items have turned up in the pool. Ducks and even alligators have been found, and many times the waters have frothed and foamed when boxes of detergent or bubble bath were added.

On May 22, 1952, the University community experienced its first panty raid, a fad that had a big build-up in national magazines and full coverage in newspapers over the nation. Throughout the 1950s and into the 1960s, these raids occurred periodically when students were bored or wanted to find excitement. The one pictured here occurred on October 11, 1962, before the big O.U. weekend.

Student interest on the campus is often gauged by "spirit" shown at the big rallies before football games. At the turn of the century nightshirt parades and rallies in the auditorium were popular. Pregame rallies reached a height in popularity about 1923–1925. Student reporters spoke of regular triweekly rallies, attended by as many as two thousand to three thousand on special occasions.

Students still hold pregame rallies, led by the cheerleaders (earlier called rooters, then yell leaders). At a pregame rally in 1967, students were giving the "hook 'em" sign.

The 1975–1976 cheerleaders enter Memorial Stadium in their 1930s vintage Chevrolet.

The Texas Union ballroom has often had capacity crowds to see and hear prominent guest performers. These four students are late arrivers.

The popular Longhorn Singers, represented here by the 1963 ensemble, have entertained numerous groups.

The 1965 Glee Club members sing for a student audience.

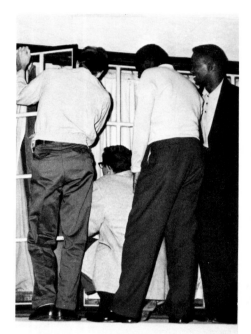

The Department of Drama productions are widely praised for their quality. *A Cry of Players* was one of the 1962 presentations.

Some activities are only fads and soon disappear, but chess always remains popular.

The powder puff football game between the Pi Beta Phis and the Kappa Kappa Gammas was a big event in the 1960s.

Bored Martyrs, a spoof on Mortar Board, enjoy a meeting at Scholz's.

The annual auction of student and faculty art has become popular. Income provides scholarships for art students. Professor Don Weismann is the auctioneer in this 1963 photograph.

Student elections are being held on a sunny day in March 1968.

When eighteen-year-olds received the right to vote in 1971, the student vote became a force in local politics. The University began to remove all traces of *in loco parentis* that still existed in University policies.

The women's liberation movement aroused students at U.T. Consciousness-raising sessions and assertiveness training were "in" during the early 1970s.

The new freedom on campus in the 1970s is somehow exemplified; to each his own . . .

Even a frisbee fling on the South Mall is representative of the new spirit.

Professor Parker Fielder of the School of Law mediates a discussion when University Co-Op workers petitioned the Co-Op Board in September 1970. To his immediate right are Bob Heath and Jim Arnold.

The Texas Student Publications Board members vote to go to court to protect their interests in 1971. Bob Binder, at the end of the table, was board chairman and president of the Students' Association. He was later an Austin city councilman.

A group of politically concerned students jam the Students' Association office in March 1970.

In 1969 graffiti boards were placed on the West Mall so that students could express their feelings in writing.

Each year for ten years (1962–1972), the Texas Union sponsored "Challenge," an in-depth, three-day discussion of some topic, such as "American Character in Transition," "Freedom and Responsibility," "Campus in Ferment," "Creation Excites Creation," and "The Black Experience." Here, students sign to attend the 1970 event.

The University "Y" first sponsored a model United Nations. Later, the Texas Union assumed sponsorship of the event. A student delegate is making an appeal in 1967.

A panel discusses the "generation gap" in 1967. Bob Breihan, director of the Methodist Student Center (now United Campus Ministries) since about 1950, has often served as a catalyst in heated student discussions.

Flower children and interested bystanders gather on the Texas Union patio in 1968 for a "Gentle Thursday" celebration.

In the Round-Up parade of 1947, one float is a satire on the "separate but equal" Negro Law School the University had established to accommodate black applicants.

A group discusses the University's segregation policies in the early 1960s (*center left*). On the far left is Lowell Lebermann, later an Austin city councilman.

The Program for Educational Opportunity (PEO) was an attempt in 1969 to provide assistance to qualified minority students. Here (*bottom left*), a group discusses the program.

Gwen Jordan, in 1962, smiles happily after her election to the Student Assembly from the College of Arts and Sciences. Gwen was the first black ever to hold an elected student government office.

Hector De Leon (*center right*) served as ombudsman from 1971 to 1973. Other ombudsmen have been Wayne McCormick (for Arts & Sciences only), 1968–1969; Carnegie Mims, 1969–1970; Jack Strickland, 1970–1971; Jim Osborn, 1973–1975; Linda Perine, 1975–1976; Clare Buie, 1977–1980; and Cheryl Ann Zaremba, 1980–present.

Jim Boyle was the first students' attorney, not only at U.T. but also in the nation (*bottom right*). During his two-year term, 1970–1972, Boyle handled approximately 2,500 cases. Mid-law and senior law students assisted him as clerks. Other students' attorneys have been Frank Ivy, 1972–1976, and Ronald W. Shortes, 1976–present.

In 1975, Carol Ann Crabtree was the first woman elected president of the student body.

Absurdism dominated the student elections in 1976 when Jay Adkins (*right*) was elected president and Skip Slyfield was elected vice-president. Their successful "Arts and Sausages" campaign preceded by two years the vote to abolish the Students' Association.

PRESIDENTS OF THE STUDENTS' ASSOCIATION

1902	W. T. Bartholomew	1950–1951	Lloyd Hand
1903–1904	Charles W. Ramsdell	1951–1952	Wales H. Madden and Wilson Foreman
1904–1905	Edward Crane		
1905–1906	Frank M. Ryburn	1952–1953	Rush Moody
1906–1907	L. W. Parrish	1953–1954	Franklin Spears
1907–1908	J. J. D. Cobb	1954–1955	Jerry Wilson
1908–1909	H. B. "Tick" Seay	1955–1956	Roland Dahlin
1909–1910	Towne Young	1956–1957	Lloyd Leroy Hayes
1910–1911	L. S. Hoffman	1957–1958	Harley Clark
1911–1912	Richard Ernest Seagler	1958–1959	William Howard Wolf
1912–1913	Hugh Potter	1959–1960	Frank Claude Cooksey
1913–1914	A. Garland Adair	1960–1961	Robert Cameron Hightower and Maurice S. Olian
1914–1915	E. H. Lawhon		
1915–1916	Francis J. Lyons	1961–1962	Maurice S. Olian
1916–1917	Raymond Myers	1962–1963	Lowell Lebermann and Marion Sanford
1917–1918	Virgil P. Lee		
1918–1919	Reagan R. Huffman	1963–1964	Julius Glickman
1919–1920	Wallace Hawkins	1964–1965	Gregory Owen Lipscomb
1920–1921	J. Benton Morgan	1965–1966	John Mack Orr
1921–1922	C. Read Granberry	1966–1967	Clif Drummond
1922–1923	Archie D. Gray	1967–1968	Lloyd Doggett
1923–1924	F. F. "Rube" Leissner	1968–1969	Rostam Kavoussi
1924–1925	S. Eldon Dyer	1969–1970	Joseph R. Krier
1925–1926	Richard W. Blalock	1970–1971	Jeff Jones
1926–1927	Ed Gossett	1971–1972	Bob Binder
1927–1928	Robert Eikel	1972–1973	Dick Benson
1928–1929	Byron Skelton	1973–1974	Sandy Kress
1929–1930	Robert M. "Bob" Payne	1974–1975	Frank Fleming
1930–1931	Hugh G. Dunlap	1975–1976	Carol Crabtree
1931–1932	Wilson H. Elkins	1976–1977	Jay Adkins
1932–1933	Allan Shivers	1977–1978	Judy Spalding
1933–1934	Hill Hodges		
1934–1935	John J. Bell		
1935–1936	Jenkins Garrett		
1936–1937	Jimmie Brinkley		
1937–1938	J. J. "Jake" Pickle		
1938–1939	John B. Connally		
1939–1940	Sydney Reagan		
1940–1941	J. Ward Fouts		
1941–1942	Fred Niemann		
1942–1943	William Arthur "Bill" Barton		
1943–1944	T. Lawrence "Larry" Jones		
1944–1945	Malcolm E. "Mac" Wallace		
1945–1946	Clayton Blakeway		
1946–1947	James W. "Jim" Smith		
1947–1948	Bradley Bourland and John Fry		
1948–1949	Barefoot Sanders		
1949–1950	Ellis Brown		

Forms of recreation are affected by life-styles, but some activities have changed little through the years. A picnic in the hills west of Austin is an activity that most students remember. Whether the food was bacon or wieners broiled on a stick or steaks broiled on a grill, the pleasure was the same. A warm fire on a chilly afternoon in the hills rejuvenates the soul.

Warm sun during the winter brings out students who want an early tan.

The Turtle Club performs in February 1964.

Dancing to the music of a rock band in 1966 was far different from the waltzes and two-steps at the turn of the century. Dean T. U. Taylor announced before the engineers' dance in 1913 that "no one will be allowed to do the Boston Dip, Open Boston, Tanglefoot, Turkey-Trot, Bunny Hug, Walking John, Still Dance, Walking, or any of the dances of the rag variety."

At a fraternity party in 1967, the frug was "in."

In September 1973, a rock concert by Z. Z. Top completely filled Memorial Stadium. Al Lundstedt, U.T. business manager of athletics, commented that, though the Students' Association profited from the venture, it took his staff two years to get the stadium back to its former condition.

The Longhorn Band, "Show Band of the Southwest," has twice marched in presidential inauguration parades. In 1961, the band marched at the inauguration of President John F. Kennedy. In the box with President and Mrs. Kennedy are Vice-President Lyndon B. Johnson and daughter Lynda, later a U.T. student. Vincent R. Di Nino was director of the Longhorn Band. The second inauguration parade in which the band participated was that of President Johnson in 1965. Chancellor and Mrs. Harry Ransom sat in the box with President and Mrs. Johnson.

An exchange of U.T. students with students from Chile was arranged with the State Department in the late 1950s and in the 1960s. This group of U.T. students was in Washington for State Department orientation before the trip to Chile in 1961. Senator Ralph Yarborough is on the front row; on the extreme right is Calvin P. "Pat" Blair, professor of international trade and resources, faculty adviser of the 1961 group. The Department of State initiated the exchange after Vice-President Richard Nixon was mobbed by angry students while on a "good will" tour of Latin America in 1958. Several universities were enlisted for exchange programs with the various countries, but the University's program was the only one that lasted for several years.

The International Club arranges an exhibit of native artifacts in 1964. Left to right are Micky Harada of Japan; Janet Di Rienzo, chairman of the Union Hospitality Committee; Yuichi Ozawa of Japan, president of the International Club; and Sally Sneed, exhibit chairman.

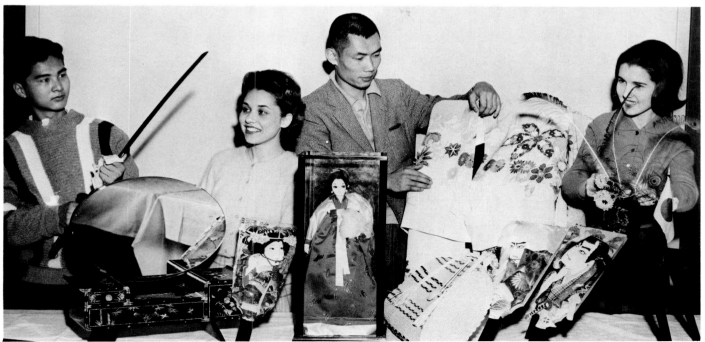

U.T. Austin currently has approximately two thousand students from other lands. Rostam Kavoussi (*top left*) was the first to be chosen as president of the student body (1968–1969). Here, he is with Joe Neal, director of the International Office, who is presenting Kavoussi an award from his home government in Iran.

Governor Allan Shivers presents honorary Texas citizenship certificates to a group of foreign students in the early 1950s.

The International Club, one of the largest groups on campus, enjoys an outing in September 1967.

Lorrin Kennamer (*center*) moderates a panel of international students in 1962. Left to right are Cecilia Ubilla from Chile, Mahdi Ali-Al-Najjar from Iraq, Hellmut Ammerlahn from West Germany, and Ram Sharma from India.

Reading for blind students is a volunteer program that has been of significance for at least twenty-five years.

Student groups often support various charities. These women are donating toys to the U.S. Marines "Toys for Tots" program in 1962.

Celebrating publication of the *Guide to The University of Texas for the Mobility Impaired* are (*left to right*) William Wilcox, Agnes Edwards, Jack Emmott, Jack Maguire, and Ronald M. Brown. Emmott was president of Mobility Impaired Grappling Hurdles Together (MIGHT).

Cap and Gown for senior women and the Kane Club for senior men were formed in the teens to perpetuate University traditions. The Kane Club terminated about 1925, but Cap and Gown remained active until the mid-sixties.

Members of Spooks, a women's service organization formed in 1941, are shown working on a service project in 1955.

Karate became popular as a student activity in the mid-1960s. These two students perform in 1965.

Riata, a student literary magazine, was first published in 1963. It last appeared in the spring of 1972.

Some interpretative dancers rehearse in 1962.

Harvey Schmidt (*at the piano*) and Tom Jones formed a duo of talent which first found harmony at U.T. in the 1950s. Their first full-length musical, *The Fantasticks*, was the longest-running show in off-Broadway history. They have since had other Broadway successes.

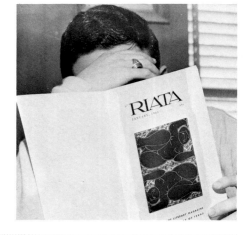

Students have watched games on television in the Texas Union since the early 1950s. Before TV, they listened to radio accounts, and before radio, they gathered on Guadalupe to hear telegraph reports of a game's progress. Beginning in 1979, closed-circuit television broadcasts of selected out-of-town games were available for a fee in the Special Events Center.

Innervisions of Blackness was organized in 1974 when a small group gathered around a piano in Jester Center. Almetris Marsh Duren helped the group organize.

Large classes exist and serve an important function, but many class activities are individualized so that learning becomes fun.

Computer-assisted and self-paced instruction are permitting students to determine their own schedules. These two students, Don Hadd and Lynda Barmore, are studying Chinese (*top left*).

Newspapers are conveniently available on microfilm in the University library.

James Daily, Jr., studies architectural design in 1967.

A student teacher works with her class in 1966.

Two 1962 award-winning students, Norma Newton and Carolyn Heafner, look on as opera coach Wilhelm Loibner instructs.

Moot court competition in Law School is serious business. A panel of law professors listen as a student pleads a case in 1966.

Combined music groups present a program of Christmas music in December 1963.

The end of a semester or school year is filled with mixed emotions. Whether cramming for exams, taking finals, or saying good-bye to friends, one's pulse beat somehow quickens.

Pamela Marie Bodemuller prepares for final exams in May 1965.

The libraries are filled during the days and nights before exams begin.

In today's modern lecture hall, as in one of the poorly lighted classrooms in Old Main, students write examinations with the same fervor or, perhaps, carelessness.

Time was that student grades were posted outside the professor's office—with names or initials listed. No more! The right to privacy protects the individual but often prolongs the anguish. Here, some students register a feeling of relief: "I passed!"

Or, in another instance, "Whee! The semester is over, and I'm graduating!"

The U.T. Austin student culture is still primarily "collegiate," with its orange-and-white-flag-waving students still predominant.

Texas Fight! Texas Fight!
And it's good-bye to A&M.
Texas Fight! Texas Fight!
And we'll put over one more win.
Texas Fight! Texas Fight!
For it's Texas that we love best!
Hail! Hail! The gang's all here,
And it's good-bye to all the rest!

7. Ex-Students and the Ex-Students' Association

Organized on Commencement Day, June 17, 1885, The University of Texas Alumni Association had as its sole purpose the maintenance of a contact with former students after they left the University. Twenty lawyers and one "academ" of the class of 1885 joined with the three law graduates of the class of 1884 to form the organization. R. C. Walker and J. H. Cobb of the class of 1884 and Yancey Lewis of the class of 1885 drew up the Association's first constitution. John S. Stone was elected the first president.

For almost a quarter of a century, the Association was without a headquarters; its home was wherever its officers happened to be. In 1910 a new era began. Under the guidance of Edwin B. Parker, the alumni structure underwent its first major reorganization. John A. Lomax accepted the position of secretary of the Alumni Association. Room 47 of the Old Main Building was designated by the regents as Alumni Headquarters in 1913. In 1914, the Association underwent its second major reorganization and was renamed "The Ex-Students' Association of The University." Lomax left in 1917, and the Association almost folded because of lack of staff and funds.

On March 1, 1919, the organization moved into the YMCA, a place it had helped to build earlier. Space was limited. After the Association was incorporated on February 8, 1924, the headquarters office moved again, this time to a house at 2300 San Antonio. Offices moved again and again before the beautiful Lila B. Etter Alumni Center on Waller Creek opened in 1965.

Among approximately 300,000 alumni are numerous prominent people. Many of these were also outstanding while they were students at the University. A few in this category were selected to introduce this chapter. Each year, since 1958, the Association honors distinguished alumni. Those who have been honored so far are shown in the latter part of the chapter.

These came to the University as students and distinguished themselves as

. . . holder of the longest term as Speaker of the House of Representatives: Sam Rayburn, 1907–1908 (*top left*).

. . . chairman of the Senate Foreign Relations Committee: Tom Connally, LL.B., 1897 (*top right*).

. . . leader in the breakthrough of women in education: Annie Webb Blanton, B.Lit., 1899, M.A., 1923 (*center*).

. . . football star, Rhodes scholar, chancellor of the University of Maryland: Wilson Elkins, B.B., M.A., 1932 (*bottom left*).

. . . dean of student life at the University: Arno Nowotny, B.A., 1922, LL.B., 1925, M.A., 1927 (*bottom center*).

. . . holder of the second-longest Methodist pastorate in the United States: Edmund Heinsohn, LL.B., 1911 (*bottom right*).

254

. . . First Lady of the United States: Lady Bird Johnson, B.A., 1933, B.J., 1934 (*top left*).

. . . justice of the United States Supreme Court: Tom Clark, B.A., 1921, LL.B., 1922 (*top right*).

. . . student body president and holder of the longest term as governor of Texas: Allan Shivers, B.A., 1931, LL.B., 1933 (*center*).

. . . student body president and United States congressman: J. J. "Jake" Pickle, B.A., 1938 (*bottom left*).

. . . dean of U.T. Law School and father of Austin's first woman mayor and one of Houston's top lawyers: Page Keeton, B.A., LL.B., 1931 (with Carole, B.A., 1961, and Richard, B.A., 1959, LL.B., 1963).

Many who were outstanding students have continued to excell in the state and nation.

Tom Law, B.A., 1939, LL.B., 1942 (*top left*), was an athlete and scholar and president of several important student groups; today he is a prominent Fort Worth lawyer and U.T. regent.

John Connally, LL.B., 1941 (*top right*), former president of the student body, has been governor of Texas, U.S. secretary of the navy, U.S. secretary of the treasury, and a candidate for the Republican nomination for the presidency.

Joe Greenhill, B.A., B.B.A., 1936, LL.B., 1939 (*center*), was editor of the *Cactus* and a Phi Beta Kappa. Today he is chief justice of the Texas Supreme Court.

Jerry McAfee, B.S., 1937 (*bottom left*), succeeded Bob Dorsey, B.S., 1940, as head of the Gulf Oil Corporation.

John Ben Shepperd, LL.B., 1941 (*bottom right*), became national president of the Junior Chamber of Commerce, attorney general of Texas, president of the Ex-Students' Association, and a leading West Texas oil man and historic preservationist.

Frank Erwin, LL.B., 1948 (*top left*), influential as a student, is still influential on the University as a whole, on U.T. athletics, and on state and national politics. He has been a member and chairman of the Board of Regents and has served as the University's chief lobbyist.

Liz Sutherland, B.J., 1942 (*top right*), vice-president of the student body while on the campus, became Liz Carpenter, press chief to Lady Bird Johnson in the White House, author of a best-seller, leader in the women's movement, and assistant secretary of education for public affairs.

John Hill, LL.B., 1947 (*center*), became Texas attorney general and candidate for governor.

Lloyd Hand, B.A., 1952, LL.B., 1957 (*bottom left*), became chief of protocol for the Department of State and lawyer-adviser to Hollywood stars.

Bobby Layne, 1944–1947 (*bottom right*), an all-American football player at U.T., became a professional football star and author of the book *Always on Sunday*.

Still others were outstanding while on the campus and have become nationally prominent.

Denton A. Cooley, B.A., 1941 (*top left*), was a basketball player who made Phi Beta Kappa. He became one of the foremost heart surgeons in the world, a pioneer in open heart surgery and heart transplants.

Kathryn Grandstaff, B.F.A., 1955 (*top right*), a graduate of the Drama Department, became Kathy Grant in the movies and the wife of Bing Crosby.

Walter Cronkite, 1933–1935 (*center*), has been called "the most trusted man in America."

Tom Landry, B.B.A., 1949 (*bottom left*), prominent as a U.T. athlete, became the calm, indefatigable, well-dressed coach of the Dallas Cowboys.

Alan Bean, B.S. in Ae.E., 1955 (*bottom right*), a graduate of the U.T. College of Engineering, was one of the U.S. astronauts who went to the moon.

Bob Strauss, LL.B., 1941 (*top left*), became national chairman of the Democratic Party, President Jimmy Carter's chief troubleshooter, and chairman of his re-election committee for 1980.

Ronnie Dugger, B.A., 1950 (*top right*), editor of the *Daily Texan*, became editor and publisher of the *Texas Observer* and author of *Our Invaded Universities*.

Willie Morris, B.A., 1956 (*center*), crusading editor of the *Daily Texan*, became the youngest editor ever of *Harper's Magazine* and author of several best-sellers.

Dolph Briscoe, B.B.A., 1943 (*bottom left*), *Cactus* editor, became governor of Texas.

Hazel Harrod, B.A., 1942, M.A., 1944 (*bottom right*), gave up a promising teaching career to marry a future chancellor of the University, Harry Ransom.

Shelby Reed, B.A., 1953 (*top left*), Mortar Board president, became Shelby Hearon and has made a national reputation as a novelist.

Lloyd Doggett, B.B.A., 1967, J.D., 1970 (*center left*), a former student body president, is a Texas state senator.

Janie Slaughter, B.S., 1971, M.Ed., 1972 (*bottom left*), became First Lady of Texas as Mrs. Dolph Briscoe.

Farrah Fawcett, 1965–1967 (*right*), a student in the mid-1960s, became one of "Charlie's Angels" on national television and a poster girl of the 1970s.

Earl Campbell, B.S., 1979 (*bottom*), winner of the Heisman Trophy, became Rookie-of-the-Year of the American Football Conference as a player for the Houston Oilers.

The first project of the Alumni Association was the erection of a YMCA building adjacent to the campus. After some delay, the University "Y" was built in 1912 across Guadalupe from the Forty Acres. Before the Texas Union, the "Y" was the center of student life to generations of students. It was razed in the late 1960s.

Beginning in 1913, the Alumni Association produced the *Alcalde*, its first direct line of communication to Association members. The magazine now serves to keep former students aware of the changing campus and to involve them in programs and concerns of the University.

During its early history, the Association held only an annual meeting at commencement. This picture was made at a barbecue in 1908, when alumni celebrated the twenty-fifth anniversary of the University. More than seventy years later, the Alumni Center is still serving barbecue to alumni.

John A. Lomax (*center right*), raconteur and folklorist, who had been secretary of the Association, was executive director from 1919 to 1926.

John A. McCurdy served as executive director of the Ex-Students' Association from 1926 to 1956. He was highly visible on campus as a friend of students and ex-students alike.

Thomas Watt Gregory (*bottom left*) was the first ex-student appointed to the Board of Regents. In 1907, he proposed erection of a modern gymnasium, and after one year, he had collected $29,000. When he left Texas to serve in Woodrow Wilson's cabinet, interest in building the gymnasium lagged. Gregory served as president of the Ex-Students' Association from 1926 to 1928, and in 1932 he was chairman of the University Union Committee as plans were completed to open the Texas Union.

After Gregory rejoined the Association's activities in 1926, he immediately revitalized his 1907 plans to construct a gymnasium. In the spring of 1928, campaigns were waged on the campus, in the city, and across the state to raise funds for what became the Union Project. Following this big alumni drive, the regents agreed to accept the Union Project as part of the University's building program and to supply whatever additional funding would be needed. This picture was taken at a student luncheon for the project.

General Gregory breaks ground for the auditorium-gymnasium (to be Gregory Gymnasium) in June 1929.

Gregory Gymnasium, Anna Hiss Gymnasium, the Texas Union, and Hogg Auditorium were included in the big Union Project.

Gregory Gymnasium (1930), part one in the Union Project, served as home for U.T. basketball and swimming teams, was used for registration until Bellmont Hall was built, and has been an auditorium for such big events as graduations and Round-Up. In 1963 an annex containing excellent recreational facilities was opened.

Anna Hiss Gymnasium (1931), formerly called the Women's Gymnasium, was renamed in 1974 to honor a former director of physical training for women. This building, which cost approximately $400,000, was part two in the Union Project.

Hogg Memorial Auditorium (1933) was originally a part of the Union plan but became a separate building. At the suggestion of ex-students, the regents named it for former Governor James S. Hogg and his son, Will. The 1,399-seat auditorium has been used for theatrical productions, convocations, examinations, and even large lecture classes.

The Texas Union (1933) was part four of the Union Project. Students and Texas alumni raised more than $400,000 for its construction. An addition was completed in 1959 at a cost of $2.15 million, and in 1977 a renovation project costing over $6 million was completed (see p. 73).

The Ex-Students' Association organized the first Round-Up in 1930. The first spring reunion on April 10 was a spectacular success. Between 2,000 and 2,500 persons attended meetings, athletic events, and a Round-Up ball. Visitors registered in the foyer of the Texas Union. Here, Orange Jackets register Beauford Jester, a member of the Board of Regents, in the mid-1930s.

More than 1,000, including members of the Legislature, attended the Round-Up barbecue in 1931.

A long generation of fraternity and sorority members will never forget those wearying pledge days of making floats. They started months in advance and then worked feverishly the last weeks before the parade to make ready. Those who watched the parades thought the products were well worth the effort (*bottom, left, 1934; right, 1950s*).

O.U. weekends in Dallas are not only popular among students, but Texas Exes also celebrate. Today celebrations usually take place at private parties. In 1957, these alumni enjoy a gala dinner dance at the Adolphus Hotel the night before the big game.

After Jack Maguire became executive director of the Association, Joe C. Thompson of Dallas, president of the Southland Corporation and founder of the chain of 7-Eleven convenience stores, became the first life member of the Association for $250. The money started a Permanent Endowment Fund, the principal of which will never be spent. Today the Alumni Center halls are lined with scrolls bearing the names and numbers of more than nine thousand life members, and the Association's endowment is more than $2 million. Judge Herman Jones, then president of the Texas Exes, admires the life membership of Elsie M. Beard.

Each Christmas since the Alumni Center was built, a Christmas party is given for students from other lands and their families.

Jack Maguire, as the third executive director, in 1956 began looking once again for a permanent home for the Association. Association officers offered to lease the George W. Littlefield Home and make it a campus showplace. The Littlefield Home was not available at that time, and the alumni organization moved into new temporary headquarters in the basement of the Home Economics Building in 1958. Three years later, the regents canceled the Association's lease on the Littlefield Home and offered instead a site on San Jacinto Boulevard between Twenty-first and Twenty-second Streets. Along with the site, the University offered the Association $110,000 from the Lila B. Etter Fund to help with construction. Holding plans for the new cen-

ter are (*left to right*) Sterling Holloway, Governor Allan Shivers, Chancellor Harry Ransom, and Jack Maguire.

Ground for the new Alumni Center was broken in April 1963 by (*left to right*) Governor John Connally, Regent W. W. Heath, President Joe Smiley, and Dean Arno Nowotny.

Staff members and alumni officers have greeted numerous visitors at the entrance to the Alumni Center. In the bottom picture, Jack Maguire, wearing the suit, talks to Roy Vaughan, current director. The woman on the step is Sara Jane English, then editor of the *Alcalde.*

The main lounge of the Alumni Center is sufficiently spacious to accommodate large groups for meetings and parties.

In 1940, Lila Belle Etter added a codicil to her will naming the University a beneficiary of her estate. The $110,000 which the regents granted from her estate paid about half the cost of the alumni headquarters. Mrs. Etter, daughter of Leslie Waggener, first president of U.T., attended the University from 1888 to 1892.

The concept of a fifty-year reunion was introduced in 1962 to honor fifty-year graduates. At an annual breakfast, the former graduates are presented Golden Anniversary Diplomas and a yearbook, *Re-Cap and Gown*, which includes current pictures of the class and a brief summary of their accomplishments since graduation (*top*). The bald man to the right of center is Richard T. Fleming, who acted as secretary at several of the fifty-year convocations.

The annual breakfast for life members was also organized in the early 1960s. In front (*left*) is Wales Madden; three persons back is Tom Sealy, one-time chairman of the Board of Regents; with his elbow on the table is Jitter Nolen. Today, because of the number of life members, the breakfast is held in a larger place.

Vincent R. DiNino, director of the Longhorn Band, receives an oversized check for $20,000 from the president of the Ex-Students' Association in May 1957. The check, a gift from the Association, set up a permanent endowment fund to provide scholarships for the band.

Pat Maguire, editor of the *Alcalde* at the time, conducts members of the fifty-year class of 1974 on a tour of the campus. W. Conner Cole and Martha Lee Cole occupy the front seat on the right.

"Alumni Fun," nationally televised game show in the 1960s, puts a question to U.T. representatives Allan Shivers; C. R. Smith, president of American Airlines; and actor Rip Torn. The unseen opposition was from George Washington University.

Operation Brainpower, a program conducted during the 1960s, was an effort to attract academically superior students to the University. Today a comparable committee works to recruit National Merit Scholars.

In this picture (*top right*), Colorado County Exes discuss Operation Brainpower with a student team from the campus: (*left to right, seated*) Judye Galeener, junior; and Clay Dowell, superintendent of Weimar schools; (*standing*) Truman McMahan, editor-publisher of the *Columbus Citizen*; Lowell Lebermann, senior; Rob See, junior; and Greg Lipscomb, law student and president of the student body.

U.T. did not have a drama department until 1937, but the Curtain Club was a popular organization for those interested in acting. Eli Wallach, a history major, was an active Curtain Club member who became successful on Broadway and in films. Here (*center left*), he receives the Distinguished Achievement Award, given annually to alumni by the New York Club, from J. Donald Hill; Mrs. Jackson Dawson watches.

President Stephen H. Spurr presents a scholarship check, made possible by an ex-students' club, to Kenneth Lenard in 1974 (*center right*). Wales Madden, president of the Texas Exes, observes the presentation.

A banquet is held each fall to honor recipients of approximately 125 scholarships currently being awarded by ex-students. Ronald M. Brown, vice-president for student affairs, is the second man from the left.

Roy Vaughan (*top left*) became executive director of the Ex-Students' Association in 1976. Membership growth under his leadership has been phenomenal. His involvement of students in program planning and program implementation develops interest among recent graduates.

Neal Spelce (*right*) and Jack Blanton (*center*) congratulate Carnegie Mims for a great job in the ex-students' minority recruitment program.

The first letterman awards dinner was held in 1938. The event has become popular as teams have won conference and national honors. Below, Scott Appleton, 1962 all-American, receives an award from sportswriter Lou Maysel as Coach Darrell Royal looks on.

Over 135 organized clubs of Texas Exes meet on March 2 each year to salute the University, to reminisce about student days, and to extend a helping hand. University administrators, faculty, and students often participate as speakers at these celebrations. In the late 1950s (*left to right*), Loraine Jackson, Harry Ransom, John A. Focht, Jack Holland, and Arno Nowotny are looking at a map of Texas that shows the location of clubs.

At the March 2 events, door prizes are often given. Pat Rutherford, Jr., and Weldon H. Smith, 1963 and 1964 presidents, respectively, of the Houston club, are presenting a door prize.

Congressman Jack Brooks, a U.T. alumnus, speaks at a Texas Exes meeting in Washington, D.C., on March 2, 1960.

Continuing education programs, begun in the 1960s, remain popular. Retreats, seminars, and trips are planned for those interested in specific topics. Lectures by professors are also scheduled on Saturdays before home football games. The first Alumni College was held for a week in 1977, when families returned to the campus for a week of lectures sponsored by the Division of Continuing Education and the Ex-Students' Association. William S. Livingston addresses an Alumni College class in the summer of 1979.

The first International Ex-Students' Conference was held in 1970. Alumni from throughout the world returned to Austin to examine the problems of today's world. They met again in 1976 to study world energy problems.

The Flying Longhorns, Inc., is an Association subsidiary to assist University ex-students in arranging travel plans. The first trip, in April 1961, was to Europe. Seventy-nine Texas Exes visited London, Paris, and other points of interest. Today, University alumni are given opportunities to travel to all parts of the globe.

Annually since 1958 (except in 1959), the Association has formally honored former University students who have been recognized in their professions and as outstanding citizens. At a Distinguished Alumnus Awards gala, those chosen for the honor are presented. Pictured on the next several pages are recipients of the award from 1958 through 1979.

The first recipients of the Distinguished Alumnus Award, in 1958, were (top, left to right) Ramón Beteta (B.A., 1923), former director general of *Novedades*, national newspaper of Mexico; Sam Rayburn (U.T. Law School, 1907–1908), former Speaker of the U.S. House of Representatives; Walter Prescott Webb (B.A., 1915, M.A., 1920, Ph.D., 1932), Distinguished Professor of History at U.T. and noted author; and (far right) Robert B. Anderson (LL.B., 1932), former U.S. secretary of the treasury. Fess Parker is the Texas Ex who acted as master of ceremonies for the first presentation.

In 1960, Logan Wilson (M.A., 1927), former president of U.T., former president of the American Council on Education, and now living in Austin, was the sole honoree (bottom left).

The only honoree in 1961 was Secretary of the Navy John B. Connally (LL.B., 1941). The temporary eye injury was incurred as he inspected the Naval ROTC Honor Guard on his arrival at the Austin airport. With him is Mrs. Connally, the former Idanell Brill, who became a recipient in her own right in 1972.

Recipients of the award in 1962 were (*top, left to right*) Allan Shivers (B.A., 1931, LL.B., 1933), former governor of Texas, and former chairman of the Board of Regents, U.T. System; Tom C. Clark (B.A., 1921, LL.B., 1922), former justice of the U.S. Supreme Court; James A. Elkins (LL.B., 1901), former senior partner of Vinson, Elkins, Searls, and Connally; and Gus S. Wortham (U.T., 1908–1911), founder of American General Insurance Group, from Houston.

Honored in 1963 were (*bottom, left to right, seated*) James I. McCord (M.A., 1942), president of Princeton Theological Seminary; Ima Hogg (U.T., 1899–1901), philanthropist; and Hines H. Baker (B.A., LL.B., 1917), former president of Humble Oil and Refining Company (now Exxon); (*standing*) Rex G. Baker (B.A., J.D., 1917), former vice-president of Humble Oil and Refining Company; and C. R. Smith (U.T., 1921–1924), former consultant to International Banking House of Lazard Freres and Company, New York, and president-founder of American Airlines.

Awardees in 1964 were (*top, left to right*) Walter Cronkite (U.T., 1933–1935), managing editor for CBS Evening News, New York; Mrs. Lyndon Baines Johnson, *née* Claudia Alta Taylor (B.A., 1933, B.J., 1934), former First Lady of the United States, now living in Austin; and Charles I. Francis (B.A., 1915, LL.B., 1917), founder and former counsel to the president, Texas Eastern Transmission Corporation.

Recipients of the award in 1965 were (*bottom, left to right*) Homer Thornberry (B.B.A., 1932, LL.B., 1936), judge of the Fifth Circuit Court of Appeals, Austin; John B. Holmes (B.B.A., 1943), independent oil operator, Houston; Leonard F. McCollum (B.S. in Geology, 1925), former chairman of United States Continental Oil Company, Houston; and C. W. (Tex) Cook (B.S. in Engineering, 1930), past chairman of the executive committee of General Foods Corporation, now living in Austin.

In 1966, recipients of the award were (*top, left to right*) Harding L. Lawrence (B.B.A., 1942), chairman of the board, president, and chief executive officer of Braniff International, Dallas; Thomas R. Sealy, Jr. (LL.B., 1931), senior partner of Stubbeman, McRae, Sealy, Laughlin, and Browder, Midland; Denton A. Cooley, M.D. (B.A., 1941), surgeon-in-chief of Texas Heart Institute, Houston; and D. Harold Byrd (U.T., 1919–1921), D. H. Byrd Enterprises, Dallas. Master of ceremonies was John B. Connally.

Honored in 1967 were (*bottom, beginning second from left*) William B. Bates (LL.B., 1915), senior partner of Fulbright, Crooker, Freeman, Bates, and Jaworski, Houston; Edward A. Clark (U.T. Law School, 1928), for-

mer ambassador to Australia and senior partner of Clark, Thomas, Winters, and Shapiro, Austin; and Dause L. Bibby (B.B.A., 1933), president of Stromberg-Carlson Corp., New York. Presenting the awards was Charles S. Coates, Sr. (*left*), president of the Ex-Students' Association in 1967. Also receiving the award was R. Ewing Thomason (LL.B., 1900), U.S. district judge (not pictured).

Receiving the award in 1968 were (*left to right, seated, beginning second from left*) Fess Parker (B.A., 1950), television and film star, Santa Barbara, California; William W. Heath (U.T. Law School, 1922–1923), former ambassador to Sweden; and Bob R. Dorsey (B.S. in Ch.E., 1940), former chairman of the board and chief executive officer of Gulf Oil Corporation, now living in Austin; and (*standing*) Gail Whitcomb (B.A., LL.B., 1931), attorney of Whitcomb and Whitcomb and civic leader, Houston. John Connally sits at extreme left, while Jack Maguire stands beside Whitcomb.

An awardee in 1969 was Fernando Beláunde-Terry (M. Arch., 1935), former president of Peru and visiting professor of regional planning at George Washington University (*bottom left*).

Also an awardee in 1969 was Mrs. Bing Crosby, *née* Kathryn Grandstaff (B.F.A., 1955), actress and author, Hillsborough, California (*bottom center*).

Another 1969 awardee was Roy Crane (U.T., 1919–1922), cartoonist for King Features Syndicate, with worldwide distribution, Orlando Beach, Florida (*bottom right*).

Two additional recipients in 1969: Benno Charles Schmidt (B.A., L.L.B., 1936), managing partner of J. H. Whitney and Company, New York (*top left*); and O. Pendleton Thomas (M.B.A., 1941), chairman of the board and chief executive officer of B. F. Goodrich Co. (*center left*).

The 1970 awardees were (*top right, left to right*) Luis Flores-Arias (B.S. in C.E., 1923), former president of Concreto, S.A., and consulting engineer, Mexico City; Herbert James Frensley (U.T., 1927–1929), former chief executive of Brown and Root, Inc.; Captain Alan L. Bean (B.S. in Ae.E., 1955), U.S. Navy on duty with NASA at Johnson Space Center; Joseph Jay Deiss (B.A., 1933, M.A., 1934), author and former vice-director of

the American Academy in Rome; and Merton Melrose Minter (B.A., 1925, M.A., 1928), physician.

Recipients in 1971 were (*bottom right, left to right*) John S. Redditt (LL.B., 1921), attorney and civic leader; Charles S. Coates, Sr. (U.T. 1931–1936), consultant and rancher; Miguel R. Cárdenas (LL.B., 1917), senior partner of Cárdenas-Sepúlveda Law Offices, Mexico, represented here by his daughter; and George John Beto (M.A., 1944, Ph.D., 1955), former director of Texas Department of Corrections and Distinguished Professor of Criminology, Sam Houston State University.

The 1972 recipients included (*bottom left*) Wilson H. Elkins (B.A., M.A. 1932), chancellor of the University of Maryland, College Park.

Also recipients in 1972 were (*left, top to bottom*) Jack S. Josey (B.S. in Petr. Prod. Engr., 1939), president of Josey Oil Company, Houston; DeWitt C. Reddick (B.A., 1925, M.A., 1928), Jesse H. Jones professor of Journalism at U.T. Austin; and David Thomas Searls (LL.B., 1929), former senior member of Vinson, Elkins, Searls, and Smith, Houston. Mrs. John B. Connally, *née* Idanell Brill (U.T., 1935–1940), former First Lady of Texas, Houston (pictured with the 1961 recipient, her husband, on p. 274), was another 1972 recipient.

Distinguished alumni in 1973 (*right*) were (*left to right, top*) Mauricio B. Madero (U.T., 1930–1933), president of Pesquera Atlántida, S.A., Mexico City (with Mrs. Madero); and George R. Brown (U.T., 1918–1919),

former chairman of the board, Brown and Root, Inc., Houston (with Mrs. Brown); (*bottom*) Thomas W. Landry (B.B.A., 1949), head coach of the Dallas Cowboys Club (with Mrs. Landry); Vernon F. (Doc) Neuhaus (U.T., 1918–1920), owner of Neuhaus Properties, Mission (with Mrs. Neuhaus); and Margaret Cousins (B.A., 1926), author and editor, San Antonio.

Honored in 1974 were (*top, left to right*) Arno Nowotny (B.A., 1922, LL.B., 1925, M.A., 1927), former dean of student life at U.T. Austin; Joe R. Greenhill (B.A., B.B.A., 1936, LL.B., 1939), chief justice of the Supreme Court of Texas (retired), Austin; Leroy Jeffers (LL.B., 1932), senior partner of Vinson, Elkins, Searls, Connally, and Smith, Houston; Bernice Milburn Moore (B.A., 1924, M.A., 1932), executive associate of the Hogg Foundation for Mental Health (retired), Austin; and William S. White (U.T., 1923–1926), author and columnist, Austin.

Receiving the awards in 1975 were (*bottom, left to right*) Maurice F. Granville (B.S. in Ch.E., 1937), chairman of the board and chief executive officer of Texaco, Inc., New York; Mario Efraín Ramírez, M.D. (U.T., 1942–1945), physician and Starr County Judge; Jack Wrather (B.A., 1939), executive and investor in hotel, entertainment, ranching, real estate, and oil and gas businesses, Los Angeles; Elizabeth (Liz) Sutherland Carpenter (B.J., 1942), former White House press secretary and staff director to the First Lady, 1963–1969, author, and now assistant secretary of education for public affairs, Washington, D.C.; Harry Huntt Ransom (U.T., 1935–1937), chancellor emeritus of The University of Texas and director of the University History Project; and Ben Fooshee Love (B.B.A., 1947), chief executive officer of Texas Commerce Bank, Texas Bancshares, Inc., Houston.

Recipients in 1976 were (*top, left to right*) Ralph Spence (B.B.A., 1942), independent oil operator, Tyler; Lorene L. Rogers (M.A., 1946; Ph.D., 1948), biochemist and president of U.T. Austin, 1974–1979; Marvin Collie (B.A., LL.B., 1941), partner in law firm of Vinson, Elkins, Searls, Connally, and Smith and former president of National Bank of Commerce, Houston; and W. Page Keeton (B.A., LL.B., 1931), dean of the U.T. Law School, 1949–1974, Austin.

The 1977 awards were presented to (*bottom, left to right*) Rex G. Baker, Jr. (B.A., 1941, LL.B., 1947), president of Southwestern Group Financial, Inc., Houston, and partner of Baker, Sharman, and Wise law firm; L. L. (Tex) Colbert (B.B.A., 1925), former president and chairman of the board of Chrysler Corporation; Margaret Milam (Mrs. Eugene) McDermott (U.T., 1932–1933), philanthropist, Dallas; and H. Frank Connally, Jr., M.D. (B.A., 1933; M.D., 1937), physician and civic leader, Waco.

Receiving the award in 1978 were (*top, third from left*) John Randolph Hubbard (B.A., 1938, M.A., 1939, Ph.D., 1950), then president of the University of Southern California, Los Angeles; (*fifth from left*) Kraft W. Eidman (B.A., LL.B., 1935), senior partner in Fulbright and Jaworski, Houston; (*fourth from right*) Jack S. Blanton (B.A., 1947, LL.B., 1950), president of Scurlock Oil Company, Houston; and (*third from right*) Nancy Lee (Mrs. Perry R.) Bass (B.A., 1937), philanthropist, Fort Worth.

The 1979 recipients were (*bottom, left to right*) Frank C. Erwin, Jr. (LL.B., 1948), attorney, Austin; J. J. "Jake" Pickle (B.A., 1938), U.S. congressman from the Tenth District, Texas; Robert L. Parker (B.S., 1944),

president and chairman of the board of Parker Drilling Company, Tulsa; and Wales H. Madden, Jr. (B.A., 1950, LL.B., 1952), partner in the legal firm of Selecman and Madden, Amarillo.

The 1980 recipients (not pictured) were Senator Lloyd Bentsen, Jack S. Gray, Dan Krausse, and Mark Martin.

The Eyes of Texas Are Upon You

8. Seals, Signs, Symbols, and Statues

The artifacts of a campus are important to an understanding of its culture and the social behavior of its students. Traditions grow up around such artifacts, and these traditions form cultural patterns endemic to the institution. Each college or university develops its own traditions, customs, symbols, and ways of life consistent with or opposed to the outside social forces.

The colors, the alma mater, the seal, the mascot, and other symbols are tangibles that provide the nostalgia that binds former students together. The pageantry of the stadium on a cool November afternoon or the quiet contentment felt when walking across the campus on a spring evening as the chimes peel a few strains of the alma mater are subtleties of the culture developed gradually by generations of students.

Artifacts appear and disappear; new conditions produce new signs and symbols; social change often kills off an old custom. Nevertheless, the pervasive traditions that are difficult to identify establish norms and relationships that are instrumental in making each college unique.

The University of Texas has its own patterns of culture developed during its first century.

"The Eyes of Texas" is the alma mater
of The University of Texas.

The University Act of the Legislature of 1881 provided that "the Regents . . . and their successors . . . shall have the right of making and using a common seal and of altering the same at pleasure." The first, designed before the University opened, was seldom used. On October 31, 1905, the regents adopted another, designed by J. W. Battle. Altered only when "at Austin" was added in the late 1960s, that seal is still used today. In 1949, Hulon W. Black, secretary of the Development Board, asked Leonard F. Kreisle, then assistant professor of mechanical engineering, to prepare a color rendition of the seal. Here, Kreisle holds a framed copy. The rendition was not officially adoped by the regents until May 4, 1957.

The University of Texas maces were designed and constructed under the supervision of Carl J. Eckhardt while he was professor of mechanical engineering and director of the University's physical plant. Eckhardt began the project in 1956. Some of the wood, mostly walnut and oak, was taken from former University buildings or campus trees. The maces are on display in the Academic Center lobby.

The University of Texas mace (*right*), made entirely of brass and weighing thirty-two pounds, is intended for stationary use at important meetings and convocations. On one side of the head of the mace is the seal of The University of Texas, and on the reverse side is a map of the state of Texas.

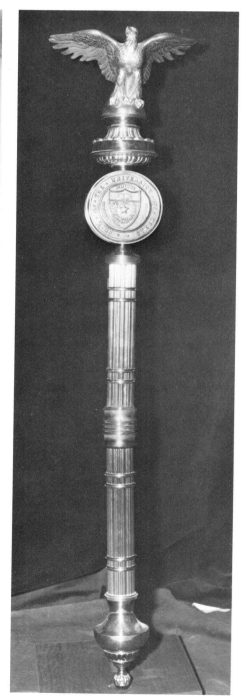

This stained glass window, a memorial to Colonel Ashbel Smith, was presented to the University on October 23, 1908, by the Ashbel Literary Society and adorned the west entrance to Old Main. Dollie Bell Rutherford made the presentation, and President Sidney Mezes accepted the gift, which was designed by H. E. Goodhue of Cambridge, Massachusetts. On the top was the seal of The University of Texas in orange and white, and on either side were emblems of art and science. The window was installed in the new Main Building, but it was mistakenly marked with a plaque designating it as a gift of the Sidney Lanier Literary Society. The lower portion of the window may be seen at the west end of the Main Building on the landing between the third and fourth floors.

The first Chuck Wagon in the Texas Union occupied the southwest corner of the building. A head of Bevo appropriately marked the entrance. For years, the Chuck Wagon was the place to go for coffee and conversation between classes.

March 2, Texas Independence Day, has been celebrated at U.T. Austin since 1897. University students had asked for a holiday so they could celebrate the signing of the Declaration of Independence of Texas sixty-one years before. President George T. Winston, who had just come to Texas from the University of North Carolina, refused the students' request. Not to be brushed off, the senior law students and most of the juniors went to the Capitol grounds and "borrowed" a cannon, which they took back to the campus. Firing began with such intensity that some windows in Old Main were shattered. The cannon was moved to old Clark Field, where the entire student body of approximately four hundred joined the fun. President Winston finally joined the group and made his famous speech:

I was born in the land of liberty, rocked in the cradle of liberty, nursed on the bottle of liberty, and I've had liberty preached to me all of my life, but Texas University students take more liberty than anyone I've ever come in contact with.

On this page are three celebrations: March 2, 1897 (*top*); March 2, 1909 (*bottom left*); and March 2, 1922 (*bottom right*).

ROTC guns were used for the 1952 celebration (*top*).

During the 1950s, members of Kappa Sigma fraternity added a new dimension. Their house on Nineteenth Street at the end of tree-lined University Avenue faced Littlefield Fountain. The guns were traditionally fired at 11:45 A.M. on March 2 toward the south, down University Avenue. The ceremony included a five-minute concert by the Longhorn Band and the raising of the Texas flag. In 1951 the Kappa Sigs dressed themselves as Mexicans and returned the cannon fire from the top of their big house. This tradition continued until the early 1970s, when some groups complained of ethnic prejudice. Shown below are Kappa Sig participants in 1959.

In 1979, U.T.'s oldest tradition was revived with a worldwide salute to Texas excellence. A large group celebrated on campus, before a backdrop formed by a big Texas flag draped on the front of the Main Building. At a cue from Smokey, a quad-service ROTC color guard raised the Texas flag. With hands uplifted in the familiar "Hook 'em Horns" position, the crowd, accompanied by the Longhorn Band, joined in singing "The Eyes of Texas" and then toasted the University and its continued excellence with orange tea in true Texas tea-sipper style.

Bevo, a Longhorn steer, is the University mascot. Stephen Pinckney (1911) spearheaded a movement to provide a live mascot for U.T., collecting $1.00 each from 124 alumni and purchasing a steer from "somewhere in the Texas Panhandle." On Thanksgiving Day 1916, the frightened Bevo I (*top left*) was dragged onto the field by two determined cowboys and formally presented to the students in a short speech by T. B. Buffington (1892). This first mascot was forthwith branded by Texas A&M pranksters with "13–0," the score of the A&M victory from the year before. A humiliated group of Texas students tried to save face by altering the numerals "13–0" to read "BEVO," the Longhorn's name in the first place. ("Bevo" was the

brand name of a popular near-beer made by Budweiser.) On January 20, 1920, Bevo I attained immortality when he was barbecued and served to more than 100 guests, primarily men and women who had won letters in athletics. A group of Aggies attended by invitation, shared the barbecue, and were given the half of Bevo I's hide that had been branded.

Bevo II (*top right*) was presented to University students by W. A. Boyett, father of Lynwood Boyett, former head yell leader, and Jack Boyett, yell leader in 1932.

Bevo VII (*bottom, left and right*), the most beloved of the U.T. Longhorns, was acquired in 1957 when he was only four months old. He was mascot for eight years.

The Silver Spurs, honorary service organization, are Bevo's official custodians. Each year, members of this group sponsor a birthday party for Bevo. Below, Bevo IX, with three of his Silver Spur friends, is having his cake and eating it, too. Acquired in 1966, Bevo IX was turned out to pasture in 1976. He was usually well behaved, but, unfortunately, he didn't like women.

Bevo X made his debut on Saturday, September 18, 1976, at Memorial Stadium. He is on loan from John Hardin III, a member of the Silver Spurs. Born on the Hardin ranch on March 2, 1972, he was a gift to John from his father, Dr. John Hardin, Jr. He weighed one thousand pounds and had a horn span of forty-three inches when he was presented.

The University colors, orange and white, were officially adopted by the regents on May 10, 1900, after a student vote. As early as 1885, students had displayed orange and white ribbons on special occasions. The exact shade of orange, not officially adopted until July 31, 1970, is "focal orange," a medium shade, but the long-disputed issue is unimportant to those who purchase T-shirts, stuffed animals, pennants, stickers, and other orange-and-white items.

John Lang Sinclair (*top right*) was author of "The Eyes of Texas." The song had its debut in the old Hancock Opera House on May 12, 1903, at a minstrel show given as a benefit for the varsity track team. Lewis Johnson, director of the band and Sinclair's roommate, decided the show needed one more peppy song to put it over and asked Sinclair to write one. Sinclair tore a strip of paper from a Bosche's laundry bundle and wrote the words, which were fitted to the tune "I've Been Working on the Railroad." The original hangs in the Alumni Center.

The song was a great success when first sung at the minstrel show by the University quartet whose mem-bers were J. D. Kivlehen (*center left*), Ralph A. Porter (*center right*), W. D. Smith (*bottom left*), and Jas. R. Cannon (*bottom right*).

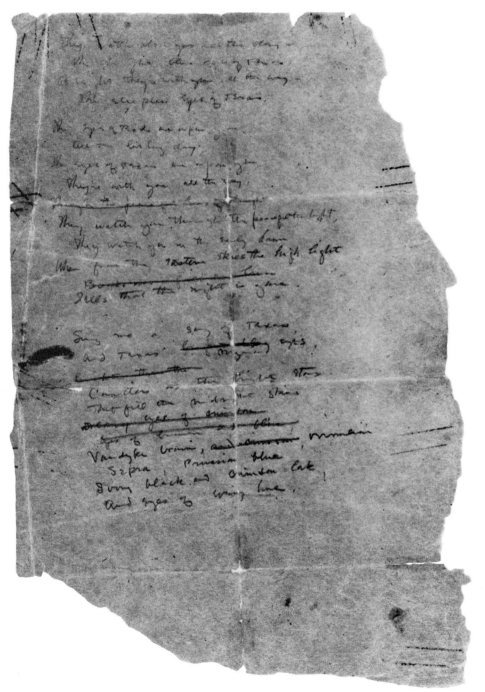

Senior Week first featured a program called "Swing-Out" in 1922. Even though Senior Week included activities for both men and women, Swing-Out was for women only and had as the major portion of the ceremony a revival of the Bluebonnet Chain tradition begun earlier. The Bluebonnet Chain ceremony was first pictured in *The Cactus* in 1917 and showed senior and junior women of 1916 participating in the simple ceremony, during which seniors passed a handmade chain of real bluebonnets, representing responsibility, to the new junior leaders.

The Swing-Out ceremony was held in front of Old Main in 1923 (*top*) when the University's fortieth anniversary was celebrated.

The 1937 Swing-Out (*bottom*) was the first held in front of the new Main Building.

During the 1960s, students tended to rebel against traditions, and Swing-Out and the Bluebonnet Chain were victims. The 1963 ceremony was the last.

At the north end of Memorial Stadium, built to honor Texas men and women killed in World War I, a tablet bearing an inscription and the names of those killed in the war was unveiled on January 14, 1931, by Governor Dan Moody. In the middle of the tablet is a statue of Columbia carrying an upraised olive branch as a sign of peace. The tablet is decorated with corps insignia and some of the names of the important battles of the war. Plaques bearing names of individual Texas men and women are placed alongside exits from the stadium. Each plaque gives the name, rank, place and date of death, and the unit of each person honored. On November 12, 1977, the stadium was rededicated "in memory of all American veterans of all wars."

Over the main entrance gates to Memorial Stadium hangs the head of a Longhorn.

"Big Bertha," reportedly the world's largest drum, became a fixture of the Longhorn Band during the 1955 season. Presented to the band by Colonel (now Brigadier General) D. Harold Byrd of Dallas, the drum is eight feet in diameter and forty-four inches wide, weighs five hundred pounds, and stands ten feet tall on its four-wheel cart. It was originally constructed for the University of Chicago in 1922.

"Smokey," a cannon fired when U.T. makes a score or an unusually good play at football games, was built in U.T.'s mechanical engineering laboratory in 1953. Operated by the Texas Cowboys, a service organization, "Smokey" is brought onto the field and taken to out-of-town games in its own special orange-and-white trailer.

The "Hook 'em Horns" signal was introduced at a Friday night pep rally in Gregory Gymnasium before the Texas Christian University football game in 1955. Harley Clark, head yell leader, and his friend Henry Pitts of Beaumont decided that the sign, made by extending the index and little fingers and tucking the middle and ring fingers beneath the thumb, would be appropriate for U.T. students because it resembled the head of a Longhorn. In the picture, Harley Clark (*center of the top row*) is with five other 1955 cheerleaders. "Hook 'em Horns," Coach Royal!

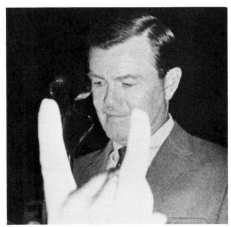

One of the memorable ceremonies associated with the annual gridiron tussle between Texas and Texas A&M is the big bonfire and pep rally preceding the game. The Cowboys usually sponsor the collection of wood for the bonfire, and a contest is staged to see which organization can gather the most wood. The location of the bonfire has been moved several times as Austin has grown, but the event preceding the big game has always attracted a large crowd. The first game between the two schools was played in 1894; Texas won, 38 to 0.

The red-candle tradition began in November 1941, when the Longhorns were scheduled to play the Aggies at College Station. Students say the candles will hex the "other" team and give U.T. the advantage. Several good examples of how they have worked are cited by former students. This 1966 photograph shows Kathy Dulan (*front center*), a sophomore from Fayetteville, Arkansas, surrounded by friends holding red candles.

Alpha Phi Omega members have been "running the flag" at football games since January 1, 1962, when Governor Ross Barnett of Mississippi gave Governor Price Daniel a big Texas flag used by the Mississippi band at half-time in the Cotton Bowl. The original flag, not very durable, was soon replaced. A third flag, made of nylon, was acquired in 1972, with financial help from the Athletics Department. The fourth, purchased with contributions to the APO flag fund, was unfurled at the Texas–Texas A&M game in 1978. It is hauled in its own trailer, built and financed by APO.

The first Round-Up parade was held in 1934 with only a few floats. This was the beginning of an annual tradition that climaxed in the late 1950s, declined during the 1960s, and was revived in the 1970s.

One of the floats in the 1950 parade featured a butterfly being driven by a sorority member.

The twenties were characterized by an increase in automobiles on the campus. During the 1925–1926 school year, all roads leading to the campus except the one on the south at the end of University Avenue were blocked. Bill B. Neans (*top left*), the "campus cop," became guardian to the entrance to the campus and a little house was built to protect him from the cold. The entrance was moved to Twenty-fourth and Whitis in 1932. Today five entrances to the campus are marked by attractive, air-conditioned buildings, constructed in the 1960s (*top center*). University police staff the entrances.

Pig Bellmont (*bottom left*) was a campus pet from 1914 to 1923. When Pig died in 1923, students mourned at his funeral (*bottom center*).

A 150-foot water tower was erected on the campus before the beginning of the 1904 session because of a water shortage caused by the flood and dam break in 1900. The tower, often called "Prexy's Pot," became a symbol, a new temptation to class groups desiring to display their numerals. The tank was the scene of numerous student protests, class fights, and other rebellious incidents. Finally, in 1918, a man from Houston paid $2,000 for the landmark and it was removed from the campus.

A pushball was ordered by the Student Council at the suggestion of Dean H. Y. Benedict in 1911 after a student had been shot following the annual March 2 tug-of-war. Dean Benedict suggested that the pushball be substituted for the tug-of-war, which usually ended in a class rush. The huge pushball, six feet in diameter, cost approximately $200. The first contest was held on Clark Field on March 2, 1912. An admission fee of fifteen cents was charged to defray the cost of the ball. The band accompanied the ball on the field, and the Globraskers, a new stunt organization, performed between halves. The first game ended in a draw for the freshmen and sophomores. On each March 2 during the teens and early twenties the pushball contest was part of the annual celebration of Texas Independence Day. The picture below was made in the mid-1920s.

Eeyore's Birthday Party was first held in Eastwoods Park on a "hummy sort of day" in the spring of 1964, when Lloyd W. Birdwell, Jr., and some of his friends decided to celebrate just as Christopher Robin would have done (Eeyore was the Great Grey Donkey in A. A. Milne's books). The event has grown so big that each year sponsors threaten that the celebration will not occur again. In 1980, followers of the original group celebrated Eeyore's birthday at Windedale Inn near Round Top, while the University "Y" sponsored a party in Pease Park near the University. Even ex-students' groups hold Eeyore parties in cities over the state.

Alexander Fredericke Claire is the patron saint of U.T. engineering students. A small group of carousing sophomore engineers "borrowed" the statue of a little fat-bellied fellow holding a glass of beer from Jacoby's Beer Garden early on April Fool's Day 1908. On April 1, 1909, Alf Toombs christened him Alexander Fredericke Claire. In this 1914 picture, he is flanked by (*left to right*) Joe Moore, Harry Fritz, and Glenn Vaughan.

Since 1901, the sunflower has been worn by law students at commencement. Today at the Sunflower Ceremony, law graduates present sunflowers to their nearest relatives and friends, and the associate dean pins a sunflower on each senior. Below, former dean, Page Keeton, holds a sunflower.

The Peregrinus (*bottom left*) is the patron saint of U.T. law students. Drawn on the blackboard in Judge W. S. Simkin's class by Russell Savage after Jim L. Mc-Call, center on the famous 1900 football team, identified the Peregrinus as "some kind of animal," the rendition was later made into a banner and, still later, a papier-mâché figure.

Beginning in 1959, Round-Up planners decided to tell the University's story with displays in the main ballroom of the Texas Union. Staff member Brucie Taylor coordinated the event. By the last one in 1974, more than seventy areas of study were represented in Showcase. Regent Edward Clark stands at the lectern in the 1971 picture.

301

Stump speaking became popular during and immediately following the protest period of the late 1960s,
and a special area was designated on campus where one
could speak on any topic. In the picture below, student
body president Bob Binder (1971–1972) debates President Stephen H. Spurr.

Seniors bought University rings for the first time in
the spring of 1927. The ring, designed by Mrs. Darrell
Jackson, technician in the Department of Zoology, was
of 10-karat gold and had a garnet stone. Today rings are
available in a wide variety of styles, with or without
stones, at most jewelry stores in Austin and at book-
stores near the campus.

Littlefield Memorial Fountain was turned on for the first time on March 26, 1933. It was part of the Littlefield Memorial Entrance Gate, a gift of Major George W. Littlefield, and was designed by Pompeo Coppini and arranged in place by consulting architect Paul P. Cret. The intention of the memorial was to honor the men and women of the Confederacy, "who fought with valor and suffered with fortitude that states' rights be maintained," and the men and women of the nation, "who gave of their possessions and of their lives that free government be made secure to the peoples of the earth."

Seventeen bells (not a complete carillon) hang in the square colonnaded belfry that rests on the clock-story and forms the crowning feature of the Tower of the Main Building. The bells, which weigh 40,000 pounds, were cast by the Old Meneely Bell Foundry of Watervliet, New York, and were installed in 1936. They are made of "bell metal," 78 percent copper and 22 percent tin. The hammers are iron and, like the bells, are covered with bronze.

Until 1968, the carillonneur played in the Tower on a mechanical keyboard, a clavier, open to the sky (*bottom right*, Tom Anderson in 1967). Today the chime room is a small room on the third floor of the Main Building. The area is bare of all furniture except a keyboard that resembles a small electric organ.

Six statues were included in the Littlefield Memorial Entrance Gate: John H. Reagan (*top center*), James Stephen Hogg (*top right*), Woodrow Wilson (*opposite page*), Robert E. Lee (*bottom center*), Albert Sidney Johnston (*bottom right*), and Jefferson Davis (*left*). Reagan, Hogg, and Johnston are the only ones closely associated with Texas.

Woodrow Wilson (*top left*) is the only twentieth-century person commemorated in the Littlefield Memorial Entrance Gate group.

Jefferson Davis, president of the Confederacy (*bottom left*), holds a jack-o-lantern placed in his hand by some wag.

The Tower of the Main Building, completed in 1937, is an identity symbol for U.T. Austin. The 27-story tower, 59 feet square and 307 feet tall, is crowned by what is sometimes called a Greek outhouse. Above the observation deck rises the portion of the Tower that supports four faces of a huge clock, twelve feet in diameter. The clock, which marks the quarter-hour by four bells of the Westminster chime and strikes the hours on a bell that weighs three and a half tons, serves as the principal time piece for the campus community.

The *Torchbearers*, a sculpture that stands in front of the Academic Center, was created by Charles Umlauf, the first Leslie Waggener Professor in Fine Arts.

Umlauf's statue in front of the Graduate School of Business represents the family, the basic unit of our society and economic system.

The statue of George Washington, not a part of the original Littlefield Memorial Entrance Gate group, was requested and financed by the Daughters of the American Revolution. Pompeo Coppini's last, it was at one time the only statue of Washington west of the Mississippi River.

In front of Texas Memorial Museum stands the statuary group known as *Mustangs*—a stallion, five mares, and a colt scrambling down the side of a mountain. The sculptor was A. Phiminster Proctor, one of the greatest sculptors of Western life. Ralph R. Ogden, Austin oilman and cattleman, donated the funds to pay for the *Mustangs* and the statue was unveiled on Commencement Day in 1948. It was the first statue on campus that in any real way identified with Texas life. Even J. Frank Dobie approved it.

A sign in a residence hall window occasionally announces a special event. This one in a Kinsolving window in September 1975 announces an engagement.

A bulletin board in the Texas Union is interesting to read, even when you aren't looking for a bargain.

An armadillo painted orange was removed from the football field by a U.T. band member during half-time at a Texas–Texas A&M game. During the early 1970s, a proposal that the U.T. mascot be changed to the armadillo was scorned by some and applauded by others.

Signs of the times appear on doors, walls, and even buttons. Regent Frank Erwin, often the target of protesters in the late 1960s, once referred to a group of student protesters as "dirty nothin's."

The grille above the gates to the two north entrances to the Main Building embodies a modified form of the University seal.

Class insignia at the School of Military Aeronautics in 1918 are displayed over the entrance to one of the Little Campus buildings. The school made a modest beginning on the University campus early in May 1917, with a class of twenty-five cadets organized under the Aviation Section of the Signal Corps and later taken over by the Division of Military Aeronautics of the Air Service. It became one of the six ground schools for the preliminary training of American army airmen during World War I.

The student or faculty/staff identification card is one's admission to numerous places on campus. The card bears one's picture, name, Social Security number, and record of optional fees purchased. It has replaced the old blanket tax, first issued in 1916, which served as admission to athletic and cultural events.

Among the numerous logos and other signs and symbols are those that are peculiarly U.T.; social groups, honor societies, and University divisions are identified by their own signs. Rabbit Foot, Friar Society, Visor, Texas Cowboys, Orange Jackets, Silver Spurs, Phi Beta Kappa, Tau Beta Pi, and many others may be identified by a pin, a key, a logo. A few special logos are shown on these two pages. They represent (*top row*) University of Texas Press (first symbol designed by Tom Lea in 1950; second, by Richard Hendel in 1975; and third, by George Lenox in 1978); (*center*) The University of Texas System (*left*), Division of Extension (*middle*), and Correspondence Study (*right*); (*bottom*) Texas Student Publications (*left*), Institute of Latin American Studies (*middle*), and Hogg Foundation for Mental Health (*right*).

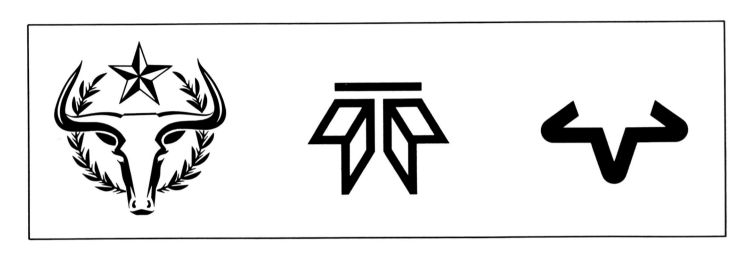

Other logos are for (*top*), University Publications (*left*), Center for Energy Studies (*middle*), and Intramural Sports for Men, 1970–1971 (*right*); (*center*) The University of Texas at Austin Graduate School (*left*; this is a wood engraving done about 1800 by Thomas Bewick), *Graduate Journal* (*middle*); and The University of Texas Ex-Students' Association (*right*); and, finally, the Eyes. Someone has said that, if one looks at the Tower from the right angle, the two faces of the big clock look like the Eyes themselves!

9. Unforgettable Incidents

Each student who attends the University has a special list of unforgettable incidents. Among these special memories are events related to classroom occurrences, athletic events or celebrations, local and national political events, extracurricular activities, personal crises, and campus happenings not anticipated in the *General Information Bulletin.* Certain unforgettable moments are personal but are as important to individuals as any described here. Those personal incidents, whether recalled with pleasure or pain, become a part of the nostalgia that binds former students to their alma mater.

The incidents described in this chapter may be repetitive, but they are of sufficient significance to have had an effect on the University's history and its cultural milieu. They are highlighted because they usually affected the entire campus.

The University Ad Hoc Strike Committee on Monday, May 4, 1970, called for a boycott of classes to protest U.S. involvement in Cambodia, the trial of Black Panther Bobby Seale, the city's denial of a solicitation permit to the Community United Front, the arrest of ten anti-ROTC demonstrators, and the four Kent State University deaths. After a series of incidents, the faculty, in an emergency meeting on Thursday, May 7, voted to suspend classes, but the regents refused to close the University. Thousands gathered on the Main Mall, engaged in teach-ins, and listened to speakers. Hundreds even spent the night on the mall.

Carry Nation brought her booze-hating, hatchet-carrying campaign to the U.T. campus twice—in October 1902 and November 1904. Students had a great time telling her stories about the "general depravity" of the campus, how prominent faculty members were corrupting the morals of students, and how the campus was a "den of iniquity." Then they watched her publicly embarrass those whose names she had been given.

The first U.S. president to visit the campus was William McKinley, who came on May 3, 1901. In honor of the occasion, the University put on its gaudiest attire. The U.S. flag was on the Main Tower, and the Texas flag flew from the tower of each wing. The front of the old Main Building was decorated in flags and bunting, interspersed here and there with orange and white as well as the colors of Baylor, Add-Ran (later became Texas Christian University), Southwestern, and other Texas colleges. President McKinley and his party drove north along Congress Avenue, Colorado Street, University Avenue, and the east drive to the University. When directly in front of the Main Building, the carriage halted, and the president spoke to the assembled crowd.

President Theodore Roosevelt visited the campus in 1905 (*bottom, left*) and again in 1911 (*right*).

On May 26, 1906, a Charity Circus served as a benefit for the Athletic Council. The second benefit, called Varsity Circus, featured the election of a queen (her float pictured below) and a parade on May 17, 1909. The Varsity Circus occurred biennially until after the one in 1925. Before the Students' Association officially abolished it, a student editor called it a "white elephant." The circus, however, had its heyday. The three held in the 1920s were spectacular affairs that required extensive planning. Coronation of a queen, selected in a popular campus campaign, and her king was an elaborate ceremony the night before the circus began. In 1930, the celebration was reborn as Varsity Carnival and continued as a project sponsored by Panhellenic and the Interfraternity Council.

In 1923, the Varsity Circus was part of the University's fortieth anniversary celebration. Maria Taylor was crowned as Queen of Varsity for two years (*center*). Her escort, the King of Varsity, was John Bullington. The parade down Congress Avenue featured decorated cars, the band, and groups of marchers.

The inauguration of the governor has always been an important event in Austin. An example of this special event is the inauguration of Governor Dan Moody on January 18, 1927 (*top*). Students joined in the excitement because he was Texas' youngest governor, a graduate of U.T., and an honor student.

The inauguration of W. Lee O'Daniel as governor of Texas in 1939 afforded Austin and the entire state a great deal of excitement and celebration. O'Daniel, relatively unknown in state politics, entered the Democratic race for governor against twelve opponents in 1938. He won without a runoff and was inaugurated in Memorial Stadium on the University campus (*bottom*).

James E. Ferguson was inaugurated as governor of Texas on January 12, 1915. During the same year, he launched his unexpected attack on the University. Dr. Robert E. Vinson was elected U.T. president in April 1916. The governor called for the dismissal of President Vinson and several other faculty members in May 1917, saying he would veto the appropriations bill if his demands were not carried out. He also demanded abolition of all fraternities. Approximately one hundred faculty members adopted a resolution emphatically declaring that the regents should be a free and autonomous board. A collage of 1917 headlines about the University-Ferguson controversy tells part of the story.

Students met in protest on Monday morning, May 28, 1917, led by George Peddy, president-elect of the Students' Association and a member of the Legislature and the officers' training camp at Leon Springs (*center*).

At the end of Peddy's speech, students marched to the Capitol and down Congress Avenue (*bottom*), proclaiming that the University's future was threatened. Outraged, Governor Ferguson vetoed the appropriations bill on June 2, 1917, but the attorney general declared the veto to be invalid because the governor had failed to veto the totals on the bill.

A report in 1916 by John A. Udden, University geologist, started the search for oil on U.T. land in West Texas. On Monday morning, May 28, 1923, Santa Rita #1 blew in. The discovery well on the University's extensive properties in West Texas, this oil strike precipitated a trend in oil mining on University lands that brought the total amount of the Permanent Fund on August 31, 1979, to $1,143,845,761. This amount included investments and cash in the amount of $1,133,818,377 and land carried at a nominal value of $10,027,384.

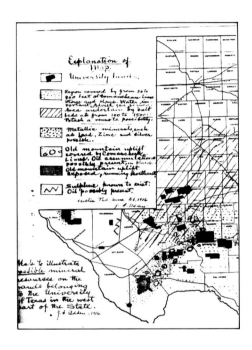

The Constitution of 1876 provided an endowment of approximately one million acres in West Texas for the support of the University. The Legislature in 1883 added another million acres to this endowment. The income from this land and the land itself (approximately 2 million acres) form the state endowment, called the Permanent University Fund. All of the income, most notably oil royalties since 1923, must be invested through the Permanent University Fund. Only the income from this principal may be expended, not the direct revenues from the land or the principal itself, and this earned income forms what is known as the Available University Fund.

Because Texas A&M University was originally established as part of The University of Texas, it has received each year since 1934 one-third of the Available Fund, except income from grazing leases. The remaining two-thirds goes to The University of Texas System, but not to all of its component institutions. Originally, only U.T. Austin, U.T. El Paso, and the U.T. Medical Branch at Galveston benefited from the fund. In 1956, the constitution was amended to include Southwestern Medical School at Dallas, the Dental School at Houston, and M.D. Anderson Hospital and Tumor Institute at Houston. The map shows the location of University lands in West Texas.

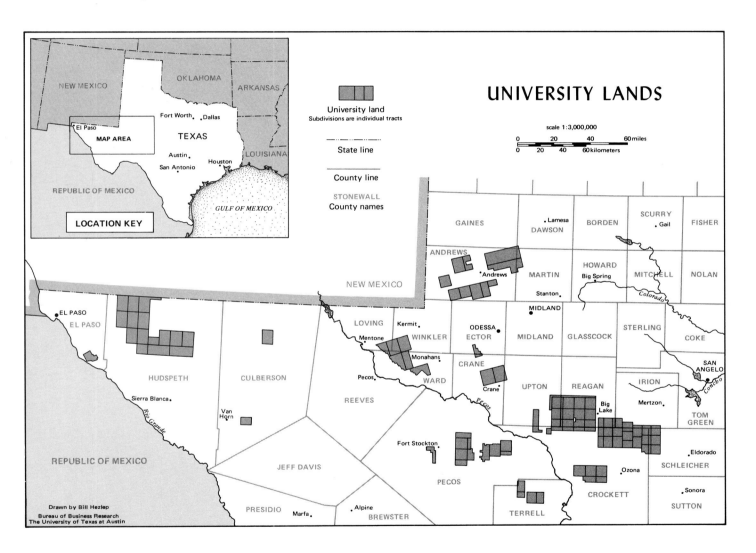

Standing in front of the discovery well of the Big Lake pool in West Texas about 1934 with the University president and several members of the Board of Regents are some of the personnel related to U.T. oil interests. In the picture are (*left to right, front row*) W. M. Griffith, Jess Conklin, Ed Warren, Frank Friend, J. S. Posgate, Charles I. Francis, Robert L. Holliday, Dr. K. H. Aynesworth, Beauford Jester, Hal P. Bybee, and C. R. Johnson; (*top row*) Lutcher Stark, W. V. Stell, Nalle Gregory, Charles E. Boyer, President H. Y. Benedict, and E. J. Compton.

The old Santa Rita rig was dismantled in January 1940 and shipped to Austin. Eighteen years later, in 1958, it was placed on the campus at the corner of Mar-tin Luther King Boulevard and Trinity and was memorialized on Thanksgiving Day just before kick-off time for the Texas-A&M game.

Fires have on several occasions caused a considerable amount of loss on the U.T. campus. Some of the most destructive ones are pictured here.

In the early morning hours on January 23, 1959, the Drama Building burned (*top left*). Originally the Woman's Building, it was in 1903 the first women's dormitory on the campus.

On August 10, 1965, a fire in the Tower apparently started from sparks of molten metal from cutting tools used by men installing an air-conditioning unit in the building (*top right*). The Tower's basic structure was not affected, but considerable replacement and repair were necessary on ceilings, partitions, and fixtures on the twentieth floor and several floors above and below.

Near the flames were some of the University's valuable collections.

Early on a fall morning in 1926 the old Chemistry Laboratory, built in 1891, burned (*bottom left*). Many valuable books and instruments were lost.

A fire in Mezes Hall on November 10, 1970, caused considerable damage (*bottom right*).

The Rainey controversy with the Board of Regents resulted in the firing of Homer Price Rainey as University president on November 1, 1944. The issues centered on the relations between the governing board and the president and other administrative officers of the University. During the controversy the University was placed on probation by the Southern Association of Colleges and Schools and was censured by the American Association of University Professors.

On November 2, 1944, the morning after President Rainey was fired, a large part of the student body met in front of the Main Building and, led by Students' Association President Mac Wallace, marched to the Capitol to request Governor Coke Stevenson to invite the regents to meet with the student body on Saturday, November 4 (*top right*). Students, except naval trainees, went on strike for the remainder of the week, and large numbers remained for hours on the Main Mall.

On Friday, November 3, a group of students estimated in the press as numbering five thousand paraded through downtown Austin (*center*).

The students stopped on the Capitol grounds. On the same day, the faculty met and adopted a resolution asking for reinstatement of Dr. Rainey. He was not reinstated.

On January 10, 1958, the University officially observed its seventy-fifth anniversary at a convocation of faculty and staff, laypersons, students, and distinguished educators from other colleges and universities. The convocation procession moved up the South Mall between lines formed by the University ROTC units. On the same day and in concert with the convocation, began the Conference on Expectations for the Main University to form a charter for the next twenty-five years of University development. The year-long work of the Committee of 75 and the Conference on Expectations provided a blueprint for the future.

President Logan Wilson (*left*) and Governor Price Daniel (*right*) cut the ribbons to open the 75th Year Exhibit in the Regents' Room in the Main Building. At the extreme right, Dean L. L. Click looks as if he fears the scissors won't work.

A luncheon meeting for the Committee of 75 is held in the Texas Union Ballroom.

Heman Marion Sweatt was admitted to U.T.'s Law School after a four-year court battle. Denied entry in 1946, he sued in district court, which decided that he was being denied Fourteenth Amendment rights, but only because no law school for blacks existed in Texas. The state responded by, first, creating a law school in Houston, a one-room class above a saloon, and, later, a school in downtown Austin. Sweatt refused to attend either school. The Supreme Court held that the black school was not equal to U.T.'s and the University was ordered to admit Sweatt. Here, he is in registration line in September 1950. Eight other blacks preceded him, as graduate students in the University, by being admitted to summer terms.

Even after blacks were admitted, their troubles were not over. In the spring of 1957, Barbara Smith, a young black student, was cast in the lead of a University production of *Dido and Aeneas*. Following a meeting of "interested persons," she was taken out of the part. She graduated in January 1959, and twenty years later, Barbara Smith Conrad starred as the famous black opera singer, Marian Anderson, in ABC's mini-series "Franklin and Eleanor."

Armando Gutierrez, the first Chicano faculty member hired by the Government Department in a tenure-track position, was denied tenure in the fall of 1978. A large group of students, led by members of Alianza, a U.T. Chicano organization, protested his tenure denial.

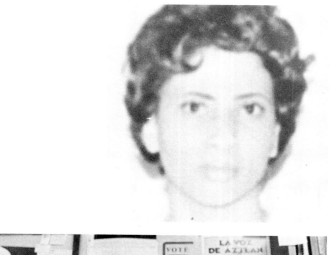

On several occasions during the past century, Austin weather has triggered unforgettable incidents. April 7, 1900, when the dam broke (see p. 27), was one of the most traumatic days in Austin's history. On May 4, 1922, a tornado struck Austin, killing thirteen and injuring forty-four. That night several hundred University students had a shirttail parade through downtown streets and into the movie houses where they gave their college yells and helped relieve the tension of frightened Austinites. Fortunately, no buildings on the University campus were damaged.

In the fall of 1962, Hurricane Carla unleashed its fury far inland, and Austin felt its effects as fallen trees and flooded streets caused problems. Amid a continuous downpour of rain, students braved the long lines of registration outside Gregory Gymnasium.

The Tower has been the site of nine deaths, seven of which were suicides. The observation deck has been closed to visitors since the last one occurred on October 28, 1974.

The most tragic incident occurred at high noon on August 1, 1966, when Charles Joseph Whitman climbed to the top of the Tower and began firing with a high-powered rifle at students and passersby on and near the campus. Before he was stopped, he took the lives of sixteen people and injured thirty-one others. The night before, the 25-year-old student had killed his mother and wife because he did not want to leave them to face the embarrassment he would cause. He had written and typed a series of notes planning his attack from the Tower. Ninety minutes after the shooting began, four police officers and one civilian reached Whitman on the Tower. One officer killed him with a shotgun blast. Classes were dismissed the following day, and flags flew at half-mast. One note left by Whitman requested an autopsy to determine if he suffered from mental illness. The autopsy revealed a brain tumor, which had caused Whitman to suffer headaches.

"Book 'em Horns!" The University's College Bowl team and their coach won national acclaim—and $10,000—on March 12, 1967, when they retired undefeated after matches with five other schools in a series of contests televised nationally. Members of the team were (*left to right*) Carl Clark, Barbara Carroll, Buford (Bill) Taylor, and Thomas Edwards (captain). Their coach (*right*) was Professor Douglas N. Morgan, professor of philosophy, who instilled the spirit to win in the Longhorn contestants. The tower turned orange five times for the champion team.

In the late 1960s the Texas Union kitchens needed extensive repair. Stimulated by the aroma pervading the first floor of the Union, a group calling themselves the "Student Onion" led a boycott of the Chuck Wagon and the Commons on November 13, 1968. The incident resulted in transferral of management of the Union food facilities to the Union Board of Directors and in improvements to the ventilation system.

On November 10, 1969, students, nonstudents, Department of Public Safety officers, and Austin police had a confrontation inside and around the Chuck Wagon. The issue was whether nonstudents should be allowed in the Chuck Wagon. In the ensuing scuffle, glass doors were shattered and tables were overturned. Eight persons, five of them students, were arrested. Later, at least twenty-two others were arrested and named in grand jury indictments.

On Monday, October 2, 1969, a small group of picketers gathered at Waller Creek to protest the proposed uprooting of trees to make way for an addition to Memorial Stadium. The next day the group, now swelled to fifty, caused a construction halt. Workers arrived on Wednesday to find protesters lodged high in the trees as a last attempt to save them. Also on the scene was Board of Regents Chairman Frank C. Erwin, Jr. City, state, and campus police were called in to remove the tree-sitters, and twenty-seven arrests were made. The trees were cut down, but students dragged their branches to the front of the Main Building in protest.

A year later, Frank Erwin planted a tree beside Waller Creek.

The late 1960s and early 1970s marked a surge of social change that manifested itself on the University campus in the form of many protests, demands, rallies, and petitions. The free speech area in the Texas Union patio often attracted those seeking to be heard.

The Main Mall was often reserved for a noon rally by a student group with a cause.

Thomas Collier and Pablo Torres (*bottom left, seated*) talk with Houston Representative Mickey Leland and Board of Regents Chairman and former Governor Allan Shivers before a regents' meeting in March 1975.

On Friday, May 8, 1970, an estimated twenty thousand marched downtown in peaceful protest of the Vietnam War, U.S. involvement in Cambodia, and the four Kent State University deaths. The march concluded on the East Mall, where many relaxed in the fountain; schedules slowly returned to normal.

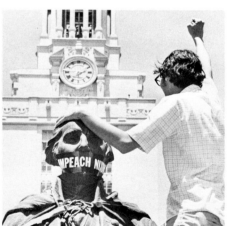

An internal University crisis occurred during the 1969–1970 session. The issues involved the relations among the regents, the president, and Dean of Arts and Sciences John R. Silber. The central question was whether the College of Arts and Sciences should be split, a matter that sharply divided students, faculty, and regents. Dean Silber protested the division of the college and was dismissed in July 1970. Students protested.

President Stephen H. Spurr came into conflict with the chancellor and the regents over a number of matters never publicly explained. In September 1974, when Spurr refused to resign, Chancellor Charles LeMaistre fired him. The Board of Regents in a divided vote con-

firmed his firing. Many students and faculty members questioned the action as being high-handed and a violation of academic freedom.

Vice-President Lorene Rogers was appointed acting president upon the dismissal of President Spurr. Almost a year later, on September 12, 1975, she was named president, the first woman president of a major state university. The faculty-student advisory committee had recommended against her, but the Board of Regents, in a divided vote, accepted Chancellor LeMaistre's recommendation that she be appointed.

Approximately six thousand students jammed the Main Mall in the noon heat shouting for President Rogers' resignation. Signs read, "Buck Rogers," "Rogers Is Revolting," and "March for Academic Freedom." Another three thousand later marched to the homes of Regents' Chairman Allan Shivers, Chancellor Charles

LeMaistre, Ex-Regent Frank Erwin, and President Rogers. The General Faculty adopted a resolution calling on faculty members to refuse to serve on standing committees appointed by President Rogers or to take part in University Council proceedings. This boycott lasted a year.

Distinguished guests are occasionally entertained at lunch on the fourth floor of the Academic Center or in the Harry Ransom Center. At this luncheon were (*left to right*) Rabbi Levi Olan, Jack Josey, former Governor John Connally, Mrs. Perry Bass, Frank C. Erwin, Jr., former President Lyndon B. Johnson, Mrs. John Connally, and Chancellor Harry Ransom.

The dedication of a new building attracts visitors and friends of the University, as well as current students. When Burdine Hall was dedicated in 1970, former Chancellor Logan Wilson (then president of the American Council on Education) was speaker.

Amid some 4,500 friends, followers, and members of the University community, former President Lyndon Baines Johnson presented the nation with its sixth presidential library on Saturday, May 22, 1971, in nationally televised ceremonies. Nothing dampened the jovial mood of the crowd, not even the muggy weather, the skies that were alternately cloudy and bright blue, the long lines at the barbecue buffet, the strict security arrangements, the chants of "no more war" from demonstrators a few blocks away, and the black balloons rising in protest. U.T. Board of Regents Chairman Frank C. Erwin, Jr. (*front row, center*), presided at the ceremony. President Richard Nixon (*at podium*) officially accepted the library for the federal government.

The Reverend Billy Graham (*not shown*) delivered the invocation. Others on the front row included (*left to right*) Chancellor Emeritus Harry Ransom, Mrs. Richard Nixon, President Johnson, and Mrs. Lyndon Johnson.

Since the Lyndon Baines Johnson Library opened, a number of scholarly symposia have been convened on major issues and problems facing the American public. The first symposium was held on January 24–25, 1972, to mark the opening of the education papers. On the platform in the LBJ Auditorium are (*left to right*) John W. Gardner (*at podium*) Harry J. Middleton, President Stephen H. Spurr, Robert L. Kunzig, and Wilbur J. Cohen.

In the fall of 1977, the Tower glowed orange for three special events.

The University of Texas Press published *The Book of Merlyn* by T. H. White, the previously unpublished conclusion of *The Once and Future King.* The manuscript was discovered in U.T.'s Humanities Research Center, a rare books and manuscript library. On October 9, 1977, the book appeared on the *New York Times* best-seller list, where it remained for several months. By December 6, 100,000 copies had been sold, as well as book club and paperback rights.

Earl Campbell, star running back of Coach Fred Akers' 1977 championship Longhorn football team, accepts the Heisman Trophy on a nationally televised program. With him here are his mother and Coach Akers. Earl was the first U.T. student to receive a Heisman. In tribute to him, the team, and the coach, the Tower—marked by an eleven-story "one" on each side—was solid orange for four nights, beginning December 8, 1977.

On Tuesday night, October 11, 1977, the Tower was orange because Ilya Prigogine, professor of physics and chemical engineering and director of the Center for Studies in Statistical Mechanics, was named winner of the 1977 Nobel Prize in chemistry.

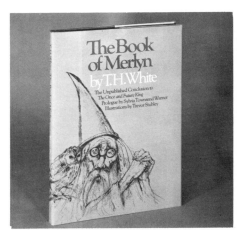

Through the years, commencement has been a memorable event. The day itself was the grand official climax to the school year—even for the first session, when only thirteen Law School students graduated. Oratory, long and dull for many, marked the event that was usually preceded by a week filled with social events.

In 1919, graduation was held outside the Old Main Building.

Nowadays, ceremonies are held on the Main Mall in front of the Tower, which traditionally turns orange when the president declares that degrees have been awarded.

Rain has occasionally marred the outdoor commencement ceremonies. On this occasion, in 1970, a few umbrellas began to appear before the ceremonies were over.

The 1971 graduates march to their seats. The state Capitol looms in the background.

During the Vietnam protests, a few graduates wore armbands.

The faculty procession in 1963 is led, as it has been for years, by the chief marshal, Professor H. Malcolm Macdonald. On either flank of Karl Dallenbach (*center, hand on tassel*) are President Joseph Smiley (*left*) and Chancellor Harry Ransom (*right*).

Only four honorary degrees have been awarded by U.T. in modern times: a Doctor of Laws degree to Robert E. Vinson in 1923 when he retired as U.T. president after seven years; a Doctor of Laws degree in 1935 to John Nance Garner, a Texan who was then vice-president of the United States; a Doctor of Laws degree to President Lyndon B. Johnson and a Doctor of Letters degree to Mrs. Johnson in 1964. Judge W. W. Heath,

chairman of the Board of Regents, hoods Mrs. Johnson on May 30, 1964.

President Lyndon B. Johnson delivered the commencement address when he and Mrs. Johnson received honorary degrees. A torrential downpour caused ceremonies to be moved to the Austin Municipal Auditorium. Seated on the front row are (*right to left*) President Norman Hackerman, Mrs. Johnson, Chancellor Harry Ransom, Dr. Lanier Cox, and Dr. H. Malcolm Macdonald, bearing the new commencement mace.

10. Athletics

Beginning with the founding of The University of Texas in 1883, when athletic programs on the campus were nonexistent and students had to provide for their own recreation, steady growth proceeded in the magnitude, scope, and influence of athletic affairs. Sandlot baseball was played from the start, and a tennis club and a track club soon appeared on the campus. Early programs were organized and controlled primarily by students, but as athletic affairs increased in popularity and became revenue producing, the University began to regulate and reorganize them through a faculty-dominated Athletic Council.

By 1933 when U.T. celebrated its fiftieth anniversary, the University maintained a $2 million athletic plant, including the stadium with a seating capacity of 40,000. Despite excellent programs for physical training and intramurals, intercollegiate athletics, bound up intimately with the culture of the entire campus, dominated the scene.

Today the University has superb athletic and recreational facilities. Included are Memorial Stadium, which now seats 80,000 and contains track and field facilities; the Special Events Center with more than 16,000 arena seats; Disch-Falk Field that seats 5,000 for baseball; and the 50-meter-long Swimming Center, designed to accommodate all known events in competitive swimming, diving, and water polo. Also available are the Penick-Allison tennis courts, the intramural fields, and the indoor facilities of Gregory Gymnasium and Bellmont Hall.

The Athletic Council today is composed of nine members—one each from the student body and the Ex-Students' Association, two appointed by the Board of Regents, and five members of the General Faculty Standing Committee on Intercollegiate Athletics. The chairman of the faculty committee serves as chairman of the council and also as the institution's faculty representative in the Southwest Conference.

One of U.T.'s most cherished athletic traditions is the Longhorn Hall of Honor. The governing body, the Longhorn Hall of Honor Council, is made up exclusively of men who have lettered at U.T. Through 1979, 118 men have been enshrined in the Longhorn Hall of Honor since the first four were so honored in 1957.

MEMBERS OF THE LONGHORN HALL OF HONOR

1957	L. Theo Bellmont
	William J. (Uncle Billy) Disch
	Louis Jordan
	Daniel A. Penick
1958	Gus (Pig) Dittmar
	Wilson H. (Bull) Elkins
	Arnold Kirkpatrick
	H. J. Lutcher Stark
1959	K. L. Berry
	James A. (Pete) Edmond
	George (Hook) McCullough
	Harrison Stafford
1960	Dana X. Bible
	David (Skippy) Browning
	Jack Gray
	Ernie Koy
1961	Frank "Pinky" Higgins
	Pete Layden
	Clyde Littlefield
	Oscar Eckhardt
1962	Charley Coates
	Jack Crain
	Bibb Falk
	Slater Martin
1963	Hub Bechtol
	C. L. (Ox) Higgins
	Bobby Layne
	Ed Olle
1964	Wilmer Allison
	Bohn Hilliard
	Bobby Moers
	A. M. G. (Swede) Swenson
1965	Maxey Hart
	Joe Ward
	Mal Kutner
	Tex Robertson
1966	F. T. (Star) Baldwin
	Harvey (Chink) Wallender
	Billy (Rooster) Andrews
	Gover (Ox) Emerson
1967	C. J. Alderson
	Denton Cooley
	Grady Hatton
	Edwin B. Price

1968	Blair Cherry
	Walter W. Fisher
	James H. Hart, Sr.
	Charles I. Francis
	H. C. Gilstrap
	Dexter Shelley
	Sandy Esquivel
1969	Abb Curtis
	Jerry Thompson
	Semp Russ
	Stan Mauldin
	Harvey Penick
	Lloyd Gregory
	Alva Carlton
1970	Holly Brock
	Chal Daniel
	Bowie Duncan
	Tex Hughson
	Lucian Parrish
	Jim Reese
1971	O. J. Clements
	Tom Hamilton
	Dick Harris
	Tom Landry
	W. O. Murray
	Don Robinson
1972	Len Barrell
	Gene Berry
	Bobby Dillon
	John Hargis
	Wallace Scott, Jr.
	Ed White
	Lewis White
1973	Jay Arnette
	H. J. Ettlinger
	Lewis P. McFadin
	James Saxton
	Walter Schreiner
	Eddie Southern
1974	Bobby Cannon
	Alex Cox
	Wilbur Evans
	Charley Haas
	Nelson Puett
	Bobby Robertson

1975	F. F. Rube Leissner
	Carlton Massey
	Charley Parker
	Joe Parker
	Joe Russell
	Harley Sewell
1976	Jack Collins, Sr.
	Tommy Nobis
	Darrell Royal
	C. B. Smith, Sr.
	Tom Stolhandske
1977	Randy Clay
	Bobby Lackey
	Wally Pryor
	Berry Whitaker
	Hugh Wolfe
1978	Frank Erwin
	Chris Gilbert
	Tiny Gooch
	T. Jones
	Karl Kamrach
	Frank Medina
	Murray Wall
1979	Bruce Barnes
	Ed Bluestein
	Duke Carlisle
	Wayne McDonald
	Bob Rochs
	J. Neils Thompson

In April 1892, an Athletic Association was formed; it fielded the University's first football team that autumn. In 1893, the University enjoyed an undefeated season, consisting of only four games. Members of the first team (top) were (left to right, bottom row) David S. Furman, William P. McLean, Walter J. Crawford (manager), Richard U. Lee, and Addison Day; (middle row) Victor C. Moore, Paul McLane, and J. W. Philip; (top row) Ray McLane, James Morrison (captain), J. H. (Baby) Meyers, and R. E. L. Roy. The McLane brothers (sons of District Judge McLane of Laredo), who had played football at Cornell the year before, organized the team. They were assisted by Albert Lefevre, who managed the team during the first part of the season.

The 1900 football team, known as the "Big Team," was recognized by football critics as one of the best in the South. Two members of the team won places on the "All-Southern," an honor not often received during the early history of University athletics. Caspar Whitney, a well-known sportswriter, in *Outing*, accused the University of playing two men who were not bona fide students.

Baseball, then "the national game," started earlier than did football as an organized sport at U.T. After the players had tried sandlot ball for three years, they formed a varsity team in 1886. The 1898 team is shown here.

While women had organized their own athletic association with basketball and tennis as the principal sports and had played their first intercollegiate game against Baylor in the spring of 1904, with only women as spectators, the spirit of "athletics for all" did not reach women in the University until about 1916.

The women's basketball team in 1902 . . .

Women's tennis in 1907 . . .

Fencing in 1909 . . .

Daniel A. Penick and the 1901 tennis team. Fifty-five years later, Penick was still coaching the tennis team. A professor of Greek, he would not accept pay for coaching championship tennis teams until he was persuaded, in retirement as a professor, to supplement his income by coaching. He also served as a choir director and was on the YMCA board of directors for more than half a century.

Little interest was shown in track in the early days. The first organized team is pictured in the 1896 *Cactus*.

Progress in track was slow until 1902, when the Texas team took first honors at the State Collegiate Meet.

The Texas teams, not referred to as "Longhorns" until the fall of 1904, competed in football, baseball, and track that year. The regents hired Ralph Fielding Hutchinson, a Princeton man, as director of outdoor athletics in 1904 when they decided to abolish the plan of having temporary coaches obtained by the students themselves to train teams.

In 1904, the football team made a northern trip to play Washington University in St. Louis and the University of Chicago. The team was defeated at Chicago, 60–0. A cartoon in a Chicago newspaper heralded the Texas invasion.

The original Clark Field, located where Taylor Hall now stands, was constructed in 1897. It was not named until 1904, and no bleachers were built until 1907. In the fall of that year, the football team played Missouri and saw new bleachers on that campus that students had built. The team returned home and sparked a campaign to build bleachers before the Thanksgiving game with A&M ten days later. The new bleachers were filled for the big game.

By 1916, Clark Field, with seating capacity for approximately fifteen thousand, had grandstands on all sides. On one side they were even covered.

Lutcher Stark gave the football team new orange-and-white blankets in 1914.

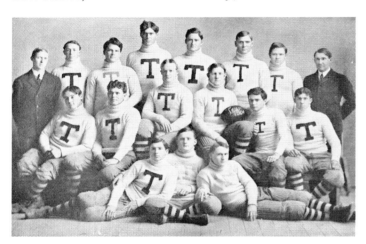

Dave Allerdice (*left*) was football coach for five years, 1911 to 1915.

In 1913, the Athletic Council was reorganized. The new council was responsible to the faculty, the president of the University, and the Board of Regents; it was not responsible to the students. L. Theo Bellmont (*center*), for whom Bellmont Hall is named, was appointed director of athletics at the beginning of the 1913–1914 session. As a result of his initial efforts, the Southwest Intercollegiate Athletic Conference became an actuality on December 8, 1914, when eight universities, one of which was The University of Texas, became charter members. Others were Texas A&M, Oklahoma, Oklahoma A&M, Arkansas, Rice, Baylor, and South-

western. The conference affiliated with the Cotton Bowl in 1940 and, in 1942, ruled that the SWC football champions must play in the Cotton Bowl.

Uncle Billy Disch (*right*) was baseball coach from 1911 to 1941. During those thirty-one years, his teams were champions twenty-five times. A former minor league professional player, Uncle Billy was a stern disciplinarian who would not permit swearing or smoking by his players.

In 1919–1920, the Women's Athletic Association (WAA) affiliated with the Athletic Conference of American College Women. Helen Marr Kirby opposed opening women's athletic events to men spectators, and they remained closed until the twenties. This women's basketball game was photographed after men were allowed to attend games.

Members of the women's field hockey team who won a "T" in 1920 were (*left to right, bottom row*) Patricia S. Davis, Genevieve Groce, Bernadine Appleby, and Anna Joe Neal; (*top row*) Martha R. Allen, Susie M. Anderson, and Lettie Mitchell.

Members of a 1922 swimming team . . .
    Members of Bit and Spur in 1924 . . .
    These were two of the intramural sports clubs that were popular when women could not compete officially in intercollegiate sports.

Louis Jordan (*top left*), the 205-pound right guard on the 1914 team, was the first football player installed in the Longhorn Hall of Honor, in 1957. He was named in 1914 to Walter Camp's all-American second team.

The University of Notre Dame team played U.T. in Austin on Thanksgiving Day, 1913. Texas guaranteed $4,000 to Notre Dame for the game; critics were silenced when receipts reached $8,000. Paul Simmons (*center in center picture*) starred in the game. Texas led at the half, but a second-half norther blew in, invigorating the Fighting Irish to such an extent that they ran over the Longhorns to an easy victory.

Jim Reese (*bottom left*), U.T.'s first NCAA champion, won the mile in 1925.

The 1915 championship basketball team included (*left to right*) Coach L. Theo Bellmont, Bob Blaine, H. C. Blackburn, Clyde Littlefield, Grady Ross, and Pete Edmond.

Key U.T. figures in athletics in the 1920s included (*left to right*) Berry Whitaker, W. J. Disch, Theo Bellmont, Doc Stewart, and Clyde Littlefield. Whitaker, who was employed as director of intramural sports in 1916, innovated a unified and organized system of intramural sports with the specific purpose of encouraging as many students as possible to take part in some type of physical activity and recreation. The program today ranks among the best in the nation.

The 1925 football team . . .

Memorial Stadium was dedicated on Thanksgiving Day, 1924. Though it was still incomplete, pledges totaling $500,000 had been made, and its completion was assured. The preliminary plans for the stadium, drawn by Herbert M. Greene, called for four ornamental towers at the ends of the east and west sides, but this last phase was never accomplished.

The baseball team moved into new Clark Field after 1927, when the Engineering Department claimed old Clark Field as the future site of Taylor Hall. This new park, north of Memorial Stadium, with its green-painted chalk hill in the outfield, remained the home of the baseball team until 1975, when Disch-Falk Field was completed.

C. J. (Shorty) Alderson will long be remembered as one who coached, taught physical education, attained academic degrees in a half-dozen fields, and announced football at Memorial Stadium.

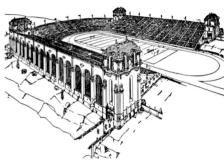

Wilmer Allison (*top left*), son of a Fort Worth physician, began playing tennis at the age of 21. The next spring, in 1927, he captured the NCAA singles championship. One of the world's ranking players during the 1930s, he teamed with Johnny Van Ryan to take the Wimbledon doubles titles in 1929 and 1930, was runnerup in singles at Wimbledon in 1930, and played on the United States Davis Cup team from 1929 through 1937. He assisted Dr. D. A. Penick as coach for ten years before taking the reins in 1957. He served as coach until 1972, producing four conference crowns.

Clyde Littlefield (*top right*), a graduate of U.T. and a four-sport athlete during his University years, was track coach from 1921 until 1961 and football coach from 1927 through 1933, during which period he won two Southwest Conference titles.

Harvey Penick (*bottom left*) became golf coach in 1931. For nearly fifty years, he was considered one of the master teachers of the game.

Coach Clyde Littlefield's 1930 football team won the Southwest Conference title. The faculty chairman of the Athletic Council and professor of German, W. E. Metzenthin (*top row left*), coached U.T. football in 1907–1908.

Bohn Hilliard (*top left*) displays the trophy he received when he was selected the most valuable football player in the Southwest Conference in 1934.

Jack Gray (*center left*) overwhelmed Southwest Conference basketball opponents with his one-hand push shot in the early 1930s. U.T.'s first all-American basketball player, he later served as the University's basketball coach.

Jack Chevigny (*bottom left*) was football coach from 1934 through 1936.

Nelson Puett, Jr., flings himself across the goal line against Texas A&M in 1938 in an effort that probably delayed Texas from being defeated by the Aggies for the first time in Memorial Stadium.

The *Life* cover marks the first time that magazine had ever shown an entire starting football team individually. On the Saturday following the appearance of *Life* on the nation's newsstands, a Baylor team tied Texas 7–7 in Waco, and TCU later beat the Longhorns, 14–7.

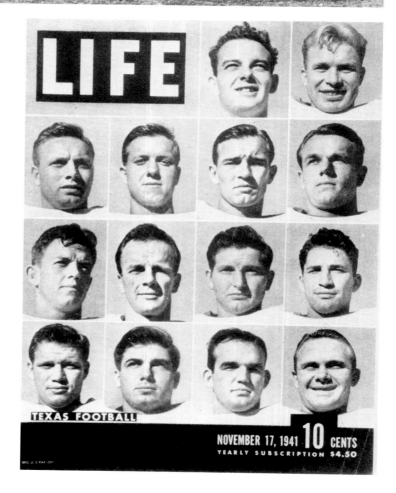

In 1940, the Athletic Council, with J. C. Dolley as chairman, had six other members. Clockwise from the left front are A. E. Cooper, faculty representative from applied mathematics; Clyde La Motte, student representative; Ed Olle, a former three-sport star athlete who became business manager of athletics; Dolley; coach Dana X. Bible; W. H. Richardson, who represented ex-students; and Read Granberry, faculty representative from engineering.

Dana Xenophon Bible, son of a professor, brought an articulateness to his profession that gained him wide respect as a lecturer and author. He came to Texas as football coach in the fall of 1937 and signed a contract that was a marvel in those depression years. The con-tract was for ten years at $15,000 a year, about twice the amount the president of the University was making and nearly four times the salary of the governor of Texas.

Longhorn fans argue whether this 1940 game with A&M or the Texas-Arkansas game the year before marked the turning point in U.T. athletics under Coach Bible. Texas A&M came to Austin with a team that had been named No. 1 in the nation in 1939 and was on its way to the same ranking and a Rose Bowl invitation. Texas won, 7–0.

Augustus (Bibb) Falk was one of U.T.'s most outstanding athletes. After a successful career as football and baseball player, Falk went straight from the campus to the Chicago White Sox, where he compiled a twelve-year lifetime batting average of .315, hit an average of .300 for more than eight years, and attained a career high of .352 in 1924. When Uncle Billy Disch became ill in 1941, Falk stepped in as coach and directed the Longhorns to two national baseball championships and almost five hundred victories.

Denton Cooley, now a famous heart surgeon, was a first-line Texas basketball player in 1939–1941.

Billy (Rooster) Andrews (*center*), *Cactus* outstanding student in 1945, was also a baseball letterman and manager for the football squad in that year. In the 1944 Texas-A&M game, he made a conversion to help the Longhorns win 27–13.

Tennis champions Felix Kelley (*left*) and John P. Hickman in 1945.

Betsy Rawls, a Phi Beta Kappa, could out-drive, out-putt, and out-score most of the males on the golf course while she was a student. She later had an outstanding career as a pro.

Although boxing has never been an intercollegiate sport at Texas, when Berry Whitaker initiated Fite Night at Gregory Gymnasium, he packed the arena annually. This picture was made in 1944.

Jerry Thompson was a national collegiate champion in the two-mile run (9:29.9) in 1943, again in the two-mile run in 1947 (9:22.9), and in the 5,000-meter run (15:04.5) in 1948. On his right is Coach Clyde Littlefield.

The 1950 Southwest Conference championship golf team is shown here. Reece Alexander (*front left*) was the Massingill Trophy winner (low qualifier) that year.

Bobby Layne was an all-SWC back in 1944, 1945, 1946, and 1947. He was an all-American selection in 1947, played as quarterback in the 1948 all-star game, and was installed in the Longhorn Hall of Honor in 1963. He is the only U.T. football player in the National Football Hall of Fame. Layne was also an outstanding baseball pitcher, won all-Southwest Conference baseball honors for four years, and was offered an opportunity to play professional baseball.

J. Blair Cherry (*top left*) was football coach from 1947 to 1950. His teams won thirty-two games, lost ten, and tied one. His resignation produced an article in a national magazine on the pressures of big-time football.

Governor Beauford Jester presented the Orange Bowl trophy to Co-Captains Tom Landry and Dick Harris at the annual T Association banquet in 1949. Tom Landry, now coach of the Dallas Cowboys, has become a household name, while Harris became president of Austin's oldest bank.

Edwin Booth Price (*center left*), who earned eight letters with the Longhorns and played on championship teams in football, basketball, and baseball in the early 1930s, was appointed head football coach in 1951 and

held the position through the 1956 season. In the picture at the right, he is cheering his team from the sidelines at the Oklahoma game in 1953. Assistant Coach Buddy Jungmichel looks on. Price was elected to the Longhorn Hall of Honor in 1967.

Lewis (Bud) McFaddin (*bottom left*), a guard, lettered in football in 1948, 1949, and 1950, receiving all-Southwest Conference, as well as all-American honors, in 1949 and 1950. He also participated in intramural wrestling and boxing.

Darrell Royal, a former University of Oklahoma all-American football player, started an era of championship football with his arrival on campus early in 1957. When he retired as coach twenty years later, he was a national athletic legend, with a winning percentage of .778, eleven Southwest Conference championships, three national championships, and sixteen bowl teams. Here, he is shaking hands with Ed Olle, an athletic great in several sports in the 1930s and director of athletics at U.T. after D. X. Bible retired on September 1, 1957.

Royal and his young assistants when he first became coach at Texas in 1957: (*left to right*) Raymond L. Willsey, Harold Jack Swarthout, William Mike Campbell,

James Carroll T. Jones, Robert Clayburn Schulze, James N. Pittman, and Charles Norris Shira.

The Darrell Royal era was marked by huge crowds, numerous honors, and a considerable amount of national publicity. Here, his 1963 team is featured in a cover story in *Sports Illustrated.*

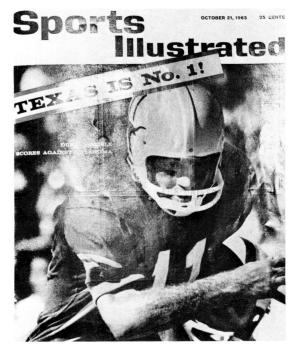

The Wishbone formation brought fame to the team and its coach. These four players caused the Wishbone to gain national acclaim as an offensive technique in 1968. They are (*left to right*) James Street, Chris Gilbert, Steve Worster, and Ernie Koy. Gilbert, in three years of varsity football, became the only man in NCAA history to gain one thousand yards in three consecutive seasons.

Spectacular rallies on the Main Mall drew huge crowds in the 1960s. This one features a burning U T in front of the Tower.

An excited basketball crowd in Gregory Gymnasium watches Larry Franks make a basket in 1964.

Harold Bradley (wearing the "T") was succeeded as basketball coach in 1968 by Leon Black, who was coach through the 1976 season.

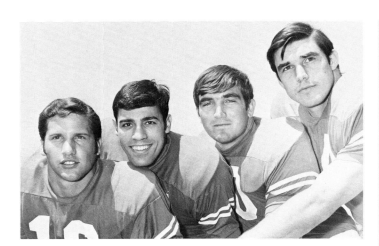

Texas' first national championship (1963) required some cooperation from the Aggies. A&M was defeating Texas before a national television audience, with time running out for the Longhorns. On its final drive, Texas recovered an intercepted pass, renewed its drive, and won in a last-minute effort, 15–13. When Texas defeated Roger Staubach and the U.S. Naval Academy in the Cotton Bowl, no one disputed the Longhorns' No. 1 status.

For its next national championship at the close of the 1969 season, Texas had to overcome early adversity again to defeat Notre Dame in the Cotton Bowl in another waning-minutes drive, 21–17. The game attracted more than usual national interest because of Texas' dramatic victory over Arkansas in the closing game of the 1969 season, because the Wishbone was still a new formation, and because Notre Dame, which hitherto had not been interested in bowl games, had decided to accept the bid to play Texas.

Tex Robertson (*top right*), swimming coach for thirteen years (1936–1943 and 1946–1950), led his swimmers to thirteen Southwest Conference titles.

Adolph Kiefer (*center right*) was a swimming champion in the late 1930s.

John (Hondo) Crouch (*bottom right*) was captain of the swimming team in 1939 and later became a raconteur of national stature.

Hank Chapman, coach, and Skippy Browning, diver, in 1951. In 1952, Texas swimmers won their nineteenth Southwest Conference championship in twenty-one years.

The University athletic program recruited its first black athletes with great care. Size, speed, and quick reactions weren't enough. James Means, whose father was a Huston-Tillotson professor and whose mother was extremely active in community action programs, became the first black letterman, in track (1967). The first black letterman in football (*top right*) was Julius Whittier (1969), son of a San Antonio physician. Both were young men of superior character and were good athletes. Within a short time, the coaches began recruiting blacks the same way they did whites.

Reporters in the press box have often described the excitement of sports events in Memorial Stadium. This scene occurs in the old press box in 1968 before the new upper deck was added.

On the centenary of the beginning of intercollegiate football (1969), Texas and Arkansas agreed to postpone their usual October meeting until the week following Thanksgiving in return for an exclusive national television audience. The game turned into a promoter's dream. Both teams entered the game undefeated, both boasted exciting offenses, and President Richard Nixon flew from Washington to witness the action in person. Playing before 50 million TV fans plus 44,000 in Razorback Stadium on an overcast afternoon, No. 1 Texas defeated No. 2 Arkansas in the final minutes of a contest some called the biggest game in college football's first one hundred years.

On national TV, President Nixon visits the Longhorn dressing room and proclaims the Horns No. 1 in the nation.

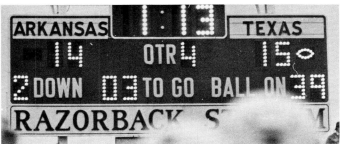

Frank Medina (*top left*), trainer for the Texas Long-horns for more than thirty years, served as trainer for many world team competitions and for three Olympic games.

Mrs. J. H. (Ma) Griffith was housemother to University athletes from 1936 to 1961, when she was 83 years of age.

Lan Hewlett (*center left*) was "brain coach" for U.T. athletes from 1957 until he retired in 1977. Coach Darrell Royal realized that recruiting quality athletes was useless if those students flunked out of school before reaching their potential. Attempting to rectify the problem, Royal created the academic counselor position that has since been widely accepted nationwide.

Al Lunstedt, business manager of athletics (*standing*), and Jones Ramsey, sports information director, hold key positions in intercollegiate athletics.

Bill Ellington (*bottom left*) came to U.T. in 1959 as backfield football coach, was freshman coach from 1966 to 1973, served as assistant to the athletic director, 1965–1968, and was assistant athletic director, 1968–1979. He was appointed director of men's intercollegiate athletics in 1980.

Coach Darrell Royal displays the 1973 Cotton Bowl trophy at the annual awards banquet.

Freddie Steinmark, the popular 1969 safety from Wheat Ridge, Colorado, was a victim of cancer. He is shown here on crutches at the Notre Dame game in the Cotton Bowl after his leg had been amputated following the Arkansas game early in December. A new scoreboard in Memorial Stadium was dedicated to his memory in the fall of 1972.

Larry Robinson dribbles in a game against TCU on January 15, 1974.

John Lee wins the 440-yard dash with a time of 46.87 seconds in 1973. (Dave Morton [1968] holds the Texas varsity track record of 45.5 seconds.)

Ben Crenshaw, who won three straight NCAA golf crowns (1971, 1972, and 1973) and all-American honors in 1971 and 1972, was the first freshman to win the individual title. He tied with Tom Kite for the 1972 championship.

George Hannon (*top left*) has been golf coach since 1964. His teams have won eleven Southwest Conference titles, eight Texas players under his coaching have won SWC individual titles, and he has coached twenty all-Americans.

Tom Kite, NCAA champion (with Ben Crenshaw) in 1972, won all-American honors in 1970, 1971, and 1972. Kite and Crenshaw have been the two most successful professional golfers from U.T.

Recreational sports have been a basic part of out-of-class life at the University for many years among both men and women. They have provided a release from the academic pressures and have given students the opportunity to compete for fun. They are under the man-

agement of a nine-member Recreational Sports Committee. Through this committee, the University seeks to promote and conduct officially organized sports activities and athletic recreation programs. Shown here are a lacrosse team in 1973 and a soccer team playing St. Mary's University in November 1966. Both men's and women's soccer teams are organized and compete with other schools, but they have not yet succeeded in achieving NCAA status for the sport.

Roosevelt Leaks, an all-American selection in 1973 who also won all-conference acclaim, is the first black football player to achieve these honors at U.T. A Brenham High School graduate, he currently plays with the Buffalo Bills in the National Football League.

Crowds cheer in old Clark Field in 1966 as Joe Gideon scores a homer and drives in three runs.

Cliff Gustafson, another former Longhorn baseball player, succeeded Bibb Falk as baseball coach in 1968. Since he became coach, his teams have won eleven conference championships and one national championship. His 1977 team won thirty-four straight games, an NCAA record, although it was Gustafson's first team to miss out on the conference championship.

A women's basketball team in 1975.

John Hernandez, a slight, bright, intense athlete from San Antonio, dominated the Southwest Conference tennis courts in 1955 because of his court finesse and speed.

Paul Craig widens his lead over a North Texas runner in a 1976 U.T. cross-country invitational meet.

Coach Leon Black, who resigned after the 1976 basketball season, exhorts his players.

Texas sprinter Julia Campbell runs the first leg of the mile relay at the Texas Relays in 1976.

Coached by Jody Conradt and paced by forward Linda Waggoner (*left*) and post Jackie Swaim, (*right*) the Uni-

versity women's basketball team finished the 1978–1979 season with a 37–4 record and was ranked fourth in the nation by the Associated Press.

Money was the principal issue and the meeting room of the University Athletic Council was the battlefield in 1974 as concerned students, fully informed about the contents of Title IX of the 1972 Education Amendments, united in an effort to end sex discrimination in intercollegiate athletics at U.T. In 1974–1975, when Donna Lopiano was chosen as director of women's athletics, women had their own intercollegiate athletics department, but with a budget of only $57,000. Nevertheless, they were able to compete and win in basketball, swimming, tennis, track, golf, and volleyball.

Fred Akers (*top center*), at 38, became head football coach on December 15, 1976. A native of Arkansas and a former back and kicker with the Razorbacks, he was an assistant coach under Royal 1966–1974 and coached for two years at Wyoming. He was the only major college coach with an undefeated regular season in 1977. In the Cotton Bowl, Notre Dame defeated Texas 24–3.

Abe Lemons (*top right*) became the twentieth basketball coach in March 1976. A renowned wit as well as a capable coach, he led his first Texas team to a Southwest Conference co-championship. The team went on to win the National Invitational Tournament (1977).

Darrell Royal resigned as coach following the December 4, 1976, victory over Arkansas. He continued to serve as athletic director until January 1, 1980, when he became special assistant to the president for athletic programs, the first such position in the country.

11. Libraries and Special Collections

The Lyndon Baines Johnson Presidential Library was built by The University of Texas. Operated as a United States archive, the building is maintained by the General Services Administration. The basis of the library is the 31 million papers produced during Lyndon Johnson's public service career. These are supplemented by personal papers of his associates and contemporaries. Available published works include government documents on the Johnson administration; books relevant to the Johnsons, the period, and the presidency; and a small reference collection. Of added interest to scholars are the microfilmed agency records, the administrative histories from the Johnson years, and an extensive collection of video and audio tapes, movies, sound recordings, and still photographs. The oral history interviews, begun by Joe B. Frantz before President Johnson left office and still in process, are another rich source of information on the personalities and perspectives of the period reflected in the library collections. The library sponsors scholarly symposia on major national and world issues.

The library possibly existed when the University was in the Temporary Capitol in the fall of 1883. Former librarian and historian E. W. Winkler wrote that it had fewer than one thousand volumes at the time, and J. E. Goodwin, also a former librarian, noted that its first recorded home was in the state Capitol, but no documentation is available that establishes its location or its actual existence as a service unit. Thirty years later, M. W. Humphreys, one of the original faculty members, stated that the University library was not available for students or faculty until after the University had moved to the completed Main Building in early 1884. Total annual expenditures for the library in 1883–1884 were $1,000 and for 1884–1885, $4,983. During these first years of operation, female students and faculty had free access to the collection, but books for male students were paged by the librarian.

From these meager beginnings, the various libraries of the University of Texas at Austin now constitute the ninth largest academic library in the United States and include the General Libraries, the Tarlton Law Library, and the Humanities Research Center. The General Libraries include the Perry-Castañeda Library, the Undergraduate Library, eleven branch libraries, the Collections Deposit Library, the Film Library, and special collections: the Nettie Lee Benson Latin American Collection, the Eugene C. Barker Texas History Center, the University Writings Collections, the Asian Collection, the Middle East Collection, and the Lyndon B. Johnson School of Public Affairs Library. In 1977, the University celebrated the acquisition of its four-millionth volume.

The Humanities Research Center Library and Academic Center Collections is a complex of rare book libraries and special collections relating primarily to the humanities but including also social science and history of science research materials. Its major strength is twentieth-century printed materials in English and American literature, but it also includes primary research material in numerous other fields.

The Tarlton Law Library, now the fifth largest academic law library in the nation, is the largest legal research facility in the Southwest, with 426,000 volumes. A new library facility, which opened in the fall of 1980, can seat 1,200 students at once, including 500 in carrels.

The archival collections of the Lyndon B. Johnson Presidential Library are limited to scholarly research, but the galleries are open daily to the public.

Ranking among the great, the University library was one of only five in the United States included in a 1970 book, *Great Libraries* by Anthony Hobson.

U.T.'s first library was located from 1884 until 1887 in an unlighted room on the fourth, or top, floor of the Old Main Building. Its dimensions were 24 feet by 27 feet, and its capacity was estimated at about three thousand volumes. In January 1884, Ashbel Smith, in his report to the Board of Regents, expressed his dissatisfaction with the location and his hopes for the future: "No sensible person will propose to lodge valuable articles [books, minerals, and objects of natural history] in any upper fourth story, who bears in mind the destruction of the library in the late capitol. A spacious library will be needed in the near future, where books, etc., can not be merely packed on inaccessible shelves, but where they can be studied."

In 1885, the library was expanded into larger quarters on the first floor, and in 1897 it was moved again to the large hall under the auditorium (*bottom*).

Sir Swante Palm, a Swedish immigrant who lived in Austin from 1850 until his death in 1899, gave his personal collection of approximately ten thousand books to the University in 1897, doubling the size of the U.T. library at the time. As a citizen of Austin, he was successively alderman, justice of peace, and postmaster, and from 1866 until his death he was vice-consul, representing the Swedish government. In the picture (*top*), he sits in the library in his home in 1894. He spent his last days as bibliographer of the collection.

Periodicals, including *Harper's Weekly, Science, Plant World*, and *Outlook*, were displayed in the reading room of the library in 1904 (*top left*). Not until 1905 was the library fitted with electric lights. After new lamps had been placed on all of the tables, students soon petitioned to have the library open at night, but without success.

The cataloguing corner of the library at the turn of the century indicates a dire need for additional space (*top right*).

Helen Marr Kirby, lady assistant and later dean of women, set up a special study hall for women students who did not at first use the library to any extent because of "false modesty that has hitherto deterred them." This study hall was a gathering place for women students as long as Mrs. Kirby was dean (*center*).

In 1898, the Law Library was moved to separate quarters in Old Main (*bottom*). The card catalogue for the Law Library was extensively revised, and the arrangement of the cases was conducive to better order in the room. Heating and lighting still left something to be desired.

The U.T. Library Science Department was located in Old Main in the 1920s.

James B. Clark (1885–1896), Benjamin Wyche (1897–1903), Phineas L. Windsor (1903–1909), Nathaniel L. Goodrich (1909–1911), and John Edward Goodwin (1911–1923) were early librarians at the University (*top left to bottom right*). Smith Ragsdale (1883–1885, not pictured here) was the first librarian, but the actual administration of the library was in the hands of a faculty committee, which created the position of assistant librarian and appointed Edwin Alonzo Hull and then Charles F. Gompertz to that position. Actual library service probably started on March 6,

1884, and Hull probably provided that service. Only 161 book loans were made during this first semester of library service.

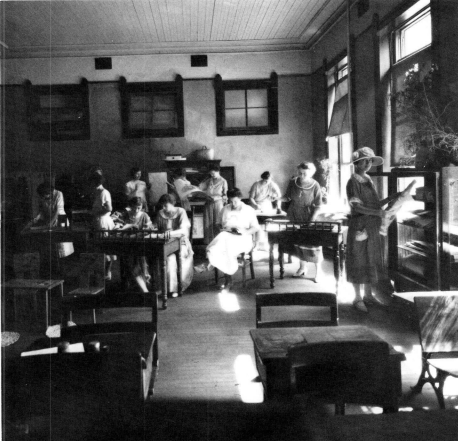

The new library building (now Battle Hall), completed in 1911 and designed by Cass Gilbert, was acclaimed as beautiful. The reading room on the second floor has a Renaissance style ceiling with decorated wooden beams. The doors leading into the reading room and research study and the arch above the loan desk have hand-carved scroll decorations.

The reading room was crowded when this 1913 picture was taken. Men were still expected to wear coats and ties in the library. On a warm day in late May 1917, a group of young male students, perspiring under the hot Texas sunshine, peeled off their coats and invaded the library. When asked to leave for violating a well-established rule, the students questioned the rule, and the librarian finally admitted that the University had no regulation prescribing the wearing of coats in the library. The students remained in comfort and were joined by others who "cast aside all chivalry and respect for time honored customs" by doffing their coats.

When the new Main Building was completed in the mid-thirties the English Room, containing the Wrenn, Stark, and Aitken collections, was moved intact from the old library to the fourth floor of the new building. The room was described then as one of the most beautiful in the world. The president's office is currently in this room, while the collections have been moved to the Harry Ransom Center.

The Wrenn Library (*left*), collected by John Henry Wrenn of Chicago, was presented to The University of Texas in 1918 by Major George W. Littlefield, who purchased it for $225,000. When the library was acquired for the University, a librarian in Chicago commented,

"It's a damned shame—that library buried down there in Texas, where nobody will ever see it."

Harold Wrenn, son of the collector, and T. E. Tallmadge, of Chicago also, made trips to Austin to supervise the installation of the books in their new home. Tallmadge supervised the design and furnishings of the room. He commented, "I have confined myself to no particular period or country. The carving is American." He considered the stained-glass windows, the work of C. J. Connick of Boston, particularly fine. Shown here are the main door, a Peter Mansbendel carving, and one of the four stained-glass windows.

The Stark Library is housed in a room furnished from Mrs. Lutcher Stark's home in 1936. This room, on the fourth floor of the Main Building, is currently used as the president's conference room.

Donald Coney (*bottom left*) was librarian and professor of library science at U.T. from 1934 to 1945.

Ernest William Winkler (*bottom right*) was librarian from July 1, 1923, to September 16, 1934. The title first selected for him by the regents was "Bibliographer," a title Winkler kept until he died in 1960. He also has an enduring reputation as a Texas historian.

At the circulation desk on the second floor of the Tower library, students checked out books for more than forty years. Coats of arms from Texas history decorate the library interior, and on the buff Indiana limestone and granite exterior are shields of historic universities and complete alphabets of the Egyptians, Phoenicians, Hebrews, Greeks, and Romans.

The large room on the east end of the second floor in the Main Building was the Humanities Reference Room (or the Hall of Noble Words) for many years. Students found it a pleasant place to study. Quotations painted on the beams are from Thomas Carlyle, Isaac Barrow, Richard Hooker, William Shakespeare, King Solomon, and others.

The wide marble stairs in the Main Building once led to the circulation desk on the second floor.

Reading rooms are good places to study or to let the mind wander and even soar. This 1963 student is taking advantage of the excellent library facilities.

Ronnie Seeliger, periodicals librarian, sits at his desk in the old periodicals reading room in the Main Building library before periodicals were moved to the new Perry-Castañeda Library in 1977. Note again the beautiful beamed ceiling at which generations of students have gazed.

Around this table the faculty held its meetings from the early days of the University until the faculty grew too large and was compelled to meet in a classroom. The table was also used for meetings of the Board of Regents, first in the Main Building, then in the southwestern part of the basement of the old library (now Battle Hall) until Sutton Hall was completed in 1918 and the regents met there. Many issues of importance in the history of the University have been discussed around the table. The most dramatic and far-reaching in its consequences was the attack of Governor James E. Ferguson, October 10, 1918, on certain members of the faculty. Walnut armchairs, upholstered in red leather, were used around the table, which is now in the main reading room of Battle Hall.

The foyer of the Academic Center, opened in the fall of 1963, has been used for exhibits, receptions, registration, and lounging.

The Academic Center has excellent study facilities.

The study of Erle Stanley Gardner, creator of Perry Mason, was presented to the University and has been installed intact on the fourth floor of the Academic Center. This picture, with Gardner at his desk, was used as a guide to those who arranged the artifacts in the restored library.

Undergraduate students often line up to check out books at the reserve desk on the first floor of the Academic Center.

Alexander Moffit joined the U.T. library staff in 1936 as associate librarian and became librarian in 1945. In 1967, he became consultant for library development in the University System. During his tenure as librarian, the University library grew from 770,000 volumes to more than 1,870,000.

Fannie E. Ratchford joined U.T. as an assistant in the Wrenn Library in 1919. She served as curator of the Rare Books Collection from 1927 to 1957 and as director of research in rare book bibliography from 1952 to 1957. She was a recognized expert on the Brontës.

The Collections Deposit Library on Martin Luther King and Red River streets was built in 1968 as a deposit library for little-used materials. At present, more than 200,000 volumes catalogued to other libraries are housed in this building. In addition, a large number of other valuable materials, books, newspapers, and reports are stored there.

In contrast to the modern storage facility above, valuable manuscripts were stored on shelves in a room in Old Main at the turn of the century.

E. W. Winkler chats with Llerena B. Friend, librarian of the Eugene C. Barker Texas History Center from 1950 until she retired in 1970 (*top left*). Like Winkler, Friend is highly regarded for her excellent books on Texas history.

C. Fred Folmer (*top right*) succeeded Alexander Moffit as librarian in 1967 and retired in 1974. He had been associate librarian since 1946.

Marcelle Lively Hamer (*center left*) was director of the Texas Collection from 1935 to 1955.

Dr. Carlos Eduardo Castañeda (*right*), professor of Latin American history and Latin American Collection librarian, and William Spence Robertson examine a map. The new general library bears Castañeda's name.

He held three degrees from the University and served it from 1927 until his death in 1958.

Richard T. Fleming (B.A., 1912, LL.B., 1915), former vice-president and general counsel for the Texas Gulf Sulphur Company in New York, returned to Austin in 1961 and became founder and volunteer curator of the University Writings Collections, a storehouse of source materials about the University. Fleming is shown here among the books and papers he collected, now located in Sid Richardson Hall next to the Barker Collection. With him is Maud Ann Armstrong, who served as secretary-curator of the collection until 1978.

Thirty carrels on each floor of the stacks in the Tower provided ample study space when the Main Building was completed in 1936, but before the move to the new Perry-Castañeda Library in 1977, the library had become overcrowded.

Nettie Lee Benson was librarian of the Latin American Collection from 1946 until she retired in 1975. She built the collection into "probably the single most important body of Latin American materials in the United States." When she became head of the collection, it contained approximately 40,000 volumes. It now contains more than 286,000 volumes of printed materials exclusive of maps and broadsides, 3,000 volumes of newspapers, 20,086 broadsides, 2,500 flat maps,

811,016 pages of manuscripts, 10,000 prints and photographs, and 2,046 titles of archival and printed materials on 6,789 reels of microfilm. Also in this photograph may be seen Harry Akin (*in crook of Benson's arm*), founder of the Night Hawk chain of restaurants and late mayor of Austin; Emma Long (*center, in horn-rimmed glasses*), first city councilwoman of Austin; and Joe Neal (*extreme right, hand on neck*), director of the International Office.

Chancellor Emeritus Harry Ransom, first director of the Humanities Research Center, continued to devote his time to the acquisition of collections. He is shown here examining some rare books in the Wrenn Room of the Stark Library in 1964. With him are Dianne Garrett (*left*) and Martha Brindley.

Warren Roberts was director of the Humanities Research Center from 1961 until 1978.

Among the valuable artifacts in the Humanities Research Center are the book *Memento of the Four Napoleons*; a decree, with Napoleon's signature and imperial seal, conferring a promotion upon an officer of the army; the marriage contract of Josephine's cousin, with signatures of Josephine, Napoleon, and others; and an imperial order with Napoleon's signature.

Another treasure among the collections is the autographed manuscript and corrected typescript of Ernest Hemingway's *Death in the Afternoon*, along with an autographed first edition presented by Hemingway to F. Scott Fitzgerald. The manuscripts and books available to scholars provide wide research possibilities in the areas of English and American literature, photography, history of science, and history of the theater.

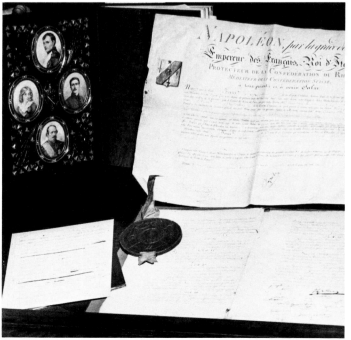

The original manuscript of "Gone, Gone, Gone" from George Gershwin's *Porgy and Bess* and the layout for the show's songs are in the Harry Ransom Center.

The Hoblitzelle silver collection, one of the many rare gifts that have been presented to the University, is exhibited in the Harry Ransom Center in the Esther Thomas Hoblitzelle Memorial Room.

In 1978, the University regents acquired a Gutenberg Bible at a cost of $2.4 million. The Chancellor's Council collected $1.4 million, and the regents committed up to $1 million to supplement the funds. The two calf-bound books comprise one of about two hundred Bibles printed by Gutenberg and one of only forty-eight Gutenberg Bibles known to exist. Only five complete copies are in the United States, and the one at U.T. is the only one south and west of Washington, D.C. The massive volumes are encased in bulletproof glass with a built-in security system and heat and humidity controls. Acquisition of a Gutenberg Bible fulfills a dream of the late Harry Ransom, who as chancellor of the U.T. System developed at U.T. Austin one of the great libraries of the Western world.

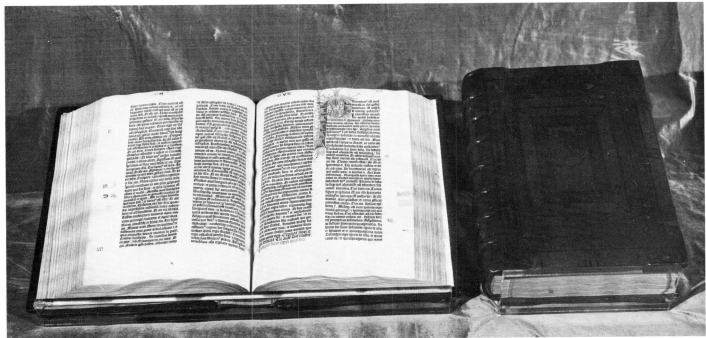

Study space in University libraries includes reading rooms such as the one shown here in the Harry Ransom Center.

The Michener Gallery in the Harry Ransom Center is the home of the James A. Michener Collection, almost three hundred American paintings dating from 1900. Called the "Art of the Americas," it includes a Latin American art section. One of the reasons Texas was chosen to house this collection was the University's specialization in Latin American studies. Renowned artists represented include Milton Avery, George Bellows, Thomas Hart Benton, Fernando Botero, Luis Cuevas, Arthur B. Davies, Stuart Davis, Raquel Forner, Carlos Merida, and Joaquín Torres-García.

Research scholars find the Humanities Research Center collections, located in the Harry Ransom Center and the Academic Center, not only a storehouse of information but also pleasantly arranged for study. Professor Norman Farmer (*top left*) works in the Iconography Collection office beneath an oil by Albert Bierstadt and a pastel by Dante Gabriel Rossetti.

Joe Coltharp (*top right*), long-time curator of the photography collection in the Harry Ransom Center, examines a 1938 E. O. Goldbeck photograph of the Seventh Cavalry Brigade Mechanized, Fort Knox, Kentucky.

In the Harry Ransom Center are several special rooms, including faithful reproductions of the study and living room from John Foster Dulles' Washington home. Shown here is the study.

The Perry-Castañeda Library opened at the beginning of the fall 1977 semester and now serves as the main library of the University, replacing the library in the Main Building (1934–1977). The new facility, dedicated on November 19, 1977, has 500,673 square feet of floor space, approximately 3,200 reader seats, and book capacity of approximately 3,250,000 volumes. It has 9.3 acres of carpeting and over 70 miles of shelving. Cost of the building was $21.7 million.

The book stacks in the Perry-Castañeda Library, located on the third, fourth, fifth, and sixth levels, are open to all. Access to the brightly lighted and spacious stack levels is by means of modern elevators or broad stairways. Lounge seating is interspersed on each stack level, and modern carrels are located along the windows.

Library materials are charged out and returned at the large Circulation Services desk on the ground level. A Reference Services Department and an information desk, also on the ground level, form a centralized information point for the U.T. Austin campus.

Reader facilities in the Perry-Castañeda Library include a seminar room on each stack level that is available for group study or discussion when not reserved for library-user education programs. Also to be found are coin-operated typewriters on each stack level, public lockers, graduate student lockers on the stack levels, and a refreshments area on the first level.

12. Laboratories, Museums, and Centers

During the summer and fall of 1891, the Chemical Laboratory was built on the campus near the site of the current Biological Laboratory. This marked the beginning of the University's long and distinguished history as a leader and innovator in scientific research. Today the facilities and special programs available at the University are among the best available in this country. The variety of research problems being investigated by the faculty of the University and the comprehensive nature of their studies offer a vital atmosphere for inquiry into many aspects of the environment, from the smallest particles in quantum physics to the global search for energy.

Research is an integral part of any educational endeavor, a strong research program being a positive influence on the teaching, service, and cultural goals of a learning environment. The general intellectual climate for research that prevails at an institution is molded by the laboratories, museums, and centers for study that are available. On this campus, scholars have long recognized the benefits to be realized from a vigorous research program. The first artificially induced mutation in a genetic system, an invaluable tool in deciphering the complexities of heredity, was accomplished here by Herman Joseph Muller in 1928. He later received the Nobel Prize for his work. University researchers have identified a multitude of metabolites and vitamins necessary for proper nutrition, and work in this field continues to be of major importance. Studies in engineering, geology, and business continue to influence the development of policy and the utilization of resources at both the state and national level.

Currently, sixty-three formally organized research units are a part of U.T. Austin, including the Center for Energy Studies, the McDonald Observatory, the Center for Theoretical Physics, the Ilya Prigogine Center for Studies in Statistical Mechanics and Thermodynamics, the Bureau of Business Research, the Humanities Research Center, the Institute of Latin American Studies, the Marine Science Institute, and the Texas Memorial Museum. Illustrated here are only a few examples of research activities and resources available to students and faculty in the past and the present. The photographs provide a small window into the world of basic research being conducted at The University of Texas.

Two research scholars at work in a University genetics laboratory in 1962.

At the turn of the century, University laboratory facilities left something to be desired. Lighting was poor, chairs were uncomfortable, and materials were scarce. On this page are two of the laboratories circa 1904.

In the geology lab, men wore coats and ties and women wore hats.

In the advanced zoology laboratory, students left their equipment neatly arranged on the long tables.

A geology laboratory in 1902 (*top left*), a physics laboratory in 1904 (*top right*), a psychology laboratory in 1903 (*center left*), and a drawing laboratory for architectural students in 1915 (*center right*) give us reasons to appreciate the facilities available to students today.

A group of engineering students depart from Old Main around the turn of the century, carrying their survey equipment.

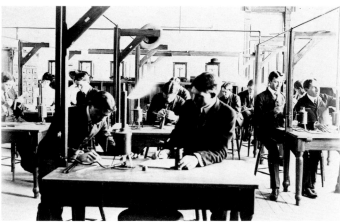

An art laboratory in 1911 and two others in use today provide a study in contrasts.

Early art classes at the University were offered in architecture and engineering. Courses in freehand drawing, design, water color, pen and pencil, perspective, and shades and shadows were typical. Few women registered for the courses, because women were not well accepted as architects and engineers and the courses were vocationally oriented. In contrast, today almost twice as many women as men are enrolled in the College of Fine Arts; almost one-third of architectural majors and approximately one-eighth of engineering majors are women.

Public attitudes toward women in the professions that were formerly dominated by males have changed, and women's education is no longer limited to certain "feminine" fields. Informal dress that is neat but comfortable is completely acceptable in today's labs.

The Archer M. Huntington Gallery is a teaching gallery in the Art Building, dedicated on November 5, 1963. Annual exhibitions of student and faculty art draw considerable attention. A portion of a faculty exhibition, featuring Charles Umlauf's sculpture and Sylvia Bialko's paintings, is pictured here.

William W. Newcomb, Jr., recently retired director of the Texas Memorial Museum (1957–1978), and Robert W. McMinn, technical staff assistant, examine materials in a museum workroom in 1975. Newcomb is a well-known authority on native America and its inhabitants.

Perhaps the most striking exhibit on the second floor of the Texas Memorial Museum is the Onion Creek

Mosasaurus—the reconstructed skeleton of a thirty-foot Cretaceous marine reptile that probably lived about seventy million years ago. The skeleton was found in Onion Creek, near Austin.

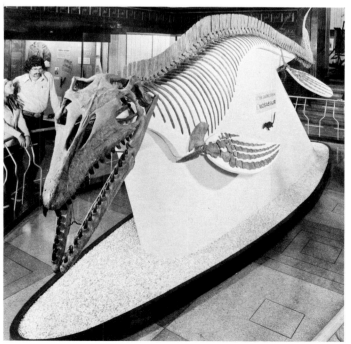

The Road Material Laboratory as it existed in the Bureau of Economic Geology in 1915. Established in 1909, the bureau, in conjunction with other state agencies, is responsible for geological surveys in Texas. Its director fills the position of state geologist.

Somparb Coompanthu (*bottom left*), a graduate student in mechanical engineering in 1967, is working on his thesis, an evaluation of ignition systems.

Students examine Austin maps in preparation for a field trip to assigned areas to observe transportation, existing land-use patterns, and zoning laws (*bottom right*).

Graduate student Mary Lou Miller, working in the Electroacoustic Research Laboratory of the College of Engineering, prepares a microphone for a calibration test in the anechoic chamber. The laboratory provides facilities and instrumentation for architectural, biomedical, electrical, mechanical, and petroleum engineering acoustical research. It also has available this anechoic room for airborne acoustic studies, an array of transducers for the generation and measurement of sound waves and vibrations, and signal analysis systems.

The faculty associated with the laboratory works closely with the staff of the Applied Research Laboratories, which is also heavily involved in underwater and nonlinear acoustics.

The Solar Energy Laboratory, located in the east wing of Taylor Hall, is working to develop systems adaptable to solar thermal input, especially general applications of solar cooling systems.

This concentrating collector array (*top*) currently provides solar heating, cooling, and hot water to a student apartment complex in Austin.

The subsonic wind tunnel, located at the Balcones Research Center, is used in the graduate teaching and research program in fluid mechanics of the Department of Aerospace Engineering and Engineering Mechanics. The tunnel can generate speeds of up to 200 mph with capabilities for architectural aerodynamic testing in addition to the usual aeronautical capabilities. The facility has been used to study natural boundary layer phenomena which occur near the surface of the earth, flow studies for the space shuttle, and the redistribution of air loads resulting from fire, explosion, or foreign-object impact on or near the wings or stabilizers of aircraft. The design allows for such other studies as the pollution dispersal from exhaust stacks at industrial sites and the effect of wind loads on mobile homes.

The Center for Research in Water Resources, located at the Balcones Research Center, is involved in wide-ranging interdisciplinary approaches to water management and contributes significantly to the education and training of students from many different departments within the University. Organized in 1963, the center coordinates water research in association with the Bureau of Economic Geology, the Marine Science Institute, and water resource centers at other Texas universities. Here, researchers simulate a hazardous-material spill in a model lake at the center to investigate the efficiency of bacterial containment methods.

The University maintains numerous special collections, including the Human Osteological Collection, which constitutes the principal repository for prehistoric humanoid skeletal material in the state. The collection offers insights into the ravages of disease on ancient humans, provides the basis for examining the skeletal morphology of various prehistoric groups, and allows for training students in the use of skeletal evidence for various medical and legal purposes. Here, a group of students examines the differences in the cranial bones of several specimens.

Allen Bard and Wendell Dunn work in a chemistry laboratory (*top left*) where Dr. Bard produced the first amino acids using sunlight.

A student in a nutrition laboratory uses an amino acid analyzer in 1975 to determine the amino acid concentrations in the plasma of severely retarded children (*bottom left*).

Louis Goodall, a graduate student in nutrition (*bottom right*), measures the enzyme levels in a rat liver as part of his research on the combined effects of alcohol and low-protein diet on metabolic function.

The Genetics Foundation, approved by the Board of Regents in 1952, and the Genetics Institute, approved in 1974, maintain a vigorous program in organismal, pop-ulation, and molecular genetics. The institute offers research support and is in the University budget, while the foundation depends on private funds. Major expansion of the genetics program at U.T. occurred in the 1920s when J. T. Patterson was a driving force in the Zoology Department. One of the institute's major responsibilities is the maintenance of a collection of many species of fruit flies, genus Drosophila, a commonly used experimental animal in genetic research. The collection is the largest available in the world and supplies requested strains to most major genetics research institutions.

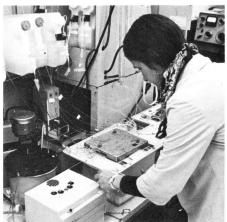

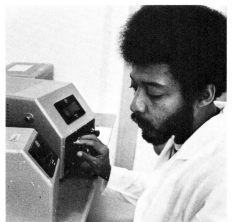

Biomedical engineering students with Professor George Thurston learn to operate an electron microscope in 1974.

The Radiobiological Laboratory of the Air Force School of Aerospace Medicine was established at the Balcones Research Center in July 1951. Among the research projects carried out was the evaluation of the performance of various animals during simulated space flight. Sam, a rhesus monkey born and trained at the center, was the first animal to be launched into space.

The Animal Resources Center was established to maintain the wide variety of animals required by researchers in the biological sciences. At the same time this uniquely designed facility complies with the spirit as well as the letter of the animal welfare laws. Graduate student Linda Keller and Professor Hugh Bonner study the physiological reactions of rats running on a treadmill in the Exercise Physiology Laboratory. They are seeking to determine the effect of consistent exercise on the occurrence of myocardial infarctions.

Psychologist Michael Gabriel is shown conducting research on the neural mechanisms of mammalian learning.

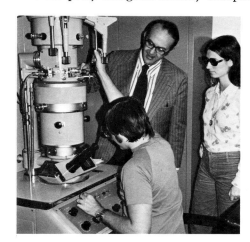

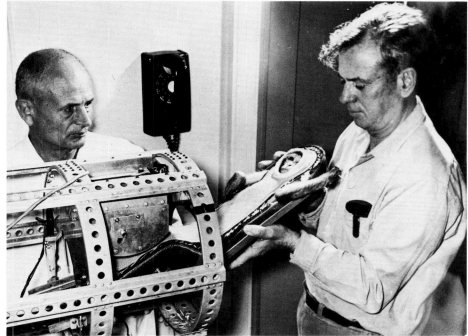

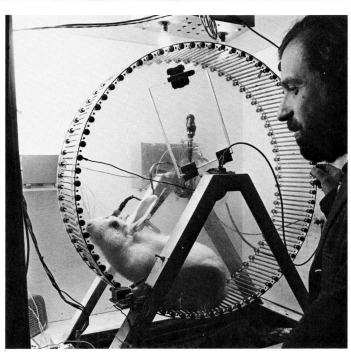

Stephen Ernst (*standing*) of the Clayton Foundation Biochemical Institute demonstrates to Marvin Hackert (*center*) and Jon Robertus (*front*) a computer-generated representation of the three-dimensional structure of a protein molecule. With the use of the Advanced Graphics Laboratory's computer, research scientists are able to develop more accurate depictions of molecular structure and to develop models of their interactions which more faithfully reflect their actual properties.

Early in 1958, the University established the Computation Center with an IBM 650 computer, a small staff, and a vision of the usefulness of such a facility. The center moved from its original home in the Experimental Science Building when a permanent facility was completed in 1961. A Control Data (CDC) Model 6600 computer system was installed in 1966 and a Model 6400 was added in 1971. Tape drives (*top right*) and a control console (*bottom*) are shown here. A Digital Equipment Corporation DEC-10 time-sharing system installed in 1975 and two Control Data Cyber 170/750 computers, which replaced parts of the early hardware, greatly increased the storage and applications capabilities of the center. In 1980, an IBM 370/158 Computer System came on line. These systems are used solely for instructional and research purposes, all other administrative computational requirements being met by equipment located elsewhere on campus.

The Center for Energy Studies was established in 1974. The primary function of the center is the coordination of the rapidly expanding energy research and educational activities of the University. Dale Klein demonstrates the Energy-Environment Simulator, used to acquaint the public with the complexities of the current energy crisis.

Nancy Weaver is shown working with a patient in the University's Speech and Hearing Center.

Using a detailed map of San Antonio, Harley L. Browning (*left*), former director of the Population Research Center, and Dudley L. Poston, former associate director, are employing statistical methods to delineate subareas of the city which are ecologically related. The center maintains vast numbers of census-related documents, both for this country and the world, and is a major resource for scholars making demographic studies.

Located some nine miles north of the University on a 476.2-acre tract of land, the Balcones Research Center has been actively developed since its inception in 1946. Component labs have taken part in much national defense research, including radar applications, nuclear physics, and industrial design. At its July 1980 meeting, the Board of Regents gave initial approval to the concept of developing the center into a "highly visible, identifiable research community," establishing the center as an "integral part of the University's pre-eminent energy-related research and educational program."

J. D. Gavenda in his laboratory in Robert Lee Moore Hall (*top*) explores the low temperature properties of solids. Samples of metals are placed between the poles of a large magnet and are cooled to very low temperatures with liquid helium. By using sound waves and their resultant ultrasonic propagation, the band structure of the metals can be determined. This property is critical in designing semiconductors.

Professor Manfred Fink is working at his scattering chamber to determine the electron distribution of certain molecules (*bottom*). Beams of high-energy electrons are focused into the chamber, which contains quantities of a specific diatomic molecule, such as nitrogen. From the resultant scattering, similar to the patterns produced in X-ray crystallography, the orbital distributions of the electrons can be determined. Earlier predictions based on the chemical nature of the molecule can be verified or corrected with this accurate method for determining actual electron orbital locations.

A TRIGA reactor in the Nuclear Reactor Training Laboratory is used by the College of Engineering for training personnel in reactor operations. It also serves as a source of neutrons for materials testing referred to as neutron activation analysis. The chemical composition of materials, especially trace elements, can be ascertained with this method. The Texas Department of Public Safety has used this facility for forensic examinations of hair and soils in the investigation of criminal cases. The regulation of the facility is controlled by the U.S. Nuclear Regulatory Commission and the Radiation Control Board of Texas.

Roger Bengtson works on the "PRETEXT" tokamak. The Texas Turbulent Torus, the University's first tokamak, became operational in 1971. The tokamak is the key element of the University's Fusion Research Center, directed by William Drummond and funded by the U.S. Department of Energy and the Texas Atomic Energy Research Foundation. In late 1977, the center began construction of the Texas Experimental Tokamak (TEXT) (*shown at the left of the bottom picture*), designed to replace the earlier machine. In March 1980, the Department of Energy chose the University as the site for the new national Institute for Fusion Studies which will bring together the world's foremost physicists and energy researchers to further investigate the potential of fusion reactions.

This well, thirty-five miles south of Houston in Brazoria County, is the first geopressured-geothermal test well to be drilled in Texas. Geothermal energy in the form of steam and hot water has been employed to melt snow on Boise, Idaho, streets; heat homes in Iceland and Japan; run paper mills in New Zealand; and generate electricity in California. The U.T. Department of Petroleum Engineering and the geothermal division of the Center for Energy Studies, both under the direction of Myron Dorfman, coordinate the activities at the well site for the Department of Energy. The project is investigating how much gas is recoverable and how much geothermal energy production is possible in the form of electric power generation or process heat for such diverse applications as frozen food packaging and gasohol processing.

The research vessel *Ida Green* is docked at the U.T. Marine Science Institute's Geophysics Laboratory at Galveston.

A research scientist at the Geophysics Laboratory is examining an ocean-bottom seismometer.

University of Texas marine biologists at Port Aransas use the *Longhorn* for research. The staff of the Marine Science Institute analyzed the recent Campeche Bay oil spill in the Gulf of Mexico to determine the extent of the damage to the Texas coastal environment and economy.

U.T. researchers help man the U.S. Antarctic Research Program satellite tracking station at McMurdo Sound, Antarctica, conducting ionospheric studies. This research is under the auspices of the Applied Research Laboratories.

From McDonald Observatory on Mount Locke in the Davis Mountains in West Texas, a 107-inch telescope sends a laser beam shooting through space to the moon. The beam then bounces off retroreflectors left on the moon's surface by Apollo astronauts and returns to earth. In this way, U.T. Austin astronomers can measure precisely the distance from earth to moon at any given time. They can then pinpoint, within an inch or two, the rate and direction of the drift of the continents.

The McDonald astronomers are developing plans for a 300-inch instrument, employing a new design which would allow construction at one-tenth the cost of a conventionally designed telescope. They hope to secure private financing for the major part of this project.

Appendix

This list includes not only individuals who actually served on the Board of Regents but also those who declined appointment or whose appointments were not confirmed by the Senate. (c) indicates individuals who have served as chairman of the Board, and (p) indicates individuals who have served as president of the Board. The period of service used here dates from the month of appointment until the month of expiration of term, resignation, rejection by the Senate, death, et cetera. Dates of service often vary on published lists of members of the Board because the appointment procedure includes four dates: date appointed, date confirmed, date of oath, and date commission was issued.

*Resigned position.
†Declined appointment.
‡Appointment not confirmed by Senate.
§Resigned while still unconfirmed by Senate.
°Died in office; not all Board members who died in office are marked.

1. Served as secretary from 1897 to 1908.
2. Removed from the Board in May 1917 and officially resigned his position in October 1917.
3. Enjoined.

Dec. 1885	–Jan. 1887	Alexander, L. C.
Jan. 1917	–Oct. 1917*	Allen, Wilbur Price (c)
Jan. 1933	–Oct. 1944°	Aynesworth, Kenneth H. M.D.
Feb. 1891	–Feb. 1899	Ball, Frank W.
Jan. 1927	–Jan. 1933	Batts, Robert Lynn (c)
Mar. 1965	–Jan. 1971	Bauer, William H.
Jan. 1973	–Jan. 1979	Bauerle, James E., M.D.
Apr. 1881	–Nov. 1881	Bell, James Hall
Mar. 1942	–Nov. 1944*	Bickett, John H., Jr. (c)
Jan. 1937	–Jun. 1942	Blackert, E. J.
Jan. 1977	–	Blumberg, Jane W. (Mrs. Roland)
Sep. 1910	–Jan. 1911	Bonner, John T.
Nov. 1886	–Jan. 1911	Brackenridge, George W. (c)
Jan. 1911†		
Aug. 1917	–Jan. 1919*	
Nov. 1920	–Dec. 1920°	
Jan. 1940	–Jun. 1942	Branson, Fred C.
Mar. 1961	–Jan. 1967	Brenan, Walter P. (Spike)
Dec. 1916	–May 1921	Brents, William R.
Jan. 1903	–Jan. 1907	Browning, James Nathan
Jan. 1895	–Jan. 1907	Bryan, Beauregard
Jan. 1957	–Mar. 1963	Bryan, J. P.
Jan. 1941	–Jan. 1947	Bullington, Orville
Feb. 1947‡		
Jan. 1911	–May 1914*	Burges, William Henry
Mar. 1882†		Burroughs, James M.
Jan. 1917	–May 1917*	Butler, James W.
Jan. 1903	–Jan. 1907	Cain, Benjamin B.
Jun. 1923	–Mar. 1924‡	Caldwell, Clifton M.
Jan. 1907	–Jan. 1909	Calvin, Elvis A.
Sep. 1881	–Apr. 1882	Camp, J. L.
Jan. 1903	–Jan. 1907	Chapman, H. M.
Jan. 1973	–Jan. 1979	Clark, Edward A.
Mar. 1883	–Jun. 1885	Clark, James Benjamin[1]
Oct. 1921	–May 1924*	Cochran, Sam Poyntz
Mar. 1961	–Jan. 1967	Connally, H. Frank, Jr., M.D.
Jan. 1911	–Sep. 1923	Cook, Fred W. (c)
May 1893	–Jan. 1903	Cowart, Robert E.
Jun. 1927	–Jan. 1933	Crane, Edward E.
1925†		Crane, M. M.
Mar. 1882	–Jul. 1883	Crawford, M. L.
Feb. 1947	–Jan. 1953	Darden, William E.
Jan. 1925†		Dealey, E. M. (Ted)

Feb. 1955 –Mar. 1961	Devall, Lyde (Mrs. Charles)
Apr. 1881 –Mar. 1882	Devine, Thomas J.
Feb. 1911*	Dibrell, Joseph Burton
Aug. 1917 –Nov. 1920	Dougherty, W. H.
Apr. 1881 –Apr. 1882	Edwards, Amasa N.
Mar. 1963 –Jan. 1975	Erwin, Frank C., Jr. (c)
Feb. 1915 –Nov. 1916*	Faber, M.
Jan. 1935 –Feb. 1945	Fairchild, Marguerite S. (Mrs. I. D.)
Apr. 1911 –Sep. 1913*	Faust, Joseph
Jan. 1907 –Sep. 1909	Finley, Newton Webster
Jan. 1909 –Jan. 1911	Fly, Ashlew Wilson, M.D.
Jul. 1913 –Aug. 1917‡	
Jan. 1977 –	Fly, Sterling, M.D.
Oct. 1920 –Jun. 1923	Folts, W. H.
Jan. 1925 –Jan. 1931	Foster, Marcellus E.
Sep. 1932 –Feb. 1935	Francis, Charles I.
Mar. 1883 –Aug. 1883	Garnett, M. W.
Jan. 1969 –Jan. 1975	Garrett, Jenkins
Jul. 1899 –Jan. 1903	Garwood, Hiram Morgan
Jan. 1963‡	Garwood, W. St. John
Jan. 1909 –Sep. 1910	Gary, Hampson
Sep. 1913 –Jan. 1915	Graham, J. Walter
Jan. 1907 –Jan. 1911	Greenwood, Thomas B.
Feb. 1899 –Jan. 1907	Gregory, Thomas Watt
Jan. 1883 –Nov. 1885	Hadra, Berthold Ernest, M.D.
May 1924 –Jan. 1925‡	Hankamer, Earl C.
Jan. 1957 –Jan. 1963	Hardie, Thornton (c)
May 1914 –Jan. 1917	Harrell, David H.
May 1921 –Oct. 1921*	Harrington, H. H.
Jan. 1941 –Nov. 1944*	Harrison, Dan J.
Oct. 1881 –Jan. 1895	Harwood, Thomas M.
Jan. 1977 –	Hay, Jess
Jan. 1959 –Apr. 1967	Heath, W. W. (c)
Jan. 1895 –Jan. 1911	Henderson, Thomas S. (c)
Nov. 1909 –Jan. 1911	Henry, Will Thomas
Jun. 1923 –Dec. 1923	Hicks, Marshall
Aug. 1913 –Jan. 1917	Hogg, William Clifford
Jan. 1927†	
Feb. 1927 –Jan. 1933	Holliday, Robert L.
Apr. 1898†	House, E. M.
Feb. 1925 –Apr. 1929	Howard, Edward
Apr. 1881 –Mar. 1882	Hubbard, Richard B.
Apr. 1965 –Jan. 1973	Ikard, Frank N.

Jan. 1953 –Jan. 1959	Jeffers, John Leroy (c)
Jun. 1929 –Mar. 1935	Jester, Beauford H. (c)
Jan. 1971 –Jan. 1977	Johnson, Claudia T. (Mrs. L. B.)
Feb. 1955 –Mar. 1961	Johnson, J. Lee, III
Jan. 1963 –Jan. 1969	Johnson, Ruth Carter (Mrs. J. Lee, III)
Oct. 1909 –Jan. 1911	Johnson, W. A.
May 1921 –May 1924*	Jones, Frank C.
Apr. 1882 –Jan. 1883	Jones, James Henry
Feb. 1915 –May 1917 –Oct. 1917*	Jones, Samuel J.²
Mar. 1965 –Jan. 1971	Josey, Jack S.
Mar. 1917 –Jun. 1923	Kelley, C. E.
Oct. 1917 –May 1921	Kemp, Joseph Alexander
Jul. 1967 –Jan. 1973	Kilgore, Joe M.
Jan. 1911 –Apr. 1911†	Kirby, John Henry
Jan. 1945 –Jan. 1951	Kirkpatrick, E. E.
Dec. 1905 –Jan. 1907	Kleberg, Marcellus E.
Sep. 1907 –Jul. 1908	Lanham, Samuel Willis Tucker
Jan. 1975 –	Law, Thos. H.
Jan. 1917‡	Lawrence, David H., M.D.
Jan. 1911 –Jan. 1920*	Littlefield, George W.
Jan. 1953 –Jan. 1959	Lockwood, Lee
Jun. 1917 –Aug. 1917‡	Love, William G.
Jul. 1882 –Jan. 1883	McKinney, Andrew Todd
Jan. 1907 –Nov. 1909	McLaughlin, James Wharton, M.D.
Jan. 1959 –Jan. 1965	McNeese, A. G., Jr. (c)
Jan. 1971 –Jan. 1977	
Dec. 1914 –May 1917	McReynolds, George S., M.D.
Jan. 1959 –Jan. 1965	Madden, Wales H., Jr.
Oct. 1924 –Jan. 1925‡	Marsh, Charles E.
Jan. 1900 –Jan. 1903	Marsh, Henry B.
Jan. 1907 –1909	Marx, M.
May 1917 –Jul. 1917§	Mathis, John M.
Feb. 1955 –Mar. 1961	Minter, Merton M., M.D. (c)
1883†	Moore, George F.
Feb. 1935 –Jan. 1941	Morgan, George D.
Feb. 1925 –Jan. 1931	Neathery, Sam
Jan. 1971 –Jan. 1977	Nelson, Joe T., M.D.
Jan. 1979 –	Newton, Jon
Jan. 1951 –Jan. 1957	Oates, Laried Stephen, M.D.

Apr. 1929 –Sep. 1932*	Odell, Willmot Mitchell	Jan. 1924 –Apr. 1929	Storey, Robert Gerald
May 1921 –Apr. 1929	O'Hair, Mary M. (Mrs. H. J.)	Jun. 1942 –Dec. 1946	Strickland, D. F.
Jan. 1963 –Jan. 1969	Olan, Levi A.	Jan. 1933 –Jan. 1935	Sulak, L. J.
Jan. 1911 –Aug. 1914*	Ousley, Clarence (c)	Oct. 1947 –Jan. 1953	Swenson, A. M. G.
Jan. 1925 –Sep. 1926*	Padelford, Silas Catchings	Nov. 1944°	Taylor, Judson Ludwell, M.D.
Mar. 1935 –Jan. 1941	Parten, Jubal Richard (Jube)	Jan. 1909 –Jan. 1911	Terrell, Alexander Watkins
Sep. 1967 –Jan. 1973	Peace, John (c)	Nov. 1944 –Jan. 1951	Terrell, C. O., M.D.
May 1882†	Peeler, A. J.	Feb. 1957 –Jun. 1961	Thompson, Joe C. (Jody)
Jan. 1921 –Apr. 1921	Perry, E. H.	Feb. 1887 –Apr. 1898	Thompson, T. C., M.D.
Jan. 1979 –	Powell, James L.	Apr. 1881 –Oct. 1881	Throckmorton, James Webb
Feb. 1887 –Nov. 1899	Prather, William Lambdin(c)	Feb. 1947 –Jan. 1955	Tobin, Margaret Batts
Jan. 1907 –Sep. 1907	Pressler, James M.		(Mrs. Edgar)
Apr. 1881 –Jul. 1882	Ragsdale, Smith	Jul. 1883 –Aug. 1893	Todd, George T.
Apr. 1929 –Jan. 1940*	Randall, Edward, Sr., M.D.(c)	Jan. 1925†	Truett, L. J.
Mar. 1961 –Dec. 1964*	Redditt, John S.	Jan. 1945 –Jan. 1951	Tucker, Edward B.
Jan. 1979 –	Richards, Howard	May 1917[3]	Tucker, James P.
Nov. 1961 –Jan. 1963	Robertson, French M.	Aug. 1917*	
Feb. 1947 –Jan. 1953	Rockwell, James W.	Jan. 1925 –Jan. 1927*	Tyler, George W.
Jan. 1887 –Feb. 1887*	Rose, A. J.	Jan. 1951 –Jan. 1957	Voyles, Claude W.
Oct. 1923 –Jan. 1925	Royall, Tucker	Jan. 1931 –Mar. 1942*	Waggener, Leslie C., Jr. (c)
Feb. 1925 –Jan. 1927	Royston, Mart H.	Jun. 1917 –Jul. 1917[3]	Ward, John L.
Jan. 1911 –Jan. 1917	Sanger, Alexander	Aug. 1917‡	
Feb. 1913 –Aug. 1913	Sayers, Joseph Draper	Nov. 1944 –Jan. 1955	Warren, David M.
Feb. 1945 –Feb. 1947‡	Scherer, W. H., M.D.	Nov. 1933 –Nov. 1944*	Weinert, Hilmer H.
Jun. 1942 –Sep. 1947*	Schreiner, W. Scott	May 1924 –Jan. 1925‡	Whaley, W. S.
Jan. 1931 –Dec. 1936	Scott, John T.	Jan. 1969 –	Williams, Dan C. (c)
Sep. 1917 –May 1919*	Sealy, John, II	Nov. 1944 –Jan. 1955	Woodward, Dudley K., Jr. (c)
1925†		Jun. 1923 –Jan. 1925‡	Wooten, Joe S., M.D.
Jan. 1951 –Jan. 1957	Sealy, Tom (c)	Nov. 1881 –Jul. 1899	Wooten, Thomas D., M.D.
Aug. 1883 –Jan. 1891	Shepard, Seth		(p) (c)
Jan. 1973 –Jan. 1979	Shivers, Allan (c)	Jan. 1919 –Jun. 1923	Wortham, Lewis J.
Aug. 1882 –Jan. 1895	Simkins, Elred James	Jan. 1920 –Feb. 1925	Wroe, H. A.
Apr. 1881 –Jan. 1886	Smith, Ashbel, M.D. (p)	Oct. 1926 –Jan. 1927	
May 1903 –Dec. 1905	Smith, R. Waverley	Jul. 1967 –Jan. 1971	Ximenes, E. T., M.D.
Jan. 1953 –Jan. 1959	Sorrell, James Robert (Bob)(c)	Jan. 1931 –Nov. 1933	Yount, Miles Frank
May 1898 –Apr. 1903	Spencer, Frank M.		
May 1919 –Jan. 1931	Stark, H. J. Lutcher (c)		
Jan. 1933 –Feb. 1945			
Jan. 1911 –Jan. 1915	Stark, William H.		
Aug. 1893 –Apr. 1895	Starr, Amory J.		
1881†	Starr, James H., M.D.		
Mar. 1911 –Nov. 1912*	Stedman, Nathan Alexander		
Oct. 1917 –Oct. 1920	Steiner, Ralph, M.D.		
Jan. 1975 –	Sterling, Walter G.		

1895–1896	Leslie Waggener, M.A., LL.D., ad interim
1896–1899	George Tayloe Winston, M.A., LL.D.
1899–1905	William Lambdin Prather, B.L., LL.D.
1905–1908	David Franklin Houston, M.A., LL.D.
1908–1914	Sidney Edward Mezes, Ph.D., LL.D.
1914–1916	William James Battle, Ph.D., D.C.L., LL.D., ad interim
1916–1923	Robert Ernest Vinson, D.D., LL.D.
1923–1924	William Seneca Sutton, M.A., LL.D., ad interim
1924–1927	Walter Marshall William Splawn, Ph.D., LL.D.
1927–1937	Harry Yandell Benedict, Ph.D., LL.D.
1937–1939	John William Calhoun, M.A., LL.D., ad interim
1939–1944	Homer Price Rainey, Ph.D., LL.D.
1944–1946	Theophilus Shickel Painter, Ph.D., D.Sc., LL.D., M.N.A.S., acting president
1946–1952	Theophilus Shickel Painter, Ph.D., D.Sc., LL.D., M.N.A.S.
1952	James Clay Dolley, Ph.D., acting president
1953–1960	Logan Wilson, Ph.D., LL.D.
1960–1961	Harry Huntt Ransom, Ph.D., Litt.D., LL.D., L.H.D.
1961	Harry Huntt Ransom, Ph.D., Litt.D., LL.D., L.H.D., acting president
1961–1963	Joseph Royall Smiley, Ph.D.
1967–1970	Norman Hackerman, Ph.D.
1970–1971	Bryce Jordan, Ph.D., ad interim
1971–1974	Stephen Hopkins Spurr, Ph.D.
1974–1975	Lorene Lane Rogers, Ph.D., D.Sc., F.A.I.C., ad interim
1975–1979	Lorene Lane Rogers, Ph.D., D.Sc., F.A.I.C.
1979–	Peter Tyrrell Flawn, Ph.D.

Index